The Constitution of
The State of Texas:
A Quick Reference Guide

Bootblack Budget Books
Copyright 2018 ©
ISBN-13: 978-1723247835
ISBN-10: 1723247839

Contents:

Article 2: the Powers of Government – Page 58

Section 1. Separation of Powers of Government Among Three Departments

6

Article 3: Legislative Department – Page 59

6

11

Section 49-D-12. State Water Implementation Fund for Texas

Section 49-D-13. State Water Implementation Revenue Fund for Texas

Section 49-E. Texas Park Development Fund; Bonds

Section 49-F. Bonds for Financial Assistance to Purchase Farm and Ranch Land and for Rural Economic Development

Section 49-G. Superconducting Super Collider Fund

Section 49-G. Economic Stabilization Fund; Allocation of Certain Oil and Gas Production Tax Revenue

Section 49-H. Bond Issuance for Correctional and Statewide Law Enforcement Facilities and for Institutions for Persons With Intellectual and Developmental Disabilities

Section 49-I. Texas Agricultural Fund; Rural Microenterprise Development Fund

Section 49-J. Limit on State Debt Payable from General Revenue Fund

Section 49-K. Texas Mobility Fund

Section 49-L. Financial Assistance to Counties for Roadway Projects to Serve Border Colonias

Section 49-M. Short-Term Notes and Loans for Texas Department of Transportation Functions

Section 49-N. Public Securities and Bond Enhancement Agreements Payable from State Highway Fund for Highway Improvement Projects

Section 52-A. Programs and Loans or Grants of Public Money for Economic Development

Section 52-B. Loan of State's Credit, Grant of Public Money, or Assumption of Debt for Toll Road Purposes

Section 52-C. Blank

Section 52d. County or Road District Tax for Road and Bridge Purposes in Harris County

Section 52e. County Payment of Medical Expenses of Law Enforcement Officials

Section 52f. Private Road Work by Counties With Population of 7,500 or Less

Section 52g. Dallas County Bond Issues for Roads and Turnpikes

Section 52h. Donations by Municipalities of Outdated or Surplus Fire Fighting Equipment to Underdeveloped Countries

Section 52i. Donations by Municipalities of Surplus Fire Fighting Equipment for Rural Fire Protection

Section 52j. Sale of Real Property Acquired Through Eminent Domain

Section 52k. County or Municipal Bonds or Notes to Acquire Land Adjacent to Military Installations

Section 53. Payment of Extra Compensation or Unauthorized Claims Prohibited

Section 54. Repealed

16

Article 5: Judicial Department – Page 180

Article 6: Suffrage – Page 206

Article 7: Education – Page 210

Section 16. County Taxation of Certain University of Texas Lands

Section 16-A. Terms of Office of Educational Officers

Section 17. Funding to Support Agencies and Institutions of Higher Education not Supported by Available University Fund

Section 18. Funding to Support Texas A&M University System and University of Texas System; Available University Fund

Section 19. Texas Tomorrow Fund

Section 20. National Research University Fund

25

Article 8: Taxation and Revenue – Page 241

Section 1. Equality and Uniformity of Taxation; Taxation of Property in Proportion to Value; Occupation and Income Taxes; Exemption of Certain Tangible Personal Property and Small Mineral Interests from Ad Valorem Taxation; Valuation of Residence Homesteads for Tax Purposes

Section 1-A. County Tax Levy for Roads and Flood Control

Section 1-B. Residence Homestead Tax Exemptions and Limitations

Section 1-B-1. Repealed

Section 1-C. Repealed

Section 1-D. Assessment for Tax Purposes of Lands Designated for Agricultural Use

Section 1-D-1. Taxation of Certain Open-Space Land

Section 1-E. State Ad Valorem Taxes Prohibited

Section 1-F. Ad Valorem Tax Relief

Section 1-G. Development or Redevelopment of Property; Ad Valorem Tax Relief and Issuance of Bonds and Notes

Section 1-H. Validation of Assessment Ratio

Section 1-I. Mobile Marine Drilling Equipment; Ad Valorem Tax Relief

Section 1-J. Exemption from Ad Valorem Taxation of Certain Tangible Personal Property Temporarily Located in this State

Section 1-K. Exemption from Ad Valorem Taxation of Property Owned By Nonprofit Corporations Supplying Water or Providing Wastewater Services

Section 1-L. Exemption from Ad Valorem Taxation of Property Used for Control of Air, Water, or Land Pollution

Section 1-M. Property on Which Water Conservation Initiative Has Been Implemented; Ad Valorem Tax Relief

Section 1-N. Exemption from Ad Valorem Taxation of Raw Cocoa and Green Coffee

Section 1-N. Exemption from Ad Valorem Taxation of Tangible Personal Property Held Temporarily for Certain Commercial Purposes

Section 1-O. Rural Economic Development; Limitation on Ad Valorem Tax Increase

Section 2. Equality and Uniformity of Occupation Taxes; Additional Exemptions from Ad Valorem Taxation

Section 3. Taxation By General Law for Public Purposes

Section 4. Surrender or Suspension of Taxing Power Prohibited

Section 5. Repealed

Section 6. Withdrawal of Money from Treasury; Duration of Appropriation

Section 7. Borrowing, Withholding, or Diverting Special Funds Prohibited

Section 7-A. Use of Revenues from Motor Vehicle Registration Fees and Taxes on Motor Fuels and Lubricants

28

Section 19. Exemption from Taxation of Farm Products, Livestock, Poultry, and Family Supplies

Section 19a. Exemption from Ad Valorem Taxation of Implements of Husbandry

Section 20. Ad Valorem Taxation of Property At Value Exceeding Fair Cash Market Value Prohibited; Discounts for Advance Payment

Section 21. Increase in Total Amount of Property Taxes Imposed Prohibited Without Notice and Hearing; Calculation and Notice to Property Owners

Section 22. Restriction on Rate of Growth of Appropriations

Section 23. Statewide Appraisal of Real Property for Ad Valorem Tax Purposes Prohibited; Enforcement of Appraisal Standards and Procedures

Section 24. Personal Income Tax; Dedication of Proceeds

Section 29. Transfer Tax on Transaction Conveying Fee Simple Title to Real Property

Article 9: Counties – Page 280

Section 1. Creation and Modification of Counties

Section 1-A. Authority of Coastal Counties to Regulate Motor Vehicles and Littering on Beaches

Section 2. Removal of County Seats

Section 3. Repealed

Section 4. County-Wide Hospital Districts in Certain Large Counties

Section 5. Creation and Funding of Hospital Districts in City of Amarillo, Wichita County, and Jefferson County

Section 6. Repealed

Section 7. Repealed

Section 8. Creation and Funding of Hospital District in County Commissioners Precinct No. 4 of Comanche County

Section 9. Creation, Operation, and Dissolution of Hospital Districts

Section 9a. Hospital Districts: Regulation of Health Care Services

Section 9b. Hospital Districts in Counties with Population of 75,000 or Less

Section 10. Blank

Section 11. Creation and Funding of Hospital Districts in Ochiltree, Castro, Hansford, and Hopkins Counties

Section 12. Airport Authorities

Section 13. Participation of Municipalities and other Political Subdivisions in Establishment and Operation of Mental Health, Mental Retardation, or Public Health Services

Section 14. County Facilities for Indigent Inhabitants

Article 10: Railroads – Page 295

Section 1. Repealed

Section 2. Railroads as Public Highways and Common Carriers; Regulation

Section 3. Repealed

Section 4. Repealed

Section 5. Repealed

Section 6. Repealed

Section 7. Repealed

Section 8. Repealed

Section 9. Repealed

Article 11: Municipal Corporations – Page 296

Section 1. Counties as Legal Subdivisions

Section 2. Jails, Courthouses, Bridges, and Roads

Section 3. County or Municipal Investment in or Donation or Loan to Private Corporation or Association Prohibited

Section 4. Cities and Towns with Population of 5,000 or Less: Chartered by General Law; Taxes; Fines, Forfeitures, and Penalties

Section 5. Cities of More Than 5,000 Population: Adoption or Amendment of Charters; Taxes; Debt Restrictions

Section 6. Repealed

Section 7. Counties and Cities on Gulf of Mexico; Tax for Sea Walls, Breakwaters, and Sanitation; Bonds; Condemnation of Right of Way

Section 8. Donation of Public Domain to Aid in Construction of Sea Walls or Breakwaters

Section 9. County or Municipal Property Held for Public Purpose Exempt from Forced Sale and Taxation

Section 10. Repealed

Section 11. Term of Office Exceeding Two Years in Home Rule and General Law Cities; Vacancies

Section 12. Expenditures for Relocation or Replacement of Sanitation Sewer or Water Laterals on Private Property

Section 13. Classification of Municipal Functions

33

Article 12: Private Corporations – Page 301

Section 1. Creation of Private Corporations by General Laws Only

Section 2. General Laws for Creation of Private Corporations and Protection of Public and Stockholders

Section 3. Repealed

Section 4. Repealed

Section 5. Repealed

Section 6. Repealed

Section 7. Repealed

Article 13: Spanish and Mexican Land Titles – Page 302

Repealed

Article 15: Impeachment – Page 304

Section 1. Impeachment by House of Representatives

Section 2. Trial of Impeachment of Certain Officers by Senate

Section 3. Impartial Trial by Senate; Concurrence of Two-Thirds Required

Section 4. Judgment to Remove and Disqualify; Punishment Under Other Law Permitted

Section 5. Suspension Pending Impeachment; Provisional Appointment

Section 6. Removal of District Judges by Supreme Court

Section 7. Removal of Officers When Mode not Provided in Constitution

Section 8. Removal of Judges by Governor on Address of Two-Thirds of Each House of Legislature

Section 9. Removal of Public Officer by Appointing Governor With Advice and Consent of Senate

Article 16: General Provisions – Page 307

Section 1. Official Oath of Office

Section 2. Exclusions from Office for Conviction of High Crimes

Section 3. Repealed

Section 4. Repealed

Section 5. Disqualification from Office for Giving or Offering Bribe

Section 6. Appropriations for Private Purposes; Annual Accounting of Public Money; Acceptance and Expenditure of Certain Money for Persons with Disabilities

Section 7. Repealed

Section 8. Re-Designated

Section 9. No Forfeiture of Residence By Absence on Public Business

Section 10. Deductions from Salary of Public Officer for Neglect of Duty

Section 11. Usury; Rate of Interest In Absence of Legislation

Section 12. Ineligibility of Members of Congress and Officers of United States or Foreign Power To Hold Another Office

Section 13. Unopposed Candidate for Office

Section 13a. Unopposed Candidate for Office of Political Subdivision

39

Section 46. Repealed

Section 47. Repealed

Section 48. Existing State Laws to Continue in Force

Section 49. Protection of Personal Property from Forced Sale

Section 50. Protection of Homestead from Forced or Unauthorized Sale; Exceptions; Requirements for Mortgage Loans and Other Obligations Secured by Homestead

Section 51. Size of Homestead; Uses; Release or Refinance of Existing Lien

Section 52. Descent and Distribution of Homestead; Restrictions on Partition

Section 53. Repealed

Section 54. Repealed

Section 55. Repealed

Section 56. Repealed

Section 57. Repealed

Section 58. Repealed

Section 59. Conservation and Development of Natural Resources; Development of Parks and Recreational Facilities; Conservation and Reclamation Districts; Indebtedness and Taxation Authorized

Section 60. Repealed

Article 17: Mode of Amending the Constitution of this State – Page 368

Section 1. Proposed Amendments; Publication; Submission to Voters; Adoption

Section 2. Repealed

Preamble:

Humbly invoking the blessings of Almighty God, the people of the State of Texas, do ordain and establish this Constitution.

ARTICLE 1: BILL OF RIGHTS

Section 1. Freedom and Sovereignty of State

Texas is a free and independent State, subject only to the Constitution of the United States, and the maintenance of our free institutions and the perpetuity of the Union depend upon the preservation of the right of local self-government, unimpaired to all the States.

Section 2. Inherent Political Power; Republican Form of Government

All political power is inherent in the people, and all free governments are founded on their authority, and instituted for their benefit. The faith of the people of Texas stands pledged to the preservation of a republican form of government, and, subject to this limitation only, they have at all times the inalienable right to alter, reform or abolish their government in such manner as they may think expedient.

Section 3. Equal Rights

All free men, when they form a social compact, have equal rights, and no man, or set of men, is entitled to exclusive separate public emoluments, or privileges, but in consideration of public services.

Section 3a. Equality Under The Law

Equality under the law shall not be denied or abridged because of sex, race, color, creed, or national origin. This amendment is self-operative.

Section 4. Religious Tests

No religious test shall ever be required as a qualification to any office, or public trust, in this State; nor shall any one be excluded from holding office on account of his religious sentiments, provided he acknowledge the existence of a Supreme Being.

Section 5. Witnesses not Disqualified by Religious Beliefs; Oaths and Affirmations

No person shall be disqualified to give evidence in any of the Courts of this State on account of his religious opinions, or for the want of any religious belief, but all oaths or affirmations shall be administered in the mode most binding upon the conscience, and shall be taken subject to the pains and penalties of perjury.

Section 6. Freedom of Worship

All men have a natural and indefeasible right to worship Almighty God according to the dictates of their own consciences. No man shall be compelled to attend, erect or support any place of worship, or to maintain any ministry against his consent. No human authority ought, in any case whatever, to control or interfere with the rights of conscience in matters of religion, and no preference shall ever be given by law to any religious society or mode of worship. But it shall be the duty of the Legislature to pass such laws as may be necessary to protect equally every religious denomination in the peaceable enjoyment of its own mode of public worship.

Section 7. Appropriations for Sectarian Purposes

No money shall be appropriated, or drawn from the Treasury for the benefit of any sect, or religious society, theological or religious seminary; nor shall property belonging to the State be appropriated for any such purposes.

Section 8. Freedom of Speech and Press; Libel

Every person shall be at liberty to speak, write or publish his opinions on any subject, being responsible for the abuse of that privilege; and no law shall ever be passed curtailing the liberty of speech or of the press. In prosecutions for the publication of papers, investigating the conduct of officers, or men in public capacity, or when the matter published is proper for public information, the truth thereof may be given in evidence. And in all indictments for libels, the jury shall have the right to determine the law and the facts, under the direction of the court, as in other cases.

Section 9. Searches and Seizures

The people shall be secure in their persons, houses, papers and possessions, from all unreasonable seizures or searches, and no warrant to search any place, or to seize any person or thing, shall issue without describing them as near as may be, nor without probable cause, supported by oath or affirmation.

Section 10. Rights of Accused in Criminal Prosecutions

In all criminal prosecutions the accused shall have a speedy public trial by an impartial jury. He shall have the right to demand the nature and cause of the accusation against him, and to have a copy thereof. He shall not be compelled to give evidence against himself, and shall have the right of being heard by himself or counsel, or both, shall be confronted by the witnesses against him and shall have compulsory process for obtaining witnesses in his favor, except that when the witness resides out of the State and the offense charged is a violation of any of the anti-trust laws of this State, the defendant and the State shall have the right to produce and have the evidence admitted by deposition, under such rules and laws as the Legislature may hereafter provide; and no person shall be held to answer for a criminal offense, unless on an indictment of a grand jury, except in cases in which the punishment is by fine or imprisonment, otherwise than in the penitentiary, in cases of impeachment, and in cases arising in the army or navy, or in the militia, when in actual service in time of war or public danger.

Section 11. Bail

All prisoners shall be bailable by sufficient sureties, unless for capital offenses, when the proof is evident; but this provision shall not be so construed as to prevent bail after indictment found upon examination of the evidence, in such manner as may be prescribed by law.

Section 11a. Denial of Bail After Multiple Felonies

(a) Any person

(1) accused of a felony less than capital in this State, who has been theretofore twice convicted of a felony, the second conviction being subsequent to the first, both in point of time of commission of the offense and conviction therefor,

(2) accused of a felony less than capital in this State, committed while on bail for a prior felony for which he has been indicted,

(3) accused of a felony less than capital in this State involving the use of a deadly weapon after being convicted of a prior felony, or

(4) accused of a violent or sexual offense committed while under the supervision of a criminal justice agency of the State or a political subdivision of the State for a prior felony, after a hearing, and upon evidence substantially showing the guilt of the accused of the offense in (1) or (3) above, of the offense committed while on bail in (2) above, or of the offense in (4) above committed while under the supervision of a criminal justice agency of the State or a political subdivision of the State for a prior felony, may be denied bail pending trial, by a district judge in this State, if said order denying bail pending trial is issued within seven calendar days subsequent to the time of incarceration of the accused; provided, however, that if the accused is not accorded a trial upon the accusation under (1) or (3) above, the accusation and indictment used under (2) above, or the accusation or indictment used under (4) above within sixty (60) days from the time of his incarceration upon the accusation, the order denying bail shall be automatically set aside, unless a continuance is obtained upon the motion or request of the accused; provided, further, that the right of appeal to the Court of Criminal Appeals of this State is expressly accorded the accused for a review of any judgment or order made hereunder, and said appeal shall be given preference by the Court of Criminal Appeals.

(b) In this section:

(1) "Violent offense" means:

(A) murder;

(B) aggravated assault, if the accused used or exhibited a deadly weapon during the commission of the assault;

(C) aggravated kidnapping; or

(D) aggravated robbery.

(2) "Sexual offense" means:

(A) aggravated sexual assault;

(B) sexual assault; or

(C) indecency with a child.

Section 11b. Denial of Bail for Violation of Condition of Release

Any person who is accused in this state of a felony or an offense involving family violence, who is released on bail pending trial, and whose bail is subsequently revoked or forfeited for a violation of a condition of release may be denied bail pending trial if a judge or magistrate in this state determines by a preponderance of the evidence at a subsequent hearing that the person violated a condition of release related to the safety of a victim of the alleged offense or to the safety of the community.

Section 11c. Denial of Bail for Violation of Protective Order Involving Family Violence

The legislature by general law may provide that any person who violates an order for emergency protection issued by a judge or magistrate after an arrest for an offense involving family violence or who violates an active protective order rendered by a court in a family violence case, including a temporary ex parte order that has been served on the person, or who engages in conduct that constitutes an offense involving the violation of an order described by this section may be taken into custody and, pending trial or other court proceedings, denied release on bail if following a hearing a judge or magistrate in this state determines by a preponderance of the evidence that the person violated the order or engaged in the conduct constituting the offense.

Section 12. Habeas Corpus

The writ of habeas corpus is a writ of right, and shall never be suspended. The Legislature shall enact laws to render the remedy speedy and effectual.

Section 13. Excessive Bail or Fines; Cruel or Unusual Punishment; Open Courts; Remedy by Due Course of Law

Excessive bail shall not be required, nor excessive fines imposed, nor cruel or unusual punishment inflicted. All courts shall be open, and every person for an injury done him, in his lands, goods, person or reputation, shall have remedy by due course of law.

Section 14. Double Jeopardy

No person, for the same offense, shall be twice put in jeopardy of life or liberty; nor shall a person be again put upon trial for the same offense after a verdict of not guilty in a court of competent jurisdiction.

Section 15. Right of Trial by Jury

The right of trial by jury shall remain inviolate. The Legislature shall pass such laws as may be needed to regulate the same, and to maintain its purity and efficiency. Provided, that the Legislature may provide for the temporary commitment, for observation and/or treatment, of mentally ill persons not charged with a criminal offense, for a period of time not to exceed ninety (90) days, by order of the County Court without the necessity of a trial by jury.

Section 15-A. Commitment of Persons of Unsound Mind

No person shall be committed as a person of unsound mind except on competent medical or psychiatric testimony. The Legislature may enact all laws necessary to provide for the trial, adjudication of insanity and commitment of persons of unsound mind and to provide for a method of appeal from judgments rendered in such cases. Such laws may provide for a waiver of trial by jury, in cases where the person under inquiry has not been charged with the commission of a criminal offense, by the concurrence of the person under inquiry, or his next of kin, and an attorney ad litem appointed by a judge of either the County or Probate Court of the county where the trial is being held, and shall provide for a method of service of notice of such trial upon the person under inquiry and of his right to demand a trial by jury.

Section 16. Bills of Attainder; Ex Post Facto or Retroactive Laws; Impairing Obligation of Contracts

No bill of attainder, ex post facto law, retroactive law, or any law impairing the obligation of contracts, shall be made.

Section 17. Taking Property for Public Use; Special Privileges and Immunities; Control of Privileges and Franchises

(a) No person's property shall be taken, damaged, or destroyed for or applied to public use without adequate compensation being made, unless by the consent of such person, and only if the taking, damage, or destruction is for:

(1) the ownership, use, and enjoyment of the property, notwithstanding an incidental use, by:

(A) the State, a political subdivision of the State, or the public at large; or

(B) an entity granted the power of eminent domain under law; or

(2) the elimination of urban blight on a particular parcel of property.

(b) In this section, "public use" does not include the taking of property under Subsection (a) of this section for transfer to a private entity for the primary purpose of economic development or enhancement of tax revenues.

(c) On or after January 1, 2010, the legislature may enact a general, local, or special law granting the power of eminent domain to an entity only on a two-thirds vote of all the members elected to each house.

(d) When a person's property is taken under Subsection (a) of this section, except for the use of the State, compensation as described by Subsection (a) shall be first made, or secured by a deposit of money; and no irrevocable or uncontrollable grant of special privileges or immunities shall be made; but all privileges and franchises granted by the Legislature, or created under its authority, shall be subject to the control thereof.

Section 18. Imprisonment for Debt

No person shall ever be imprisoned for debt.

Section 19. Deprivation of Life, Liberty, Property, Etc. by Due Course of Law

No citizen of this State shall be deprived of life, liberty, property, privileges or immunities, or in any manner disfranchised, except by the due course of the law of the land.

Section 20. Outlawry or Transportation Out of State for Offense

No citizen shall be outlawed. No person shall be transported out of the State for any offense committed within the same. This section does not prohibit an agreement with another state providing for the confinement of inmates of this State in the penal or correctional facilities of that state.

Section 21. Corruption of Blood; Forfeiture of Estate; Suicides

No conviction shall work corruption of blood, or forfeiture of estate, and the estates of those who destroy their own lives shall descend or vest as in case of natural death.

Section 22. Treason Against State

Treason against the State shall consist only in levying war against it, or adhering to its enemies, giving them aid and comfort; and no person shall be convicted of treason except on the testimony of two witnesses to the same overt act, or on confession in open court.

Section 23. Right to Keep and Bear Arms

Every citizen shall have the right to keep and bear arms in the lawful defense of himself or the State; but the Legislature shall have power, by law, to regulate the wearing of arms, with a view to prevent crime.

Section 24. Military Subordinate to Civil Authority

The military shall at all times be subordinate to the civil authority.

Section 25. Quartering Soldiers in Houses

No soldier shall in time of peace be quartered in the house of any citizen without the consent of the owner, nor in time of war but in a manner prescribed by law.

Section 26. Perpetuities and Monopolies; Primogeniture or Entailments

Perpetuities and monopolies are contrary to the genius of a free government, and shall never be allowed, nor shall the law of primogeniture or entailments ever be in force in this State.

Section 27. Right of Assembly; Petition for Redress of Grievances

The citizens shall have the right, in a peaceable manner, to assemble together for their common good; and apply to those invested with the powers of government for redress of grievances or other purposes, by petition, address or remonstrance.

Section 28. Suspension of Laws

No power of suspending laws in this State shall be exercised except by the Legislature.

Section 29. Bill of Rights Excepted From Powers of Government and Inviolate

To guard against transgressions of the high powers herein delegated, we declare that everything in this "Bill of Rights" is excepted out of the general powers of government, and shall forever remain inviolate, and all laws contrary thereto, or to the following provisions, shall be void.

Section 30. Rights of Crime Victims

(a) A crime victim has the following rights:

(1) the right to be treated with fairness and with respect for the victim's dignity and privacy throughout the criminal justice process; and

(2) the right to be reasonably protected from the accused throughout the criminal justice process.

(b) On the request of a crime victim, the crime victim has the following rights:

(1) the right to notification of court proceedings;

(2) the right to be present at all public court proceedings related to the offense, unless the victim is to testify and the court determines that the victim's testimony would be materially affected if the victim hears other testimony at the trial;

(3) the right to confer with a representative of the prosecutor's office;

(4) the right to restitution; and

(5) the right to information about the conviction, sentence, imprisonment, and release of the accused.

(c) The legislature may enact laws to define the term "victim" and to enforce these and other rights of crime victims.

(d) The state, through its prosecuting attorney, has the right to enforce the rights of crime victims.

(e) The legislature may enact laws to provide that a judge, attorney for the state, peace officer, or law enforcement agency is not liable for a failure or inability to provide a right enumerated in this section. The failure or inability of any person to provide a right or service enumerated in this section may not be used by a defendant in a criminal case as a ground for appeal or post-conviction writ of habeas corpus. A victim or guardian or legal representative of a victim has standing to enforce the rights enumerated in this section but does not have standing to participate as a party in a criminal proceeding or to contest the disposition of any charge.

Section 31. Funds for Compensation to Victims of Crime

(a) The compensation to victims of crime fund created by general law and the compensation to victims of crime auxiliary fund created by general law are each a separate dedicated account in the general revenue fund.

(b) Except as provided by Subsection (c) of this section and subject to legislative appropriation, money deposited to the credit of the compensation to victims of crime fund or the compensation to victims of crime auxiliary fund from any source may be expended as provided by law only for delivering or funding victim-related compensation, services, or assistance.

(c) The legislature may provide by law that money in the compensation to victims of crime fund or in the compensation to victims of crime auxiliary fund may be expended for the purpose of assisting victims of episodes of mass violence if other money appropriated for emergency assistance is depleted.

Section 32. Marriage

(a) Marriage in this state shall consist only of the union of one man and one woman.

(b) This state or a political subdivision of this state may not create or recognize any legal status identical or similar to marriage.

Section 33. Public Access to and Use of Public Beaches

(a) In this section, "public beach" means a state-owned beach bordering on the seaward shore of the Gulf of Mexico, extending from mean low tide to the landward boundary of state-owned submerged land, and any larger area extending from the line of mean low tide to the line of vegetation bordering on the Gulf of Mexico to which the public has acquired a right of use or easement to or over the area by prescription or dedication or has established and retained a right by virtue of continuous right in the public under Texas common law.

(b) The public, individually and collectively, has an unrestricted right to use and a right of ingress to and egress from a public beach. The right granted by this subsection is dedicated as a permanent easement in favor of the public.

(c) The legislature may enact laws to protect the right of the public to access and use a public beach and to protect the public beach easement from interference and encroachments.

(d) This section does not create a private right of enforcement.

Section 34. Right to Hunt, Fish, and Harvest Wildlife

(a) The people have the right to hunt, fish, and harvest wildlife, including by the use of traditional methods, subject to laws or regulations to conserve and manage wildlife and preserve the future of hunting and fishing.

(b) Hunting and fishing are preferred methods of managing and controlling wildlife.

(c) This section does not affect any provision of law relating to trespass, property rights, or eminent domain.

(d) This section does not affect the power of the legislature to authorize a municipality to regulate the discharge of a weapon in a populated area in the interest of public safety.

ARTICLE 2: THE POWERS OF GOVERNMENT

Section 1. Separation of Powers of Government Among Three Departments

The powers of the Government of the State of Texas shall be divided into three distinct departments, each of which shall be confided to a separate body of magistracy, to wit: Those which are Legislative to one; those which are Executive to another, and those which are Judicial to another; and no person, or collection of persons, being of one of these departments, shall exercise any power properly attached to either of the others, except in the instances herein expressly permitted.

ARTICLE 3. LEGISLATIVE DEPARTMENT

Section 1. Senate and House of Representatives

The Legislative power of this State shall be vested in a Senate and House of Representatives, which together shall be styled "The Legislature of the State of Texas."

Section 2. Membership of Senate and House of Representatives

The Senate shall consist of thirty-one members. The House of Representatives shall consist of 150 members.

Section 3. Election and Term of Office of Senators

The Senators shall be chosen by the qualified voters for the term of four years; but a new Senate shall be chosen after every apportionment, and the Senators elected after each apportionment shall be divided by lot into two classes. The seats of the Senators of the first class shall be vacated at the expiration of the first two years, and those of the second class at the expiration of four years, so that one half of the Senators shall be chosen biennially thereafter. Senators shall take office following their election, on the day set by law for the convening of the Regular Session of the Legislature, and shall serve thereafter for the full term of years to which elected.

Section 4. Election and Term of Members of House of Representatives

The Members of the House of Representatives shall be chosen by the qualified voters for the term of two years. Representatives shall take office following their election, on the day set by law for the convening of the Regular Session of the Legislature, and shall serve thereafter for the full term of years to which elected.

Section 5. Meetings; Order of Business

(a) The Legislature shall meet every two years at such time as may be provided by law and at other times when convened by the Governor.

(b) When convened in regular Session, the first thirty days thereof shall be devoted to the introduction of bills and resolutions, acting upon emergency appropriations, passing upon the confirmation of the recess appointees of the Governor and such emergency matters as may be submitted by the Governor in special messages to the Legislature. During the succeeding thirty days of the regular session of the Legislature the various committees of each House shall hold hearings to consider all bills and resolutions and other matters then pending; and such emergency matters as may be submitted by the Governor. During the remainder of the session the Legislature shall act upon such bills and resolutions as may be then pending and upon such emergency matters as may be submitted by the Governor in special messages to the Legislature.

(c) Notwithstanding Subsection (b), either House may determine its order of business by an affirmative vote of four-fifths of its membership.

Section 6. Qualifications of Senators

No person shall be a Senator, unless he be a citizen of the United States, and, at the time of his election a qualified voter of this State, and shall have been a resident of this State five years next preceding his election, and the last year thereof a resident of the district for which he shall be chosen, and shall have attained the age of twenty-six years.

Section 7. Qualifications of Representatives

No person shall be a Representative, unless he be a citizen of the United States, and, at the time of his election, a qualified voter of this State, and shall have been a resident of this State two years next preceding his election, the last year thereof a resident of the district for which he shall be chosen, and shall have attained the age of twenty-one years.

Section 8. Each House Judge of Qualifications and Election of its Members; Election Contests

Each House shall be the judge of the qualifications and election of its own members; but contested elections shall be determined in such manner as shall be provided by law.

Section 9. President Pro Tempore of Senate; Lieutenant Governor Vacancy; Speaker of House of Representatives; Other Officers

(a) The Senate shall, at the beginning and close of each session, and at such other times as may be necessary, elect one of its members President pro tempore, who shall perform the duties of the Lieutenant Governor in any case of absence or temporary disability of that officer. If the office of Lieutenant Governor becomes vacant, the President pro tempore of the Senate shall convene the Committee of the Whole Senate within 30 days after the vacancy occurs. The Committee of the Whole shall elect one of its members to perform the duties of the Lieutenant Governor in addition to the member's duties as Senator until the next general election. If the Senator so elected ceases to be a Senator before the election of a new Lieutenant Governor, another Senator shall be elected in the same manner to perform the duties of the Lieutenant Governor until the next general election. Until the Committee of the Whole elects one of its members for this purpose, the President pro tempore shall perform the duties of the Lieutenant Governor as provided by this subsection.

(b) The House of Representatives shall, when it first assembles, organize temporarily, and thereupon proceed to the election of a Speaker from its own members.

(c) Each House shall choose its other officers.

Section 10. Quorum; Adjournments From Day to Day; Compelling Attendance

Two-thirds of each House shall constitute a quorum to do business, but a smaller number may adjourn from day to day, and compel the attendance of absent members, in such manner and under such penalties as each House may provide.

Section 11. Rules of Procedure; Punishment or Expulsion of Member

Each House may determine the rules of its own proceedings, punish members for disorderly conduct, and, with the consent of two-thirds, expel a member, but not a second time for the same offense.

Section 12. Journals of Proceedings; Record Votes

(a) Each house of the legislature shall keep a journal of its proceedings, and publish the same.

(b) A vote taken by either house must be by record vote with the vote of each member entered in the journal of that house if the vote is on final passage of a bill, a resolution proposing or ratifying a constitutional amendment, or another resolution other than a resolution of a purely ceremonial or honorary nature. Either house by rule may provide for exceptions to this requirement for a bill that applies only to one district or political subdivision of this state. For purposes of this subsection, a vote on final passage includes a vote on third reading in a house, or on second reading if the house suspends the requirement for three readings, on whether to concur in the other house's amendments, and on whether to adopt a conference committee report.

(c) The yeas and nays of the members of either house on any other question shall, at the desire of any three members present, be entered on the journals.

(d) Each house shall make each record vote required under Subsection (b) of this section, including the vote of each individual member as recorded in the journal of that house, available to the public for a reasonable period of not less than two years through the Internet or a successor electronic communications system accessible by the public. For a record vote on a bill or on a resolution proposing or ratifying a constitutional amendment, the record vote must be accessible to the public by reference to the designated number of the bill or resolution and by reference to its subject.

Section 13. Vacancy in Legislature

(a) When vacancies occur in either House, the Governor, or the person exercising the power of the Governor, shall issue writs of election to fill such vacancies; and should the Governor fail to issue a writ of election to fill any such vacancy within twenty days after it occurs, the returning officer of the district in which such vacancy may have happened, shall be authorized to order an election for that purpose.

(b) The legislature may provide by general law for the filling of a vacancy in the legislature without an election if only one person qualifies and declares a candidacy in an election to fill the vacancy.

Section 14. Privilege From Arrest During Legislative Session

Senators and Representatives shall, except in cases of treason, felony, or breach of the peace, be privileged from arrest during the session of the Legislature, and in going to and returning from the same.

Section 15. Disrespectful or Disorderly Conduct; Obstruction of Proceedings

Each House may punish, by imprisonment, during its sessions, any person not a member, for disrespectful or disorderly conduct in its presence, or for obstructing any of its proceedings; provided, such imprisonment shall not, at any one time, exceed forty-eight hours.

Section 16. Open Sessions

The sessions of each House shall be open, except the Senate when in Executive session.

Section 17. Adjournments

Neither House shall, without the consent of the other, adjourn for more than three days, nor to any other place than that where the Legislature may be sitting.

Section 18. Ineligibility for Other Offices; Voting for Other Members; Interest in State or County Contracts

No Senator or Representative shall, during the term for which he was elected, be eligible to

(1) any civil office of profit under this State which shall have been created, or the emoluments of which may have been increased, during such term, or

(2) any office or place, the appointment to which may be made, in whole or in part, by either branch of the Legislature; provided, however, the fact that the term of office of Senators and Representatives does not end precisely on the last day of December but extends a few days into January of the succeeding year shall be considered as de minimis, and the ineligibility herein created shall terminate on the last day in December of the last full calendar year of the term for which he was elected. No member of either House shall vote for any other member for any office whatever, which may be filled by a vote of the Legislature, except in such cases as are in this Constitution provided, nor shall any member of the Legislature be interested, either directly or indirectly, in any contract with the State, or any county thereof, authorized by any law passed during the term for which he was elected.

Section 19. Ineligibility of Persons Holding Other Offices

No judge of any court, Secretary of State, Attorney General, clerk of any court of record, or any person holding a lucrative office under the United States, or this State, or any foreign government shall during the term for which he is elected or appointed, be eligible to the Legislature.

Section 20. Eligibility of Collectors of Taxes or Persons Entrusted With Public Money

No person who at any time may have been a collector of taxes, or who may have been otherwise entrusted with public money, shall be eligible to the Legislature, or to any office of profit or trust under the State government, until he shall have obtained a discharge for the amount of such collections, or for all public moneys with which he may have been entrusted.

Section 21. Words Spoken in Debate

No member shall be questioned in any other place for words spoken in debate in either House.

Section 22. Disclosure of Personal or Private Interest in Measure or Bill; not to Vote

A member who has a personal or private interest in any measure or bill, proposed, or pending before the Legislature, shall disclose the fact to the House, of which he is a member, and shall not vote thereon.

Section 23. Vacancy Following Removal From District or County From Which Elected

If any Senator or Representative remove his residence from the district or county for which he was elected, his office shall thereby become vacant, and the vacancy shall be filled as provided in section 13 of this article.

Section 23a. Repealed

Section 24. Compensation and Expenses of Members of Legislature; Duration of Regular Sessions

(a) Members of the Legislature shall receive from the Public Treasury a salary of Six Hundred Dollars ($600) per month, unless a greater amount is recommended by the Texas Ethics Commission and approved by the voters of this State in which case the salary is that amount. Each member shall also receive a per diem set by the Texas Ethics Commission for each day during each Regular and Special Session of the Legislature.

(b) No Regular Session shall be of longer duration than one hundred and forty (140) days.

(c) In addition to the per diem the Members of each House shall be entitled to mileage at the same rate as prescribed by law for employees of the State of Texas.

Section 24a. Texas Ethics Commission; Legislative Salaries and Per Diem

(a) The Texas Ethics Commission is a state agency consisting of the following eight members:

(1) two members of different political parties appointed by the governor from a list of at least 10 names submitted by the members of the house of representatives from each political party required by law to hold a primary;

(2) two members of different political parties appointed by the governor from a list of at least 10 names submitted by the members of the senate from each political party required by law to hold a primary;

(3) two members of different political parties appointed by the speaker of the house of representatives from a list of at least 10 names submitted by the members of the house from each political party required by law to hold a primary; and

(4) two members of different political parties appointed by the lieutenant governor from a list of at least 10 names submitted by the members of the senate from each political party required by law to hold a primary.

(b) The governor may reject all names on any list submitted under Subsection (a)(1) or (2) of this section and require a new list to be submitted. The members of the commission shall elect annually the chairman of the commission.

(c) With the exception of the initial appointees, commission members serve for four-year terms. Each appointing official will make one initial appointment for a two-year term and one initial appointment for a four-year term. A vacancy on the commission shall be filled for the unexpired portion of the term in the same manner as the original appointment. A member who has served for one term and any part of a second term is not eligible for reappointment.

(d) The commission has the powers and duties provided by law.

(e) The commission may recommend the salary of the members of the legislature and may recommend that the salary of the speaker of the house of representatives and the lieutenant governor be set at an amount higher than that of other members. The commission shall set the per diem of members of the legislature and the lieutenant governor, and the per diem shall reflect reasonable estimates of costs and may be raised or lowered biennially as necessary to pay those costs, but the per diem may not exceed during a calendar year the amount allowed as of January 1 of that year for federal income tax purposes as a deduction for living expenses incurred in a legislative day by a state legislator in connection with the legislator's business as a legislator, disregarding any exception in federal law for legislators residing near the Capitol.

(f) At each general election for state and county officers following a proposed change in salary, the voters shall approve or disapprove the salary recommended by the commission if the commission recommends a change in salary. If the voters disapprove the salary, the salary continues at the amount paid immediately before disapproval until another amount is recommended by the commission and approved by the voters. If the voters approve the salary, the approved salary takes effect January 1 of the next odd-numbered year.

Section 25. Senatorial Districts

The State shall be divided into Senatorial Districts of contiguous territory, and each district shall be entitled to elect one Senator.

Section 26. Apportionment of Members of House of Representatives

The members of the House of Representatives shall be apportioned among the several counties, according to the number of population in each, as nearly as may be, on a ratio obtained by dividing the population of the State, as ascertained by the most recent United States census, by the number of members of which the House is composed; provided, that whenever a single county has sufficient population to be entitled to a Representative, such county shall be formed into a separate Representative District, and when two or more counties are required to make up the ratio of representation, such counties shall be contiguous to each other; and when any one county has more than sufficient population to be entitled to one or more

Representatives, such Representative or Representatives shall be apportioned to such county, and for any surplus of population it may be joined in a Representative District with any other contiguous county or counties.

Section 26a. Repealed

Section 27. Elections for Legislators

Elections for Senators and Representatives shall be general throughout the State, and shall be regulated by law.

Section 28. Time for Apportionment; Apportionment by Legislative Redistricting Board

The Legislature shall, at its first regular session after the publication of each United States decennial census, apportion the state into senatorial and representative districts, agreeable to the provisions of Sections 25 and 26 of this Article. In the event the Legislature shall at any such first regular session following the publication of a United States decennial census, fail to make such apportionment, same shall be done by the Legislative Redistricting Board of Texas, which is hereby created, and shall be composed of five (5) members, as follows: The Lieutenant Governor, the Speaker of the House of Representatives, the Attorney General, the Comptroller of Public Accounts and the Commissioner of the General Land Office, a majority of whom shall constitute a quorum. Said Board shall assemble in the City of Austin within ninety (90) days after the final adjournment of such regular session. The Board shall, within sixty (60) days after assembling, apportion the state into senatorial and representative districts, or into senatorial or representative districts, as the failure of action of such Legislature may make necessary. Such apportionment shall be in writing and signed by three (3) or more of the members of the Board duly acknowledged as the act and deed of such Board, and, when so executed and filed with the Secretary of State, shall have force and effect of law. Such apportionment shall become effective at the next succeeding statewide general election. The Supreme Court of Texas shall have jurisdiction to compel such Board to perform its duties in accordance with the provisions of this section by writ of mandamus or other extraordinary writs conformable to the usages of law. The Legislature shall provide necessary funds for clerical and technical aid and for other expenses incidental to the work of the Board, and the Lieutenant Governor and the Speaker of the House of Representatives shall be entitled to receive per diem and travel expense during the Board's session in the same manner and amount as they would receive while attending a special session of the Legislature.

Section 29. Enacting Clause of Laws

The enacting clause of all laws shall be: "Be it enacted by the Legislature of the State of Texas."

Section 30. Laws Passed by Bill; Amendments Changing Purpose Prohibited

No law shall be passed, except by bill, and no bill shall be so amended in its passage through either House, as to change its original purpose.

Section 31. Origination in Either House; Amendment

Bills may originate in either House, and, when passed by such House, may be amended, altered or rejected by the other.

Section 32. Reading on Three Several Days

No bill shall have the force of a law, until it has been read on three several days in each House, and free discussion allowed thereon; but four-fifths of the House, in which the bill may be pending, may suspend this rule, the yeas and nays being taken on the question of suspension, and entered upon the journals.

Section 33. Origination of Revenue Bills in House of Representatives

All bills for raising revenue shall originate in the House of Representatives.

Section 34. Defeated Bills and Resolutions

After a bill has been considered and defeated by either House of the Legislature, no bill containing the same substance, shall be passed into a law during the same session. After a resolution has been acted on and defeated, no resolution containing the same substance, shall be considered at the same session.

Section 35. Subjects and Titles of Bills

(a) No bill, (except general appropriation bills, which may embrace the various subjects and accounts, for and on account of which moneys are appropriated) shall contain more than one subject.

(b) The rules of procedure of each house shall require that the subject of each bill be expressed in its title in a manner that gives the legislature and the public reasonable notice of that subject. The legislature is solely responsible for determining compliance with the rule.

(c) A law, including a law enacted before the effective date of this subsection, may not be held void on the basis of an insufficient title.

Section 36. Revival or Amendment by Reference Prohibited; Re-Enactment and Publication at Length

No law shall be revived or amended by reference to its title; but in such case the act revived, or the section or sections amended, shall be re-enacted and published at length.

Section 37. Reference to Committee and Report

No bill shall be considered, unless it has been first referred to a committee and reported thereon, and no bill shall be passed which has not been presented and referred to and reported from a committee at least three days before the final adjournment of the Legislature.

Section 38. Signing Bills and Joint Resolutions; Entry on Journals

The presiding officer of each House shall, in the presence of the House over which he presides, sign all bills and joint resolutions passed by the Legislature, after their titles have been publicly read before signing; and the fact of signing shall be entered on the journals.

Section 39. Time of Taking Effect of Laws

No law passed by the Legislature, except the general appropriation act, shall take effect or go into force until ninety days after the adjournment of the session at which it was enacted, unless the Legislature shall, by a vote of two-thirds of all the members elected to each House, otherwise direct; said vote to be taken by yeas and nays, and entered upon the journals.

Section 40. Special Sessions; Subjects of Legislation; Duration

When the Legislature shall be convened in special session, there shall be no legislation upon subjects other than those designated in the proclamation of the Governor calling such session, or presented to them by the Governor; and no such session shall be of longer duration than thirty days.

Section 41. Elections by Senate and House of Representatives

In all elections by the Senate and House of Representatives, jointly or separately, the vote shall be given viva voce, except in the election of their officers.

Section 42. Repealed

Section 43. Revision of Laws

(a) The Legislature shall provide for revising, digesting and publishing the laws, civil and criminal; provided, that in the adoption of and giving effect to any such digest or revision, the Legislature shall not be limited by sections 35 and 36 of this Article.

(b) In this section, "revision" includes a revision of the statutes on a particular subject and any enactment having the purpose, declared in the enactment, of codifying without substantive change statutes that individually relate to different subjects.

Section 44. Compensation of Public Officials and Contractors; Extra Compensation; Unauthorized Claims; Unauthorized Employment

The Legislature shall provide by law for the compensation of all officers, servants, agents and public contractors, not provided for in this Constitution, but shall not grant extra compensation to any officer, agent, servant, or public contractors, after such public service shall have been performed or contract entered into, for the performance of the same; nor grant, by appropriation or otherwise, any amount of money out of the Treasury of the State, to any individual, on a claim, real or pretended, when the same shall not have been provided for by pre-existing law; nor employ any one in the name of the State, unless authorized by pre-existing law.

Section 45. Power of Courts to Change Venue

The power to change the venue in civil and criminal cases shall be vested in the courts, to be exercised in such manner as shall be provided by law; and the Legislature shall pass laws for that purpose.

Section 46. Uniformity in Collection of Fees

(a) In this section, "fee" means a fee in a criminal or civil matter all or a portion of which is required to be collected by local officers, clerks, or other local personnel and remitted to the comptroller of public accounts for deposit in the manner provided for in the law imposing the fee.

(b) This section applies only if the legislature enacts by law a program to consolidate and standardize the collection, deposit, reporting, and remitting of fees.

(c) A fee imposed by the legislature after the enactment of the program described by Subsection (b) of this section is valid only if the requirements relating to its collection, deposit, reporting, and remitting conform to the program.

(d) A fee to which this section applies may take effect on a date before the next January 1 after the regular session at which the bill adopting the fee was enacted only if the bill is passed by a record vote of two-thirds of all the members elected to each house of the legislature on final consideration in each house.

Section 47. Prohibition on Lotteries and Gift Enterprises; Exceptions for Charitable Bingo, Charitable Raffles, and State Lotteries

(a) The Legislature shall pass laws prohibiting lotteries and gift enterprises in this State other than those authorized by Subsections (b), (d), (d-1), and (e) of this section.

(b) The Legislature by law may authorize and regulate bingo games conducted by a church, synagogue, religious society, volunteer fire department, nonprofit veterans organization, fraternal organization, or nonprofit organization supporting medical research or treatment programs. A law enacted under this subsection must permit the qualified voters of any county, justice precinct, or incorporated city or town to determine from time to time by a majority vote of the qualified voters voting on the question at an election whether bingo games may be held in the county, justice precinct, or city or town. The law must also require that:

(1) all proceeds from the games are spent in Texas for charitable purposes of the organizations;

(2) the games are limited to one location as defined by law on property owned or leased by the church, synagogue, religious society, volunteer fire department, nonprofit veterans organization, fraternal organization, or nonprofit organization supporting medical research or treatment programs; and

(3) the games are conducted, promoted, and administered by members of the church, synagogue, religious society, volunteer fire department, nonprofit veterans organization, fraternal organization, or nonprofit organization supporting medical research or treatment programs.

(c) The law enacted by the Legislature authorizing bingo games must include:

(1) a requirement that the entities conducting the games report quarterly to the Comptroller of Public Accounts about the amount of proceeds that the entities collect from the games and the purposes for which the proceeds are spent; and

(2) criminal or civil penalties to enforce the reporting requirement.

(d) The Legislature by general law may permit charitable raffles conducted by a qualified religious society, qualified volunteer fire department, qualified volunteer emergency medical service, or qualified nonprofit organizations under the terms and conditions imposed by general law.
The law must also require that:

(1) all proceeds from the sale of tickets for the raffle must be spent for the charitable purposes of the organizations; and

(2) the charitable raffle is conducted, promoted, and administered exclusively by members of the qualified religious society, qualified volunteer fire department, qualified volunteer emergency medical service, or qualified nonprofit organization.

(d-1) The legislature by general law may permit a professional sports team charitable foundation to conduct charitable raffles under the terms and conditions imposed by general law. The law may authorize the charitable foundation to pay with the raffle proceeds reasonable advertising, promotional, and administrative expenses. A law enacted under this subsection applies only to an entity defined as a professional sports team charitable foundation under that law and may only allow charitable raffles to be conducted at games hosted at the home venue of the professional sports team associated with a professional sports team charitable foundation. In this subsection, "professional sports team" means:

(1) a team organized in this state that is a member of Major League Baseball, the National Basketball Association, the National Hockey League, the National Football League, Major League Soccer, the American Hockey League, the East Coast Hockey League, the American Association of Independent Professional Baseball, the Atlantic League of Professional Baseball, Minor League Baseball, the National Basketball Association Development League, the National Women's Soccer League, the Major Arena Soccer League, the United Soccer League, or the Women's National Basketball Association;

(2) a person hosting a motorsports racing team event sanctioned by the National Association for Stock Car Auto Racing (NASCAR), INDYCar, or another nationally recognized motorsports racing association at a venue in this state with a permanent seating capacity of not less than 75,000;

(3) an organization hosting a Professional Golf Association event; or

(4) any other professional sports team defined by law.

(d-2) Subsection (a) of this section does not prohibit the legislature from authorizing credit unions and other financial institutions to conduct, under the terms and conditions imposed by general law, promotional activities to promote savings in which prizes are awarded to one or more of the credit union's or financial institution's depositors selected by lot.

(e) The Legislature by general law may authorize the State to operate lotteries and may authorize the State to enter into a contract with one or more legal entities that will operate lotteries on behalf of the State.

Section 48. Repealed

Section 48a. Repealed

Section 48b. Repealed

Section 48c. Blank

Section 48-d. Repealed

Section 48-E. Emergency Services Districts

Laws may be enacted to provide for the establishment and creation of special districts to provide emergency services and to authorize the commissioners courts of participating counties to levy a tax on the ad valorem property situated in said districts not to exceed Ten Cents (10¢) on the One Hundred Dollars ($100.00) valuation for the support thereof; provided that no tax shall be levied in support of said districts until approved by a vote of the qualified voters residing therein. Such a district may provide emergency medical services, emergency ambulance services, rural fire prevention and control services, or other emergency services authorized by the Legislature.

Section 48-F. Jail Districts

The legislature, by law, may provide for the creation, operation, and financing of jail districts and may authorize each district to issue bonds and other obligations and to levy an ad valorem tax on property located in the district to pay principal of and interest on the bonds and to pay for operation of the district. An ad valorem tax may not be levied and bonds secured by a property tax may not be issued until approved by the qualified voters of the district voting at an election called and held for that purpose.

Section 49. State Debts

(a) No debt shall be created by or on behalf of the State, except:

(1) to supply casual deficiencies of revenue, not to exceed in the aggregate at any one time two hundred thousand dollars;

(2) to repel invasion, suppress insurrection, or defend the State in war;

(3) as otherwise authorized by this constitution; or

(4) as authorized by Subsections (b) through (f) of this section.

(b) The legislature, by joint resolution approved by at least two-thirds of the members of each house, may from time to time call an election and submit to the eligible voters of this State one or more propositions that, if approved by a majority of those voting on the question, authorize the legislature to create State debt for the purposes and subject to the limitations stated in the applicable proposition. Each election and proposition must conform to the requirements of Subsections (c) and (d) of this section.

(c) The legislature may call an election during any regular session of the legislature or during any special session of the legislature in which the subject of the election is designated in the governor's proclamation for that special session. The election may be held on any date, and notice of the election shall be given for the period and in the manner required for amending this constitution. The election shall be held in each county in the manner provided by law for other statewide elections.

(d) A proposition must clearly describe the amount and purpose for which debt is to be created and must describe the source of payment for the debt. Except as provided by law under Subsection (f) of this section, the amount of debt stated in the proposition may not be exceeded and may not be renewed after the debt has been created unless the right to exceed or renew is stated in the proposition.

(e) The legislature may enact all laws necessary or appropriate to implement the authority granted by a proposition that is approved as provided by Subsection (b) of this section. A law enacted in anticipation of the election is valid if, by its terms, it is subject to the approval of the related proposition.

(f) State debt that is created or issued as provided by Subsection (b) of this section may be refunded in the manner and amount and subject to the conditions provided by law.

(g) State debt that is created or issued as provided by Subsections (b) through (f) of this section and that is approved by the attorney general in accordance with applicable law is incontestable for any reason.

Section 49a. Financial Statements and Revenue Estimate by Comptroller of Public Accounts; Limitation of Appropriations and Certification of Bills Containing Appropriations

(a) It shall be the duty of the Comptroller of Public Accounts in advance of each Regular Session of the Legislature to prepare and submit to the Governor and to the Legislature upon its convening a statement under oath showing fully the financial condition of the State Treasury at the close of the last fiscal period and an estimate of the probable receipts and disbursements for the then current fiscal year. There shall also be contained in said statement an itemized estimate of the anticipated revenue based on the laws then in effect that will be received by and for the State from all sources showing the fund accounts to be credited during the succeeding biennium and said statement shall contain such other information as may be required by law. Supplemental statements shall be submitted at any Special Session of the Legislature and at such other times as may be necessary to show probable changes.

(b) Except in the case of emergency and imperative public necessity and with a four-fifths vote of the total membership of each House, no appropriation in excess of the cash and anticipated revenue of the funds from which such appropriation is to be made shall be valid. No bill containing an appropriation shall be considered as passed or be sent to the Governor for consideration until and unless the Comptroller of Public Accounts endorses his certificate thereon showing that the amount appropriated is within the amount estimated to be available in the affected funds. When the Comptroller finds an appropriation bill exceeds the estimated revenue he shall endorse such finding thereon and return to the House in which same originated. Such information shall be immediately made known to both the House of Representatives and the Senate and the necessary steps shall be taken to bring such appropriation to within the revenue, either by providing additional revenue or reducing the appropriation.

Section 49-B. Veterans Land Board; Bond Issues; Veterans Land and Housing Funds

(a) The Veterans Land Board shall be composed of the Commissioner of the General Land Office and two (2) citizens of the State of Texas, one (1) of whom shall be well versed in veterans' affairs and one (1) of whom shall be well versed in finances. One (1) such citizen member shall, with the advice and consent of the Senate, be appointed biennially by the Governor to serve for a term of four (4) years. In the event of the resignation or death of any such citizen member, the Governor shall appoint a replacement to serve for the unexpired portion of the term to which the deceased or resigning member had been appointed. The compensation for said citizen members shall be as is now or may hereafter be fixed by the Legislature; and each shall make bond in such amount as is now or may hereafter be prescribed by the Legislature.

(b) The Commissioner of the General Land Office shall act as Chairman of said Board and shall be the administrator of the Veterans' Land Program under such terms and restrictions as are now or may hereafter be provided by law. In the absence or illness of said Commissioner, the Chief Clerk of the General Land Office shall be the Acting Chairman of said Board with the same duties and powers that said Commissioner would have if present.

(c) The Veterans' Land Board may provide for, issue and sell bonds or obligations of the State of Texas as authorized by constitutional amendment or by a debt proposition under Section 49 of this article for the purpose of creating the Veterans' Land Fund, the Veterans' Housing Assistance Fund, and the Veterans' Housing Assistance Fund II.

(d) Said Veterans' Land Fund, to the extent of the moneys attributable to any bonds hereafter issued and sold by said Board may be used by said Board, as is now or may hereafter be provided by law, for the purpose of paying the expenses of surveying, monumenting, road construction, legal fees, recordation fees, advertising and other like costs necessary or incidental to the purchase and sale, or resale, of any lands purchased with any of the moneys attributable to such additional bonds, such expenses to be added to the price of such lands when sold, or resold, by said Board; for the purpose of paying the expenses of issuing, selling, and delivering any such additional bonds; and for the purpose of meeting the expenses of paying the interest or principal due or to become due on any such additional bonds.

(e) For purposes of this section, "veteran" means a person who satisfies the definition of "veteran" as set forth by the laws of the State of Texas.

(f) The Veterans' Housing Assistance Fund shall be administered by the Veterans' Land Board and shall be used for the purpose of making home mortgage loans to veterans for housing within the State of Texas in such quantities, on such terms, at such rates of interest, and under such rules and regulations as may be authorized by law. The expenses of the board in connection with the issuance of the bonds for the benefit of the Veterans' Housing Assistance Fund and the making of the loans may be paid from money in the fund. The principal of and interest on the general obligation bonds authorized by this section for the benefit of the Veterans' Housing Assistance Fund shall be paid out of the money of the fund, but the money of the fund which is not immediately committed to the payment of principal and interest on such bonds, the making of home mortgage loans as herein provided, or the payment of expenses as herein provided may be invested as authorized by law until the money is needed for such purposes.

(g) The Veterans Land Fund shall be used by the Veterans' Land Board to purchase lands situated in the state owned by the United States government, an agency of the United States government, this state, a political subdivision or agency of this state, or a person, firm, or corporation.

(h) Lands purchased and comprising a part of the Veterans' Land Fund are declared to be held for a governmental purpose, but the individual purchasers of those lands shall be subject to taxation to the same extent and in the same manner as are purchasers of lands dedicated to the Permanent School Fund. The lands shall be sold to veterans in quantities, on terms, at prices, and at fixed, variable, floating, or other rates of interest, determined by the Board and in accordance with rules of the Board. Notwithstanding any provisions of this section to the contrary, lands in the Veterans' Land Fund that are offered for sale to veterans and that are not sold may be sold or resold to the purchasers in quantities, on terms, at prices, and at rates of interest determined by the Board and in accordance with rules of the Board.

(i) The expenses of the Board in connection with the issuance of the bonds for the benefit of the Veterans' Land Fund and the purchase and sale of the lands may be paid from money in the Veterans Land Fund.

(j) The Veterans' Land Fund shall consist of:

(1) lands heretofore or hereafter purchased by the Board;

(2) money attributable to bonds heretofore or hereafter issued and sold by the Board for the fund, including proceeds from the issuance and sale of the bonds;

(3) money received from the sale or resale of lands or rights in lands purchased from those proceeds;

(4) money received from the sale or resale of lands or rights in lands purchased with other money attributable to the bonds;

(5) proceeds derived from the sale or other disposition of the Board's interest in contracts for the sale or resale of lands or rights in lands;

(6) interest and penalties received from the sale or resale of lands or rights in lands;

(7) bonuses, income, rents, royalties, and other pecuniary benefits received by the Board from lands;

(8) money received by way of indemnity or forfeiture for the failure of a bidder for the purchase of bonds to comply with the bid and accept and pay for the bonds or for the failure of a bidder for the purchase of lands comprising a part of the Veterans' Land Fund to comply with the bid and accept and pay for the lands;

(9) payments received by the Board under a bond enhancement agreement with respect to the bonds; and

(10) interest received from investments of money in the fund.

(k) The principal of and interest on the general obligation bonds for the benefit of the Veterans' Land Fund, including payments by the Board under a bond enhancement agreement with respect to principal of or interest on the bonds, shall be paid out of the money of the Veterans' Land Fund, but the money in the fund that is not immediately committed to the payment of principal and interest on the bonds, the purchase of lands, or the payment of expenses may be invested as authorized by law until the money is needed for those purposes.

(l) The Veterans' Housing Assistance Fund II is a separate and distinct fund from the Veterans' Housing Assistance Fund. Money in the Veterans' Housing Assistance Fund II shall be administered by the Veterans' Land Board and shall be used to make home mortgage loans to veterans for housing within this state in quantities, on terms, and at fixed, variable, floating, or other rates of interest, determined by the Board and in accordance with rules of the Board. The expenses of the Board in connection with the issuance of the bonds for the benefit of the Veterans' Housing Assistance Fund II and the making of the loans may be paid from money in the Veterans Housing Assistance Fund II.

(m) The Veterans' Housing Assistance Fund II shall consist of:

(1) the Board's interest in home mortgage loans the Board makes to veterans from money in the fund under the Veterans' Housing Assistance Program established by law;

(2) proceeds derived from the sale or other disposition of the Board's interest in home mortgage loans;

(3) money attributable to bonds issued and sold by the Board to provide money for the fund, including the proceeds from the issuance and sale of bonds;

(4) income, rents, and other pecuniary benefits received by the Board as a result of making loans;

(5) money received by way of indemnity or forfeiture for the failure of a bidder for the purchase of bonds to comply with the bid and accept and pay for the bonds;

(6) payments received by the Board under a bond enhancement agreement with respect to the bonds; and

(7) interest received from investments of money.

(n) The principal of and interest on the general obligation bonds for the benefit of the Veterans' Housing Assistance Fund II, including payments by the Board under a bond enhancement agreement with respect to principal of or interest on the bonds, shall be paid out of the money of the Veterans' Housing Assistance Fund II, but the money in the fund that is not immediately committed to the payment of principal and interest on the bonds, the making of home mortgage loans, or the payment of expenses may be invested as authorized by law until the money is needed for those purposes.

(o) The Veterans' Housing Assistance Fund shall consist of:

(1) the Board's interest in home mortgage loans the Board makes to veterans from money in the fund under the Veterans' Housing Assistance Program established by law;

(2) proceeds derived from the sale or other disposition of the Board's interest in home mortgage loans;

(3) money attributable to bonds issued and sold by the Board to provide money for the fund, including proceeds from the issuance and sale of bonds;

(4) income, rents, and other pecuniary benefits received by the Board as a result of making loans;

(5) money received by way of indemnity or forfeiture for the failure of a bidder for the purchase of bonds to comply with the bid and accept and pay for the bonds;

(6) payments received by the Board under a bond enhancement agreement with respect to the bonds; and

(7) interest received from investments of money.

(p) The principal of and interest on the general obligation bonds for the benefit of the Veterans' Housing Assistance Fund, including payments by the Board under a bond enhancement agreement with respect to principal of or interest on the bonds, shall be paid out of money in the Veterans' Housing Assistance Fund.

(q) If there is not enough money in the Veterans' Land Fund, the Veterans' Housing Assistance Fund, or the Veterans' Housing Assistance Fund II, as the case may be, available to pay the principal of and interest on the general obligation bonds benefiting those funds, including money to make payments by the Board under a bond enhancement agreement with respect to principal of or interest on the bonds, there is appropriated out of the first money coming into the treasury in each fiscal year, not otherwise appropriated by this constitution, an amount that is sufficient to pay the principal of and interest on the general obligation bonds that mature or become due during that fiscal year or to make bond enhancement payments with respect to those bonds.

(r) Receipts of all kinds of the Veterans' Land Fund, the Veterans' Housing Assistance Fund, or the Veterans' Housing Assistance Fund II that the Board determines are not required for the payment of principal of and interest on the general obligation bonds benefiting those funds, including payments by the Board under a bond enhancement agreement with respect to principal of or interest on the bonds, may be used by the Board, to the extent not inconsistent with the proceedings authorizing the bonds to:

(1) make temporary transfers to another of those funds to avoid a temporary cash deficiency in that fund or make a transfer to another of those funds for the purposes of that fund;

(2) pay the principal of and interest on general obligation bonds issued to provide money for another of those funds or make bond enhancement payments with respect to the bonds; or

(3) pay the principal of and interest on revenue bonds of the Board or make bond enhancement payments with respect to the bonds.

(s) If the Board determines that assets from the Veterans' Land Fund, the Veterans' Housing Assistance Fund, or the Veterans' Housing Assistance Fund II are not required for the purposes of the fund, the Board may:

(1) transfer the assets to another of those funds;

(2) use the assets to secure revenue bonds issued by the Board;

(3) use the assets to plan and design, operate, maintain, enlarge, or improve veterans cemeteries; or

(4) use the assets to plan and design, construct, acquire, own, operate, maintain, enlarge, improve, furnish, or equip veterans homes.

(t) The revenue bonds shall be special obligations of the Board and payable only from and secured only by receipts of the funds, assets transferred from the funds, and other revenues and assets as determined by the Board and shall not constitute indebtedness of the state or the Veterans' Land Board. The Board may issue revenue bonds from time to time, which bonds may not exceed an aggregate principal amount that the Board determines can be fully retired from the receipts of the funds, the assets transferred from the funds, and the other revenues and assets pledged to the retirement of the revenue bonds. Notwithstanding the rate of interest specified by any other provision of this constitution, revenue bonds shall bear a rate or rates of interest the Board determines. A determination made by the Board under this subsection shall be binding and conclusive as to the matter determined.

(u) The bonds authorized to be issued and sold by the Veterans' Land Board shall be issued and sold in forms and denominations, on terms, at times, in the manner, at places, and in installments the Board determines. The bonds shall bear a rate or rates of interest the Board determines. The bonds shall be incontestable after execution by the Board, approval by the Attorney General of Texas, and delivery to the purchaser or purchasers of the bonds.

(v) This Amendment being intended only to establish a basic framework and not to be a comprehensive treatment of the Veterans' Housing Assistance Program and the Veterans' Land Program, there is hereby reposed in the Legislature full power to implement and effectuate the design and objects of this Amendment, including the power to delegate such duties, responsibilities, functions, and authority to the Veterans' Land Board as it believes necessary.

(w) The Veterans' Land Board may provide for, issue, and sell general obligation bonds of the state for the purpose of selling land to veterans of the state or providing home or land mortgage loans to veterans of the state in a principal amount of outstanding bonds that must at all times be equal to or less than the aggregate principal amount of state general obligation bonds previously authorized for those purposes by prior constitutional amendments. Bonds and other obligations issued or executed under the authority of this subsection may not be included in the computation required by Section 49-j of this article. The bond proceeds shall be deposited in or used to benefit and augment the Veterans' Land Fund, the Veterans' Housing Assistance Fund, or the Veterans' Housing Assistance Fund II, as determined appropriate by the Veterans' Land Board, and shall be administered and invested as provided by law. Payments of principal and interest on the bonds, including payments made under a bond enhancement agreement with respect to principal of or interest on the bonds, shall be made from the sources and in the manner provided by this section for general obligation bonds issued for the benefit of the applicable fund.

Section 49-C. Texas Water Development Board; Bond Issue; Texas Water Development Fund

(a) The Texas Water Development Board, an agency of the State of Texas, shall exercise such powers as necessary under this provision together with such other duties and restrictions as may be prescribed by law. The qualifications, compensation, and number of members of said Board shall be determined by law. They shall be appointed by the Governor with the advice and consent of the Senate in the manner and for such terms as may be prescribed by law.

(b) The Texas Water Development Board shall have the authority to provide for, issue and sell general obligation bonds of the State of Texas as authorized by constitutional amendment or by a debt proposition under Section 49 of this article. The bonds shall be called "Texas Water Development Bonds," shall be executed in such form, denominations and upon such terms as may be prescribed by law, and may be issued in such installments as the Board finds feasible and practical in accomplishing the purpose set forth herein.

(c) All moneys received from the sale of the bonds shall be deposited in a fund hereby created in the State Treasury to be known as the Texas Water Development Fund to be administered (without further appropriation) by the Texas Water Development Board in such manner as prescribed by law.

(d) Such fund shall be used only for the purpose of aiding or making funds available upon such terms and conditions as the Legislature may prescribe, to the various political subdivisions or bodies politic and corporate of the State of Texas including river authorities, conservation and reclamation districts and districts created or organized or authorized to be created or organized under Article XVI, Section 59 or Article III, Section 52, of this Constitution, interstate compact commissions to which the State of Texas is a party and municipal corporations, in the conservation and development of the water resources of this State, including the control, storing and preservation of its storm and flood waters and the waters of its rivers and streams, for all useful and lawful purposes by the acquisition, improvement, extension, or construction of dams, reservoirs and other water storage projects, including any system necessary for the transportation of water from storage to points of treatment and/or distribution, including facilities for transporting water therefrom to wholesale purchasers, or for any one or more of such purposes or methods.

(e) Any or all financial assistance as provided herein shall be repaid with interest upon such terms, conditions and manner of repayment as may be provided by law.

(f) While any of the Texas Water Development Bonds, or any interest on any of such bonds, is outstanding and unpaid, there is hereby appropriated out of the first moneys coming into the Treasury in each fiscal year, not otherwise appropriated by this Constitution, an amount which is sufficient to pay the principal and interest on such bonds that mature or become due during such fiscal year, less the amount in the sinking fund at the close of the prior fiscal year.

(g) The Legislature may provide for the investment of moneys available in the Texas Water Development Fund, and the interest and sinking funds established for the payment of bonds issued by the Texas Water Development Board. Income from such investment shall be used for the purposes prescribed by the Legislature. The Legislature may also make appropriations from the General Revenue Fund for paying administrative expenses of the Board.

(h) From the moneys received by the Texas Water Development Board as repayment of principal for financial assistance or as interest thereon, there shall be deposited in the interest and sinking fund for the bonds sufficient moneys to pay the interest and principal to become due during the ensuing year and sufficient to establish and maintain a reserve in said fund equal to the average annual principal and interest requirements on all outstanding bonds. If any year moneys are received in excess of the foregoing requirements then such excess shall be deposited to the Texas Water Development Fund, and may be used for administrative expenses of the Board and for the same purposes and upon the same terms and conditions prescribed for the proceeds derived from the sale of such State bonds.

(i) All Texas Water Development Bonds shall after approval by the Attorney General, registration by the Comptroller of Public Accounts of the State of Texas, and delivery to the purchasers, be incontestable and shall constitute general obligations of the State of Texas under the Constitution of Texas.

Section 49-D. Development of Reservoirs and Water Facilities; Sale, Transfer, or Lease of Facilities or Public Waters

(a) It is hereby declared to be the policy of the State of Texas to encourage the optimum development of the limited number of feasible sites available for the construction or enlargement of dams and reservoirs for conservation of the public waters of the state, which waters are held in trust for the use and benefit of the public, and to encourage the optimum regional development of systems built for the filtration, treatment, and transmission of water and wastewater. The proceeds from the sale of bonds deposited in the Texas Water Development Fund may be used by the Texas Water Development Board, under such provisions as the Legislature may prescribe by General Law, including the requirement of a permit for storage or beneficial use, for the additional purposes of acquiring and developing storage facilities, and any system or works necessary for the filtration, treatment and transportation of water or waste water, or for any one or more of such purposes or methods, whether or not such a system or works is connected with a reservoir in which the state has a financial interest; provided, however, the Texas Water Development Fund or any other state fund provided for water development, transmission, transfer or filtration shall not be used to finance any project which contemplates or results in the removal from the basin of origin of any surface water necessary to supply the reasonably foreseeable future water requirements for the next ensuing fifty-year period within the river basin of origin, except on a temporary, interim basis.

(b) Under such provisions as the Legislature may prescribe by General Law the Texas Water Development Fund may be used for the conservation and development of water for useful purposes by construction or reconstruction or enlargement of reservoirs constructed or to be constructed or enlarged within the State of Texas or on any stream constituting a boundary of the State of Texas, together with any system or works necessary for the filtration, treatment and/or transportation of water, by any one or more of the following governmental agencies: by the United States of America or any agency, department or instrumentality thereof; by the State of Texas or any agency, department or instrumentality thereof; by political subdivisions or bodies politic and corporate of the state; by interstate compact commissions to which the State of Texas is a party; and by municipal corporations. The Legislature shall provide terms and conditions under which the Texas Water Development Board may sell, transfer or lease, in whole or in part, any reservoir and associated system or works which the Texas Water Development Board has financed in whole or in part.

(c) Under such provisions as the Legislature may prescribe by General Law, the Texas Water Development Board may also execute long-term contracts with the United States or any of its agencies for the acquisition and development of storage facilities in reservoirs constructed or to be constructed by the Federal Government. Such contracts when executed shall constitute general obligations of the State of Texas in the same manner and with the same effect as state bonds issued under the authority of Section 49-c of this article, and the provisions of Section 49-c of this article with respect to payment of principal and interest on state bonds issued shall likewise apply with respect to payment of principal and interest required to be paid by such contracts. If storage facilities are acquired for a term of years, such contracts shall contain provisions for renewal that will protect the state's investment.

(d) The Legislature shall provide terms and conditions for the Texas Water Development Board to sell, transfer or lease, in whole or in part, any acquired facilities or the right to use such facilities at a price not less than the direct cost of the Board in acquiring same; and the Legislature may provide terms and conditions for the Board to sell any unappropriated public waters of the state that might be stored in such facilities. As a prerequisite to the purchase of such storage or water, the applicant therefor shall have secured a valid permit from the state authorizing the acquisition of such storage facilities or the water impounded therein. The money received from any sale, transfer or lease of facilities shall be used to pay principal and interest on state bonds issued or contractual obligations incurred by the Texas Water Development Board, provided that when moneys are sufficient to pay the full amount of indebtedness then outstanding and the full amount of interest to accrue thereon, any further sums received from the sale, transfer or lease of such facilities shall be deposited and used as provided by law. Money received from the sale of water, which shall include standby service, may be used for the operation and maintenance of acquired facilities, and for the payment of principal and interest on debt incurred.

Section 49-d-1. Additional Texas Water Development Bonds

(a) The Texas Water Development Board may issue Texas Water Development Bonds as authorized by constitutional amendment or by a debt proposition under Section 49 of this article to provide grants, loans, or any combination of grants and loans for water quality enhancement purposes as established by the Legislature to political subdivisions or bodies politic and corporate of the State of Texas, including municipal corporations, river authorities, conservation and reclamation districts, and districts created or organized or authorized to be created or organized under Article XVI, Section 59, or Article III, Section 52, of this Constitution, State agencies, and interstate agencies and compact commissions to which the State of Texas is a party, and upon such terms and conditions as the Legislature may authorize by general law. The bonds shall be issued for such terms, in such denominations, form and installments, and upon such conditions as the Legislature may authorize.

(b) The Texas Water Development Fund shall be used for the purposes heretofore permitted by, and subject to the limitations in this Section and Sections 49-c and 49-d; provided, however, that the financial assistance may be made subject only to the availability of funds.

Section 49-D-2. Additional Bonding Authority of Texas Water Development Board for Flood Control

The Texas Water Development Board may issue Texas Water Development Bonds for flood control projects and for any acquisition or construction necessary to achieve structural and nonstructural flood control purposes.

Section 49-D-3. Creation and Use of Special Funds for Water Projects

(a) The legislature by law may create one or more special funds in the state treasury for use for or in aid of water conservation, water development, water quality enhancement, flood control, drainage, subsidence control, recharge, chloride control, agricultural soil and water conservation, desalinization or any combination of those purposes, may make money in a special fund available to cities, counties, special governmental districts and authorities, and other political subdivisions of the state for use for the purposes for which the fund was created by grants, loans, or any other means, and may appropriate money to any of the special funds to carry out the purposes of this section.

(b) Money deposited in a special fund created under this section may not be used to finance or aid any project that contemplates or results in the removal from the basin of origin of any surface water necessary to supply the reasonably foreseeable water requirements for the next ensuing 50-year period within the river basin of origin, except on a temporary, interim basis.

Section 49-D-4. Bond Insurance Program for Water Projects

(a) In addition to other programs authorized by this constitution, the legislature by law may provide for the creation, administration, and implementation of a bond insurance program to which the state pledges its general credit in an amount not to exceed $250 million to insure the payment in whole or in part of the principal of and interest on bonds or other obligations that are issued by cities, counties, special governmental districts and authorities, and other political subdivisions of the state as defined by law for use for or in aid of water conservation, water development, water quality enhancement, flood control, drainage, recharge, chloride control, desalinization, or any combination of those purposes.

(b) The legislature by law shall designate the state agency to administer the bond insurance program and may authorize that agency to execute insurance contracts that bind the state to pay the principal of and interest on the bonds if the bonds are in default or the bonds are subject to impending default, subject to the limits provided by this section and by law.

(c) The payment by the state of any insurance commitment made under this section must be made from the first money coming into the state treasury that is not otherwise dedicated by this constitution.

(d) Notwithstanding the total amount of bonds insured under this section, the total amount paid and not recovered by the state under this section, excluding the costs of administration, may not exceed $250 million.

(e) Except on a two-thirds vote of the members elected to each house of the legislature, the ratio of bonds insured to the total liability of the state must be two to one.

(f) Except on a two-thirds vote of the members elected to each house of the legislature, the state agency administering the bond insurance program may not authorize bond insurance coverage under the program in any state fiscal year that exceeds a total of $100 million.

(g) Unless authorized to continue by a two-thirds vote of the members elected to each house, this section and the bond insurance program authorized by this section expire on the sixth anniversary of the date on which this section becomes a part of the constitution. However, bond insurance issued before the expiration of this section and the program is not affected by the expiration of this section and the program and remains in effect according to its terms, and the state is required to fulfill all of the terms of that previously issued insurance.

Section 49-D-5. Extension of Benefits to Nonprofit Water Supply Corporations

For the purpose of any program established or authorized by this article and administered by the Texas Water Development Board, the legislature by law may extend any benefits to nonprofit water supply corporations that it may extend to a district created or organized under Article XVI, Section 59, of this constitution.

Section 49-D-6. Review and Approval of Texas Water Development Bonds

The legislature may require review and approval of the issuance of Texas Water Development Bonds, of the use of the bond proceeds, or of the rules adopted by an agency to govern use of the bond proceeds. Notwithstanding any other provision of this constitution, any entity created or directed to conduct this review and approval may include members or appointees of members of the executive, legislative, and judicial departments of state government.

Section 49-D-7. Use of Proceeds of Texas Water Development Bonds

(a) The Texas Water Development Board may use the proceeds of Texas water development bonds issued for the purposes provided by Section 49-c of this article for the additional purpose of providing financial assistance, on terms and conditions provided by law, to various political subdivisions and bodies politic and corporate of the state and to nonprofit water supply corporations to provide for acquisition, improvement, extension, or construction of water supply projects that involve the distribution of water to points of delivery to wholesale or retail customers.

(b) The legislature may provide by law for subsidized loans and grants from the proceeds of Texas water development bonds to provide wholesale and retail water and wastewater facilities to economically distressed areas of the state as defined by law, provided, the principal amount of bonds that may be issued for the purposes under this subsection may not exceed $250 million. Separate accounts shall be established in the water development fund for administering the proceeds of bonds issued for purposes under this subsection, and an interest and sinking fund separate from and not subject to the limitations of the interest and sinking fund created for other Texas water development bonds is established in the State Treasury to be used for paying the principal of and interest on bonds for the purposes of this subsection. While any of the bonds authorized for the purposes of this subsection or any of the interest on those bonds is outstanding and unpaid, there is appropriated out of the first money coming into the State Treasury in each fiscal year, not otherwise appropriated by this constitution, an amount that is sufficient to pay the principal of and interest on those bonds issued for the purposes under this subsection that mature or become due during that fiscal year.

Section 49-D-8. Texas Water Development Fund II; Additional Bonds; Sale, Transfer, or Lease of Facilities or Public Waters

(a) The Texas Water Development Fund II is in the state treasury as a fund separate and distinct from the Texas Water Development Fund established under Section 49-c of this article. Money in the Texas Water Development Fund II shall be administered without further appropriation by the Texas Water Development Board and shall be used for any one or more of the purposes currently or formerly authorized by Sections 49-c, 49-d, 49-d-1, 49-d-2, 49-d-5, 49-d-6, and 49-d-7 of this article, as determined by the Texas Water Development Board. Separate accounts shall be established in the Texas Water Development Fund II for administering proceedings related to the purposes described in Section 49-d of this article, the purposes described in Subsection (b) of Section 49-d-7 of this article, and all other authorized purposes. The Texas Water Development Board is hereby authorized, at its determination, to issue general obligation bonds for one or more accounts of the Texas Water Development Fund II in an aggregate principal amount equal to the amount of bonds previously authorized pursuant to former Section 49-d-6 and Sections 49-d-2 and 49-d-7 of this article less the amount of bonds issued pursuant to those sections to augment the Texas Water Development Fund and the amount of bonds issued to augment the Texas Water Development Fund II. Nothing in this section, however, shall grant to the Texas Water Development Board the authority to issue bonds in excess of the total amount of those previously authorized bonds or to issue bonds for purposes described in Subsection (b) of Section 49-d-7 of this article in excess of $250 million. The expenses of the Texas Water Development Board in connection with the issuance of bonds for an account of the Texas Water Development Fund II and administration of such account may be paid from money in such account.

(b) The Texas Water Development Board is hereby authorized, at its determination, to issue general obligation bonds for one or more accounts of the Texas Water Development Fund II in order to refund outstanding bonds previously issued to augment the Texas Water Development Fund, as long as the principal amount of the refunding bonds does not exceed the outstanding principal amount of the refunded bonds, and to refund the general obligation of the State of Texas under long-term contracts entered into by the Texas Water Development Board with the United States or any of its agencies under authority granted by Section 49-d of this article, as long as the principal amount of the refunding bonds does not exceed the principal amount of the contractual obligation of the Texas Water Development Board. Money and assets in the Texas Water Development Fund attributable to such refunding bonds shall be transferred to the appropriate account of the Texas Water Development Fund II, as determined by the Texas Water Development Board, to the extent not inconsistent with the proceedings authorizing any outstanding bonds issued to augment the Texas Water Development Fund and the terms of any long-term contracts entered into by the Texas Water Development Board with the United States or any of its agencies. In addition, the Texas Water Development Board may transfer other moneys and assets in the Texas Water Development Fund to the appropriate account of the Texas Water Development Fund II, as determined by the Texas Water Development Board, without the necessity of issuing refunding bonds to effect the transfer, to the extent not inconsistent with the proceedings authorizing any outstanding bonds issued to augment the Texas Water Development Fund. Further, at such time as all bonds issued to augment the Texas Water Development Fund and all such contractual obligations have been paid or otherwise discharged, all money and assets in the Texas Water Development Fund shall be transferred to the credit of the Texas Water Development Fund II and deposited to the accounts therein, as determined by the Texas Water Development Board.

(c) Subject to the limitations set forth in Section 49-d of this article, the legislature shall provide terms and conditions under which the Texas Water Development Board may sell, transfer, or lease, in whole or in part, facilities held for the account established within the Texas Water Development Fund II for administering proceedings related to the purposes described in Section 49-d of this article, and the legislature may provide terms and conditions under which the Texas Water Development Board may sell any unappropriated public waters of the state that may be stored in such facilities. Money received from any sale, transfer, or lease of such facilities or water shall be credited to the account established within the Texas Water Development Fund II for the purpose of administering proceedings related to the purposes described in Section 49-d of this article.

(d) Each account of the Texas Water Development Fund II shall consist of:

(1) the Texas Water Development Board's rights to receive repayment of financial assistance provided from such account, together with any evidence of such rights;

(2) money received from the sale or other disposition of the Texas Water Development Board's rights to receive repayment of such financial assistance;

(3) money received as repayment of such financial assistance;

(4) money and assets attributable to bonds issued and sold by the Texas Water Development Board for such account, including money and assets transferred from the Texas Water Development Fund pursuant to this section;

(5) money deposited in such account pursuant to Subsection (c) of this section;

(6) payments received by the Texas Water Development Board under a bond enhancement agreement as authorized by law with respect to bonds issued for such account; and

(7) interest and other income received from investment of money in such account.

(e) Notwithstanding the other provisions of this article, the principal of and interest on the general obligation bonds issued for an account of the Texas Water Development Fund II, including payments by the Texas Water Development Board under a bond enhancement agreement as authorized by law with respect to principal of or interest on such bonds, shall be paid out of such account, but the money in such account that is not immediately committed to the purposes of such account or the payment of expenses may be invested as authorized by law until the money is needed for those purposes. If there is not enough money in any account available to pay the principal of and interest on the general obligation bonds issued for such account, including money to make payments by the Texas Water Development Board under a bond enhancement agreement as authorized by law with respect to principal of or interest on such bonds, there is appropriated out of the first money coming into the state treasury in each fiscal year not otherwise appropriated by this constitution an amount that is sufficient to pay the principal of and interest on such general obligation bonds that mature or become due during that fiscal year or to make bond enhancement payments with respect to those bonds.

(f) The general obligation bonds authorized by this section may be issued as bonds, notes, or other obligations as permitted by law and shall be sold in forms and denominations, on terms, at times, in the manner, at places, and in installments, all as determined by the Texas Water Development Board. The bonds shall bear a rate or rates of interest the Texas Water Development Board determines. The bonds authorized by this section shall be incontestable after execution by the Texas Water Development Board, approval by the attorney general, and delivery to the purchaser or purchasers of the bonds.

(g) This section being intended only to establish a basic framework and not to be a comprehensive treatment of the Texas Water Development Fund II, there is hereby reposed in the legislature full power to implement and effectuate the design and objects of this section, including the power to delegate such duties, responsibilities, functions, and authority to the Texas Water Development Board as it believes necessary.

(h) The Texas Water Development Fund II, including any account in that fund, may not be used to finance or aid any project that contemplates or results in the removal from the basin of origin of any surface water necessary to supply the reasonably foreseeable future water requirements for the next ensuing 50-year period within the river basin of origin, except on a temporary, interim basis.

Section 49-D-9. Issuance of Additional General Obligation Bonds for Texas Water Development Fund II

(a) The Texas Water Development Board may issue additional general obligation bonds, at its determination, for one or more accounts of the Texas Water Development Fund II, in an amount not to exceed $2 billion. Of the additional general obligation bonds authorized to be issued, $50 million of those bonds shall be used for the water infrastructure fund as provided by law.

(b) Section 49-d-8 of this article applies to the bonds authorized by this section. The limitation in Section 49-d-8 of this article that the Texas Water Development Board may not issue bonds in excess of the aggregate principal amount of previously authorized bonds does not apply to the bonds authorized by and issued under this section.

(c) A limitation on the percentage of state participation in any single project imposed by this article does not apply to a project funded with the proceeds of bonds issued under the authority of

Section 49-d-8 of this article or this section.

Section 49-D-10. Additional Bonds for Financial Assistance to Economically Distressed Areas

(a) The Texas Water Development Board may issue additional general obligation bonds, at its determination, for the economically distressed areas program account of the Texas Water Development Fund II, in an amount not to exceed $250 million. The bonds shall be used to provide financial assistance to economically distressed areas of the state as defined by law.

(b) Section 49-d-8(e) of this article applies to the bonds authorized by this section.

Section 49-D-11. Continuing Authorization for Additional Bonds for Texas Water Development Fund II

(a) In addition to the bonds authorized by the other provisions of this article, the Texas Water Development Board may issue general obligation bonds, at its determination and on a continuing basis, for one or more accounts of the Texas Water Development Fund II in amounts such that the aggregate principal amount of the bonds issued by the board under this section that are outstanding at any time does not exceed $6 billion.

(b) Section 49-d-8 of this article applies to the bonds authorized by this section. The limitation in Section 49-d-8 of this article that the Texas Water Development Board may not issue bonds in excess of the aggregate principal amount of previously authorized bonds does not apply to the bonds authorized by and issued under this section.

(c) A limitation on the percentage of state participation in any single project imposed by this article does not apply to a project funded with the proceeds of bonds issued under the authority of this section or Section 49-d-8 of this article.

Section 49-D-12. State Water Implementation Fund for Texas

(a) The State Water Implementation Fund for Texas is created as a special fund in the state treasury outside the general revenue fund. Money in the State Water Implementation Fund for Texas shall be administered, without further appropriation, by the Texas Water Development Board or that board's successor in function and shall be used for the purpose of implementing the state water plan that is adopted as required by general law by the Texas Water Development Board or that board's successor in function. Separate accounts may be established in the State Water Implementation Fund for Texas as necessary to administer the fund or authorized projects.

(b) The legislature by general law may authorize the Texas Water Development Board or that board's successor in function to enter into bond enhancement agreements to provide additional security for general obligation bonds or revenue bonds of the Texas Water Development Board or that board's successor in function, the proceeds of which are used to finance state water plan projects. Bond enhancement agreements must be payable solely from the State Water Implementation Fund for Texas; provided, however, the bond enhancement agreements may not exceed an amount that can be fully supported by the State Water Implementation Fund for Texas. Any amount paid under a bond enhancement agreement may be repaid as provided by general law; provided, however, any repayment may not cause general obligation bonds that are issued under Sections 49-d-9 and 49-d-11 of this article and that are payable from the fund or account receiving the bond enhancement payment to be no longer self-supporting for purposes of Section 49-j(b) of this article. Payments under a bond enhancement agreement entered into pursuant to this section may not be a constitutional state debt payable from general revenues of the state.

(c) The legislature by general law may authorize the Texas Water Development Board or that board's successor in function to use the State Water Implementation Fund for Texas to finance, including by direct loan, water projects included in the state water plan.

(d) The Texas Water Development Board or that board's successor in function shall provide written notice to the Legislative Budget Board or that board's successor in function before each bond enhancement agreement or loan agreement entered into pursuant to this section has been executed by the Texas Water Development Board or that board's successor in function and shall provide a copy of the proposed agreement to the Legislative Budget Board or that board's successor in function for approval. The proposed agreement shall be considered to be approved unless the Legislative Budget Board or that board's successor in function issues a written disapproval not later than the 21st day after the date on which the staff of that board receives the submission.

(e) The State Water Implementation Fund for Texas consists of:

(1) money transferred or deposited to the credit of the fund by general law, including money from any source transferred or deposited to the credit of the fund at the discretion of the Texas Water Development Board or that board's successor in function as authorized by general law;

(2) the proceeds of any fee or tax imposed by this state that by statute is dedicated for deposit to the credit of the fund;

(3) any other revenue that the legislature by statute dedicates for deposit to the credit of the fund;

(4) investment earnings and interest earned on amounts credited to the fund; and

(5) money transferred to the fund under a bond enhancement agreement from another fund or account to which money from the fund was transferred under a bond enhancement agreement, as authorized by general law.

(f) The legislature by general law shall provide for the manner in which the assets of the State Water Implementation Fund for Texas may be used, subject to the limitations provided by this section. The legislature by general law may provide for costs of investment of the State Water Implementation Fund for Texas to be paid from that fund.

(g) As provided by general law, each fiscal year the Texas Water Development Board or that board's successor in function shall set aside from amounts on deposit in the State Water Implementation Fund for Texas an amount that is sufficient to make payments under bond enhancement agreements that become due during that fiscal year.

(h) Any dedication or appropriation of amounts on deposit in the State Water Implementation Fund for Texas may not be modified so as to impair any outstanding obligation under a bond enhancement agreement secured by a pledge of those amounts unless provisions have been made for a full discharge of the bond enhancement agreement.

(i) Money in the State Water Implementation Fund for Texas is dedicated by this constitution for purposes of Section 22, Article VIII, of this constitution and an appropriation from the economic stabilization fund to the credit of the State Water Implementation Fund for Texas is an appropriation of state tax revenues dedicated by this constitution for the purposes of Section 22, Article VIII, of this constitution.

(j) This section being intended only to establish a basic framework and not to be a comprehensive treatment of the State Water Implementation Fund for Texas, there is hereby reposed in the legislature full power to implement and effectuate the design and objects of this section, including the power to delegate such duties, responsibilities, functions, and authority to the Texas Water Development Board or that board's successor in function as the legislature believes necessary.

Section 49-D-13. State Water Implementation Revenue Fund For Texas

(a) The State Water Implementation Revenue Fund for Texas is created as a special fund in the state treasury outside the general revenue fund. Money in the State Water Implementation Revenue Fund for Texas shall be administered, without further appropriation, by the Texas Water Development Board or that board's successor in function and shall be used for the purpose of implementing the state water plan that is adopted as required by general law by the Texas Water Development Board or that board's successor in function. Separate accounts may be established in the State Water Implementation Revenue Fund for Texas as necessary to administer the fund or authorized projects.

(b) The legislature by general law may authorize the Texas Water Development Board or that board's successor in function to issue bonds and enter into related credit agreements that are payable from all revenues available to the State Water Implementation Revenue Fund for Texas.

(c) The Texas Water Development Board or that board's successor in function shall provide written notice to the Legislative Budget Board or that board's successor in function before issuing a bond pursuant to this section or entering into a related credit agreement that is payable from revenue deposited to the credit of the State Water Implementation Revenue Fund for Texas and shall provide a copy of the proposed bond or agreement to the Legislative Budget Board or that board's successor in function for approval. The proposed bond or agreement shall be considered to be approved unless the Legislative Budget Board or that board's successor in function issues a written disapproval not later than the 21st day after the date on which the staff of that board receives the submission.

(d) The State Water Implementation Revenue Fund for Texas consists of:

(1) money transferred or deposited to the credit of the fund by general law, including money from any source transferred or deposited to the credit of the fund at the discretion of the Texas Water Development Board or that board's successor in function as authorized by general law;

(2) the proceeds of any fee or tax imposed by this state that by statute is dedicated for deposit to the credit of the fund;

(3) any other revenue that the legislature by statute dedicates for deposit to the credit of the fund;

(4) investment earnings and interest earned on amounts credited to the fund;

(5) the proceeds from the sale of bonds, including revenue bonds issued under this section by the Texas Water Development Board or that board's successor in function for the purpose of providing money for the fund; and

(6) money disbursed to the fund from the State Water Implementation Fund for Texas as authorized by general law.

(e) The legislature by general law shall provide for the manner in which the assets of the State Water Implementation Revenue Fund for Texas may be used, subject to the limitations provided by this section. The legislature by general law may provide for costs of investment of the State Water Implementation Revenue Fund for Texas to be paid from that fund.

(f) In each fiscal year in which amounts become due under the bonds or agreements authorized by this section, the Texas Water Development Board or that board's successor in function shall transfer from revenue deposited to the credit of the State Water Implementation Revenue Fund for Texas in that fiscal year an amount that is sufficient to pay:

(1) the principal of and interest on the bonds that mature or become due during the fiscal year; and

(2) any cost related to the bonds, including payments under related credit agreements that become due during that fiscal year.

(g) Any obligations authorized by general law to be issued by the Texas Water Development Board or that board's successor in function pursuant to this section shall be special obligations payable solely from amounts in the State Water Implementation Revenue Fund for Texas. Obligations issued by the Texas Water Development Board or that board's successor in function pursuant to this section may not be a constitutional state debt payable from the general revenue of the state.

(h) Any dedication or appropriation of revenue to the credit of the State Water Implementation Revenue Fund for Texas may not be modified so as to impair any outstanding bonds secured by a pledge of that revenue unless provisions have been made for a full discharge of those bonds.

(i) Money in the State Water Implementation Revenue Fund for Texas is dedicated by this constitution for purposes of Section 22, Article VIII, of this constitution.

(j) This section being intended only to establish a basic framework and not to be a comprehensive treatment of the State Water Implementation Revenue Fund for Texas, there is hereby reposed in the legislature full power to implement and effectuate the design and objects of this section, including the power to delegate such duties, responsibilities, functions, and authority to the Texas Water Development Board or that board's successor in function as the legislature believes necessary.

Section 49-E. Texas Park Development Fund; Bonds

(a) The Parks and Wildlife Department, or its successor vested with the powers, duties, and authority which deals with the operation, maintenance, and improvement of State Parks, shall have the authority to provide for, issue and sell general obligation bonds of the State of Texas in an amount authorized by constitutional amendment or by a debt proposition under Section 49 of this article. The bonds shall be called "Texas Park Development Bonds," shall be executed in such form, denominations, and upon such terms as may be prescribed by law, shall bear a rate or rates of interest as may be fixed by the Parks and Wildlife Department or its successor, not to exceed the maximum prescribed by Section 65 of this article, and may be issued in such installments as said Parks and Wildlife Department, or its said successor, finds feasible and practical in accomplishing the purpose set forth herein.

(b) All moneys received from the sale of said bonds shall be deposited in a fund hereby created with the Comptroller of Public Accounts of the State of Texas to be known as the Texas Park Development Fund to be administered (without further appropriation) by the said Parks and Wildlife Department, or its said successor, in such manner as prescribed by law.

(c) Such fund shall be used by said Parks and Wildlife Department, or its said successor, under such provisions as the Legislature may prescribe by general law, for the purposes of acquiring lands from the United States, or any governmental agency thereof, from any governmental agency of the State of Texas, or from any person, firm, or corporation, for State Park Sites and for developing said sites as State Parks.

(d) While any of the bonds, or any interest on any such bonds, is outstanding and unpaid, there is hereby appropriated out of the first moneys coming into the Treasury in each fiscal year, not otherwise appropriated by this Constitution, an amount which is sufficient to pay the principal and interest on such bonds that mature or become due during such fiscal year, less the amount in the interest and sinking fund at the close of the prior fiscal year, which includes any receipts derived during the prior fiscal year by said Parks and Wildlife Department, or its said successor, from admission charges to State Parks, as the Legislature may prescribe by general law.

(e) The Legislature may provide for the investment of moneys available in the Texas Park Development Fund and the interest and sinking fund established for the payment of bonds issued by said Parks and Wildlife Department, or its said successor. Income from such investment shall be used for the purposes prescribed by the Legislature.

(f) From the moneys received by said Parks and Wildlife Department, or its said successor, from the sale of the bonds issued hereunder, there shall be deposited in the interest and sinking fund for the bonds authorized by this section sufficient moneys to pay the interest to become due during the State fiscal year in which the bonds were issued. After all bonds have been fully paid with interest, or after there are on deposit in the interest and sinking fund sufficient moneys to pay all future maturities of principal and interest, additional moneys received from admission charges to State Parks shall be deposited to the State Parks Fund, or any successor fund which may be established by the Legislature as a depository for Park revenue earned by said Parks and Wildlife Department, or its said successor.

(g) All bonds issued hereunder shall after approval by the Attorney General, registration by the Comptroller of Public Accounts of the State of Texas, and delivery to the purchasers, be incontestable and shall constitute general obligations of the

State of Texas under the Constitution of Texas.

Section 49-F. Bonds for Financial Assistance to Purchase Farm and Ranch Land and for Rural Economic Development

(a) The legislature by general law may provide for the issuance of general obligation bonds of the state, the proceeds of which shall be used to make loans and provide other financing assistance for the purchase of farm and ranch land.

(b) Except as provided by Subsection (g) of this section, all money received from the sale of the bonds shall be deposited in a fund created with the comptroller of public accounts to be known as the farm and ranch finance program fund. This fund shall be administered by the Texas Agricultural Finance Authority in the manner prescribed by law.

(c) Section 65(b) of this article applies to the payment of interest on the bonds.

(d) The principal amount of bonds outstanding at one time may not exceed $500 million.

(e) While any of the bonds authorized by this section or any interest on those bonds is outstanding and unpaid, there is appropriated out of the first money coming into the treasury in each fiscal year not otherwise appropriated by this constitution an amount that is sufficient to pay the principal and interest on the bonds that mature or become due during the fiscal year less the amount in the interest and sinking fund at the close of the prior fiscal year.

(f) The bonds shall be approved by the attorney general and registered with the comptroller of public accounts. The bonds, when approved and registered, are general obligations of the state and are incontestable.

(g) Notwithstanding Subsection (a) of this section, the proceeds of $200 million of the bonds authorized by this section may be used for the purposes provided by Section 49-i of this article and for other rural economic development programs, and the proceeds of bonds issued for those purposes under this subsection shall be deposited in the Texas agricultural fund, to be administered in the same manner that proceeds of bonds issued under Section 49-i of this article are administered.

Section 49-G. Superconducting Super Collider Fund

Repealed

Section 49-G. Economic Stabilization Fund; Allocation of Certain Oil and Gas Production Tax Revenue

(a) The economic stabilization fund is established as a special fund in the state treasury.

(b) The comptroller shall, not later than the 90th day of each biennium, transfer to the economic stabilization fund one-half of any unencumbered positive balance of general revenues on the last day of the preceding biennium. If necessary, the comptroller shall reduce the amount transferred in proportion to the other amounts prescribed by this section to prevent the amount in the fund from exceeding the limit in effect for that biennium under Subsection (g) of this section.

(c) Not later than the 90th day of each fiscal year, the comptroller of public accounts shall transfer from the general revenue fund to the economic stabilization fund and the state highway fund the sum of the amounts described by Subsections (d) and (e) of this section, to be allocated as provided by Subsections (c-1) and (c-2) of this section. However, if necessary and notwithstanding the allocations prescribed by Subsections (c-1) and (c-2) of this section, the comptroller shall reduce proportionately the amounts described by Subsections (d) and (e) of this section to be transferred and allocated to the economic stabilization fund to prevent the amount in that fund from exceeding the limit in effect for that biennium under Subsection (g) of this section. Revenue transferred to the state highway fund under this subsection may be used only for constructing, maintaining, and acquiring rights-of-way for public roadways other than toll roads.

(c-1) Of the sum of the amounts described by Subsections (d) and (e) of this section and required to be transferred from the general revenue fund under Subsection (c) of this section, the comptroller shall allocate one-half to the economic stabilization fund and the remainder to the state highway fund, except as provided by Subsection (c-2) of this section.

(c-2) The legislature by general law shall provide for a procedure by which the allocation of the sum of the amounts described by Subsections (d) and (e) of this section may be adjusted to provide for a transfer to the economic stabilization fund of an amount greater than the allocation provided for under Subsection (c-1) of this section with the remainder of that sum, if any, allocated for transfer to the state highway fund. The allocation made as provided by that general law is binding on the comptroller for the purposes of the transfers required by Subsection (c) of this section.

(d) If in the preceding year the state received from oil production taxes a net amount greater than the net amount of oil production taxes received by the state in the fiscal year ending August 31, 1987, the comptroller shall transfer under Subsection (c) of this section and allocate in accordance with Subsections (c-1) and (c-2) of this section an amount equal to 75 percent of the difference between those amounts. The comptroller shall retain the remaining 25 percent of the difference as general revenue. In computing the net amount of oil production taxes received, the comptroller may not consider refunds paid as a result of oil overcharge litigation.

(e) If in the preceding year the state received from gas production taxes a net amount greater than the net amount of gas production taxes received by the state in the fiscal year ending August 31, 1987, the comptroller shall transfer under Subsection (c) of this section and allocate in accordance with Subsections (c-1) and (c-2) of this section an amount equal to 75 percent of the difference between those amounts. The comptroller shall retain the remaining 25 percent of the difference as general revenue. For the purposes of this subsection, the comptroller shall adjust the computation of revenues to reflect only 12 months of collection.

(f) The legislature may appropriate additional amounts to the economic stabilization fund.

(g) During each fiscal biennium, the amount in the economic stabilization fund may not exceed an amount equal to 10 percent of the total amount, excluding investment income, interest income, and amounts borrowed from special funds, deposited in general revenue during the preceding biennium.

(h) In preparing an estimate of anticipated revenues for a succeeding biennium as required by Article III, Section 49a, of this constitution, the comptroller shall estimate the amount of the transfers that will be made under Subsections (b), (d), and (e) of this section. The comptroller shall deduct that amount from the estimate of anticipated revenues as if the transfers were made on August 31 of that fiscal year.

(i) The comptroller shall credit to general revenue interest due to the economic stabilization fund that would result in an amount in the economic stabilization fund that exceeds the limit in effect under Subsection (g) of this section.

(j) The comptroller may transfer money from the economic stabilization fund to general revenue to prevent or eliminate a temporary cash deficiency in general revenue. The comptroller shall return the amount transferred to the economic stabilization fund as soon as practicable, but not later than August 31 of each odd-numbered year. The comptroller shall allocate the depository interest as if the transfers had not been made. If the comptroller submits a statement to the governor and the legislature under Article III, Section 49a, of this constitution when money from the economic stabilization fund is in general revenue, the comptroller shall state that the transferred money is not available for appropriation from general revenue.

(k) Amounts from the economic stabilization fund may be appropriated during a regular legislative session only for a purpose for which an appropriation from general revenue was made by the preceding legislature and may be appropriated in a special session only for a purpose for which an appropriation from general revenue was made in a preceding legislative session of the same legislature. An appropriation from the economic stabilization fund may be made only if the comptroller certifies that appropriations from general revenue made by the preceding legislature for the current biennium exceed available general revenues and cash balances for the remainder of that biennium. The amount of an appropriation from the economic stabilization fund may not exceed the difference between the comptroller's estimate of general revenue for the current biennium at the time the comptroller receives for certification the bill making the appropriation and the amount of general revenue appropriations for that biennium previously certified by the comptroller. Appropriations from the economic stabilization fund under this subsection may not extend beyond the last day of the current biennium. An appropriation from the economic stabilization fund must be approved by a three-fifths vote of the members present in each house of the legislature.

(l) If an estimate of anticipated revenues for a succeeding biennium prepared by the comptroller pursuant to Article III, Section 49a, of this constitution is less than the revenues that are estimated at the same time by the comptroller to be available for the current biennium, the legislature may, by a three-fifths vote of the members present in each house, appropriate for the succeeding biennium from the economic stabilization fund an amount not to exceed this difference. Following each fiscal year, the actual amount of revenue shall be computed, and if the estimated difference exceeds the actual difference, the comptroller shall transfer the amount necessary from general revenue to the economic stabilization fund so that the actual difference shall not be exceeded. If all or a portion of the difference in revenue from one biennium to the next results, at least in part, from a change in a tax rate or base adopted by the legislature, the computation of revenue difference shall be adjusted to the amount that would have been available had the rate or base not been changed.

(m) In addition to the appropriation authority provided by Subsections (k) and (l) of this section, the legislature may, by a two-thirds vote of the members present in each house, appropriate amounts from the economic stabilization fund at any time and for any purpose.

(n) Money appropriated from the economic stabilization fund is subject to being withheld or transferred, within any limits provided by statute, by any person or entity authorized to exercise the power granted by Article XVI, Section 69, of this constitution.

(o) In this section, "net" means the amount of money that is equal to the difference between gross collections and refunds before the comptroller allocates the receipts as provided by law.

Section 49-H. Bond Issuance for Correctional and Statewide Law Enforcement Facilities and for Institutions for Persons With Intellectual and Developmental Disabilities

(a) In amounts authorized by constitutional amendment or by a debt proposition under Section 49 of this article, the legislature may provide for the issuance of general obligation bonds and the use of the bond proceeds for acquiring, constructing, or equipping new facilities or for major repair or renovation of existing facilities of corrections institutions, including youth corrections institutions, and mental health and mental retardation institutions. The legislature may require the review and approval of the issuance of the bonds and the projects to be financed by the bond proceeds. Notwithstanding any other provision of this constitution, the issuer of the bonds or any entity created or directed to review and approve projects may include members or appointees of members of the executive, legislative, and judicial departments of state government.

(b) Bonds issued under this section constitute a general obligation of the state. While any of the bonds or interest on the bonds is outstanding and unpaid, there is appropriated out of the first money coming into the treasury in each fiscal year, not otherwise appropriated by this constitution, the amount sufficient to pay the principal of and interest on the bonds that mature or become due during the fiscal year, less any amount in any sinking fund at the end of the preceding fiscal year that is pledged to payment of the bonds or interest.

(c) In addition to the purposes authorized under Subsection (a), the legislature may authorize the issuance of the general obligation bonds for acquiring, constructing, or equipping:

(1) new statewide law enforcement facilities and for major repair or renovation of existing facilities; and

(2) new prisons and substance abuse felony punishment facilities to confine criminals and major repair or renovation of existing facilities of those institutions, and for the acquisition of, major repair to, or renovation of other facilities for use as state prisons or substance abuse felony punishment facilities.

Section 49-I. Texas Agricultural Fund; Rural Micro-enterprise Development Fund

(a) The legislature by law may provide for the issuance of general obligation bonds of the state for the purpose of providing money to establish a Texas agricultural fund in the state treasury to be used without further appropriation in the manner provided by law and for the purpose of providing money to establish a rural micro-enterprise development fund in the state treasury to be used without further appropriation in the manner provided by law. The Texas agricultural fund shall be used only to provide financial assistance to develop, increase, improve, or expand the production, processing, marketing, or export of crops or products grown or produced primarily in this state by agricultural businesses domiciled in the state. The rural microenterprise development fund shall be used only in furtherance of a program established by the legislature to foster and stimulate the creation and expansion of small businesses in rural areas. The financial assistance offered by both funds may include loan guarantees, insurance, coinsurance, loans, and indirect loans or purchases or acceptances of assignments of loans or other obligations.

(b) The principal amount of bonds outstanding at one time may not exceed $25 million for the Texas agricultural fund and $5 million for the rural micro-enterprise development fund.

(c) The legislature may establish an interest and sinking account and other accounts within the Texas agricultural fund and within the rural micro-enterprise development fund. The legislature may provide for the investment of bond proceeds and of the interest and sinking accounts. Income from the investment of money in the funds that is not immediately committed to the payment of the principal of and interest on the bonds or the provision of financial assistance shall be used to create new employment and business opportunities in the state through the diversification and expansion of agricultural or rural small businesses, as provided by the legislature.

(d) Bonds authorized under this section constitute a general obligation of the state. While any of the bonds or interest on the bonds is outstanding and unpaid, there is appropriated out of the first money coming into the treasury in each fiscal year, not otherwise appropriated by this constitution, the amount sufficient to pay the principal of and interest on the bonds that mature or become due during the fiscal year, less any amounts in the interest and sinking accounts at the close of the preceding fiscal year that are pledged to payment of the bonds or interest.

Section 49-J. Limit on State Debt Payable from General Revenue Fund

(a) The legislature may not authorize additional state debt if the resulting annual debt service exceeds the limitation imposed by this section. The maximum annual debt service in any fiscal year on state debt payable from the general revenue fund may not exceed five percent of an amount equal to the average of the amount of general revenue fund revenues, excluding revenues constitutionally dedicated for purposes other than payment of state debt, for the three preceding fiscal years.

(b) For purposes of this section, "state debt payable from the general revenue fund" means general obligation and revenue bonds, including authorized but unissued bonds, and lease-purchase agreements in an amount greater than $250,000, which bonds or lease purchase agreements are designed to be repaid with the general revenues of the state. The term does not include bonds that, although backed by the full faith or credit of the state, are reasonably expected to be paid from other revenue sources and that are not expected to create a general revenue draw. Bonds or lease purchase agreements that pledge the full faith and credit of the state are considered to be reasonably expected to be paid from other revenue sources if they are designed to receive revenues other than state general revenues sufficient to cover their debt service over the life of the bonds or agreement. If those bonds or agreements, or any portion of the bonds or agreements, subsequently requires use of the state's general revenue for payment, the bonds or agreements, or portion of the bonds or agreements, is considered to be a "state debt payable from the general revenue fund" under this section, until:

(1) the bonds or agreements are backed by insurance or another form of guarantee that ensures payment from a source other than general revenue; or

(2) the issuer demonstrates to the satisfaction of the Bond Review Board or its successor designated by law that the bonds no longer require payment from general revenue, and the Bond Review Board so certifies to the Legislative Budget Board or its successor designated by law.

Section 49-k. Texas Mobility Fund

(a) In this section:

(1) "Commission" means the Texas Transportation Commission or its successor.

(2) "Comptroller" means the comptroller of public accounts of the State of Texas.

(3) "Department" means the Texas Department of Transportation or its successor.

(4) "Fund" means the Texas Mobility Fund.

(5) "Obligations" means bonds, notes, and other public securities.

(b) The Texas Mobility Fund is created in the state treasury and shall be administered by the commission as a revolving fund to provide a method of financing the construction, reconstruction, acquisition, and expansion of state highways, including costs of any necessary design and costs of acquisition of rights-of-way, as determined by the commission in accordance with standards and procedures established by law.

(c) Money in the fund may also be used to provide participation by the state in the payment of a portion of the costs of constructing and providing publicly owned toll roads and other public transportation projects in accordance with the procedures, standards, and limitations established by law.

(d) The commission may issue and sell obligations of the state and enter into related credit agreements that are payable from and secured by a pledge of and a lien on all or part of the money on deposit in the fund in an aggregate principal amount that can be repaid when due from money on deposit in the fund, as that aggregate amount is projected by the comptroller in accordance with procedures established by law. The proceeds of the obligations must be deposited in the fund and used for one or more specific purposes authorized by law, including:

(1) refunding obligations and related credit agreements authorized by this section;

(2) creating reserves for payment of the obligations and related credit agreements;

(3) paying the costs of issuance; and

(4) paying interest on the obligations and related credit agreements for a period not longer than the maximum period established by law.

(e) The legislature by law may dedicate to the fund one or more specific sources or portions, or a specific amount, of the revenue, including taxes, and other money of the state that are not otherwise dedicated by this constitution. The legislature may not dedicate money from the collection of motor vehicle registration fees and taxes on motor fuels and lubricants dedicated by Section 7-a, Article VIII, of this constitution, but it may dedicate money received from other sources that are allocated to the same costs as those dedicated taxes and fees.

(f) Money dedicated as provided by this section is appropriated when received by the state, shall be deposited in the fund, and may be used as provided by this section and law enacted under this section without further appropriation. While money in the fund is pledged to the payment of any outstanding obligations or related credit agreements, the dedication of a specific source or portion of revenue, taxes, or other money made as provided by this section may not be reduced, rescinded, or repealed unless:

(1) the legislature by law dedicates a substitute or different source that is projected by the comptroller to be of a value equal to or greater than the source or amount being reduced, rescinded, or repealed and authorizes the commission to implement the authority granted by Subsection (g) of this section; and

(2) the commission implements the authority granted by the legislature pursuant to Subsection (g) of this section.

(g) In addition to the dedication of specified sources or amounts of revenue, taxes, or money as provided by Subsection (e) of this section, the legislature may by law authorize the commission to guarantee the payment of any obligations and credit agreements issued and executed by the commission under the authority of this section by pledging the full faith and credit of the state to that payment if dedicated revenue is insufficient for that purpose. If that authority is granted and is implemented by the commission, while any of the bonds, notes, other obligations, or credit agreements are outstanding and unpaid, and for any fiscal year during which the dedicated revenue, taxes, and money are insufficient to make all payments when due, there is appropriated, and there shall be deposited in the fund, out of the first money coming into the state treasury in each fiscal year that is not otherwise appropriated by this constitution, an amount that is sufficient to pay the principal of the obligations and agreements and the interest on the obligations and agreements that become due during that fiscal year, minus any amount in the fund that is available for that payment in accordance with applicable law.

(h) Proceedings authorizing obligations and related credit agreements to be issued and executed under the authority of this section shall be submitted to the attorney general for approval as to their legality. If the attorney general finds that they will be issued in accordance with this section and applicable law, the attorney general shall approve them, and, after payment by the purchasers of the obligations in accordance with the terms of sale and after execution and delivery of the related credit agreements, the obligations and related credit agreements are incontestable for any cause.

(i) Obligations and credit agreements issued or executed under the authority of this section may not be included in the computation required by Section 49-j, Article III, of this constitution, except that if money has been dedicated to the fund without specification of its source or the authority granted by Subsection (g) of this section has been implemented, the obligations and credit agreements shall be included to the extent the comptroller projects that general funds of the state, if any, will be required to pay amounts due on or on account of the obligations and credit agreements.

(j) The collection and deposit of the amounts required by this section, applicable law, and contract to be applied to the payment of obligations and credit agreements issued, executed, and secured under the authority of this section may be enforced by mandamus against the commission, the department, and the comptroller in a district court of Travis County, and the sovereign immunity of the state is waived for that purpose.

Section 49-L. Financial Assistance to Counties for Roadway Projects to Serve Border Colonias

(a) To fund financial assistance to counties for roadways to serve border colonias, the legislature by general law may authorize the governor to authorize the Texas Public Finance Authority or its successor to issue general obligation bonds or notes of the State of Texas in an aggregate amount not to exceed $175 million and to enter into related credit agreements. Except as provided by Subsection (c) of this section, the proceeds from the sale of the bonds and notes may be used only to provide financial assistance to counties for projects to provide access roads to connect border colonias with public roads. Projects may include the construction of colonia access roads, the acquisition of materials used in maintaining colonia access roads, and projects related to the construction of colonia access roads, such as projects for the drainage of the roads.

(b) The Texas Transportation Commission may, in its discretion and in consultation with the office of the governor, determine what constitutes a border colonia for purposes of selecting the counties and projects that may receive assistance under this section.

(c) A portion of the proceeds from the sale of the bonds and notes and a portion of the interest earned on the bonds and notes may be used to pay:

(1) the costs of administering projects authorized under this section; and

(2) all or part of a payment owed or to be owed under a credit agreement.

(d) The bonds and notes authorized under this section constitute a general obligation of the state. While any of the bonds or notes or interest on the bonds or notes is outstanding and unpaid, there is appropriated out of the general revenue fund in each fiscal year an amount sufficient to pay the principal of and interest on the bonds and notes that mature or become due during the fiscal year, including an amount sufficient to make payments under a related credit agreement.

Section 49-M. Short-Term Notes and Loans for Texas Department of Transportation Functions

(a) The legislature, by law, may authorize the Texas Transportation Commission or its successor to authorize the Texas Department of Transportation or its successor to issue notes or borrow money from any source to carry out the functions of the department.

(b) Notes issued or a loan obtained under this section may not have a term of more than two years. The legislature may appropriate money dedicated by Sections 7-a and 7-b, Article VIII, of this constitution for the purpose of paying a debt created by the notes or loan.

Section 49-N. Public Securities and Bond Enhancement Agreements Payable from State Highway Fund for Highway Improvement Projects

(a) To fund highway improvement projects, the legislature may authorize the Texas Transportation Commission or its successor to issue bonds and other public securities and enter into bond enhancement agreements that are payable from revenue deposited to the credit of the state highway fund.

(b) In each fiscal year in which amounts become due under the bonds, other public securities, or agreements authorized by this section, there is appropriated from the revenue deposited to the credit of the state highway fund in that fiscal year an amount that is sufficient to pay:

(1) the principal of and interest on the bonds or other public securities that mature or become due during the fiscal year; and

(2) any cost related to the bonds and other public securities, including payments under bond enhancement agreements, that becomes due during that fiscal year.

(c) Any dedication or appropriation of revenue to the credit of the state highway fund may not be modified so as to impair any outstanding bonds or other public securities secured by a pledge of that revenue unless provisions have been made for a full discharge of those securities.

Section 49-N. General Obligation Bonds and Notes for Military Value Revolving Loan Account

(a) The legislature by general law may authorize one or more state agencies to issue general obligation bonds or notes of the State of Texas in an aggregate amount not to exceed $250 million and enter into related credit agreements. The proceeds from the sale of the bonds and notes shall be deposited in the Texas military value revolving loan account in the state treasury or its successor account to be used by one or more state agencies designated by the legislature by general law without further appropriation to provide loans for economic development projects that benefit defense-related communities, as defined by the legislature by general law, including projects that enhance the military value of military installations located in the state.

(b) The expenses incurred in connection with the issuance of the bonds and notes and the costs of administering the Texas military value revolving loan account may be paid from money in the account. Money in the Texas military value revolving loan account may be used to pay all or part of any payment owed under a credit agreement related to the bonds or notes.

(c) A defense-related community receiving a loan from the Texas military value revolving loan account may use money from the account to capitalize interest on the loan.

(d) An agency providing a loan from the Texas military value revolving loan account to a defense-related community may require the defense-related community to pay any pro rata cost of issuing the general obligation bonds and notes.

(e) Bonds and notes authorized under this section are a general obligation of the state. While any of the bonds or notes or interest on the bonds or notes is outstanding and unpaid, there is appropriated out of the first money coming into the treasury in each fiscal year, not otherwise appropriated by this constitution, the amount sufficient to pay the principal of and interest on the bonds or notes that mature or become due during the fiscal year, including an amount sufficient to make payments under a related credit agreement, less any amounts in the interest and sinking accounts at the close of the preceding fiscal year that are pledged to payment of the bonds or notes or interest.

Section 49-o. Texas Rail Relocation and Improvement Fund

(a) In this section:

(1) "Commission" means the Texas Transportation Commission or its successor.

(2) "Comptroller" means the comptroller of public accounts of the State of Texas.

(3) "Department" means the Texas Department of Transportation or its successor.

(4) "Fund" means the Texas rail relocation and improvement fund.

(5) "Improvement" includes construction, reconstruction, acquisition, rehabilitation, and expansion.

(6) "Obligations" means bonds, notes, and other public securities.

(b) The Texas rail relocation and improvement fund is created in the state treasury. The fund shall be administered by the commission to provide a method of financing the relocation and improvement of privately and publicly owned passenger and freight rail facilities for the purposes of:

(1) relieving congestion on public highways;

(2) enhancing public safety;

(3) improving air quality; or

(4) expanding economic opportunity.

(b-1) The fund may also be used to provide a method of financing the construction of railroad underpasses and overpasses, if the construction is part of the relocation of a rail facility.

(c) The commission may issue and sell obligations of the state and enter into related credit agreements that are payable from and secured by a pledge of and a lien on all or part of the money on deposit in the fund in an aggregate principal amount that can be repaid when due from money on deposit in the fund, as that aggregate amount is projected by the comptroller in accordance with procedures established by law. The proceeds of the obligations must be deposited in the fund and used for one or more specific purposes authorized by law, including:

(1) refunding obligations and related credit agreements authorized by this section;

(2) creating reserves for payment of the obligations and related credit agreements;

(3) paying the costs of issuance; and

(4) paying interest on the obligations and related credit agreements for a period not longer than the maximum period established by law.

(d) The legislature by law may dedicate to the fund one or more specific sources or portions, or a specific amount, of the revenue, including taxes, and other money of the state that are not otherwise dedicated by this constitution.

(e) Money dedicated as provided by this section is appropriated when received by the state, shall be deposited in the fund, and may be used as provided by this section and law enacted under this section without further appropriation. While money in the fund is pledged to the payment of any outstanding obligations or related credit agreements, the dedication of a specific source or portion of revenue, taxes, or other money made as provided by this section may not be reduced, rescinded, or repealed unless:

(1) the legislature by law dedicates a substitute or different source that is projected by the comptroller to be of a value equal to or greater than the source or amount being reduced, rescinded, or repealed and authorizes the commission to implement the authority granted by Subsection (f) of this section; and

(2) the commission implements the authority granted by the legislature pursuant to Subsection (f) of this section.

(f) In addition to the dedication of specified sources or amounts of revenue, taxes, or money as provided by Subsection (d) of this section, the legislature may by law authorize the commission to guarantee the payment of any obligations and credit agreements issued and executed by the commission under the authority of this section by pledging the full faith and credit of the state to that payment if dedicated revenue is insufficient for that purpose. If that authority is granted and is implemented by the commission, while any of the bonds, notes, other obligations, or credit agreements are outstanding and unpaid, and for any fiscal year during which the dedicated revenue, taxes, and money are insufficient to make all payments when due, there is appropriated, and there shall be deposited in the fund, out of the first money coming into the state treasury in each fiscal year that is not otherwise appropriated by this constitution, an amount sufficient to pay the principal of and interest on the obligations and agreements that become due during that fiscal year, minus any amount in the fund that is available for that payment in accordance with applicable law.

(g) Proceedings authorizing obligations and related credit agreements to be issued and executed under the authority of this section shall be submitted to the attorney general for approval as to their legality. If the attorney general finds that they will be issued in accordance with this section and applicable law, the attorney general shall approve them, and, after payment by the purchasers of the obligations in accordance with the terms of sale and after execution and delivery of the related credit agreements, the obligations and related credit agreements are incontestable for any cause.

(h) Obligations and credit agreements issued or executed under the authority of this section may not be included in the computation required by Section 49-j, Article III, of this constitution, except that if money has been dedicated to the fund without specification of its source or the authority granted by Subsection (f) of this section has been implemented, the obligations and credit agreements shall be included to the extent the comptroller projects that general funds of the state, if any, will be required to pay amounts due on or on account of the obligations and credit agreements.

(i) The collection and deposit of the amounts required by this section, applicable law, and contract to be applied to the payment of obligations and credit agreements issued, executed, and secured under the authority of this section may be enforced by mandamus against the commission, the department, and the comptroller in a district court of Travis County, and the sovereign immunity of the state is waived for that purpose.

Section 49-P. General Obligation Bonds for Highway Improvements

(a) To provide funding for highway improvement projects, the legislature by general law may authorize the Texas Transportation Commission or its successor to issue general obligation bonds of the State of Texas in an aggregate amount not to exceed $5 billion and enter into related credit agreements. The bonds shall be executed in the form, on the terms, and in the denominations, bear interest, and be issued in installments as prescribed by the Texas Transportation Commission or its successor.

(b) A portion of the proceeds from the sale of the bonds and a portion of the interest earned on the bonds may be used to pay:

(1) the costs of administering projects authorized under this section;

(2) the cost or expense of the issuance of the bonds; and

(3) all or part of a payment owed or to be owed under a credit agreement.

(c) The bonds authorized under this section constitute a general obligation of the state. While any of the bonds or interest on the bonds is outstanding and unpaid, there is appropriated out of the first money coming into the treasury each fiscal year, not otherwise appropriated by this constitution, an amount sufficient to pay the principal of and interest on the bonds that mature or become due during the fiscal year, including an amount sufficient to make payments under a related credit agreement.

(d) Bonds issued under this section, after approval by the attorney general, registration by the comptroller of public accounts, and delivery to the purchasers, are incontestable and are general obligations of the State of Texas under this constitution.

Section 50. Loan or Pledge of Credit of the State

The Legislature shall have no power to give or to lend, or to authorize the giving or lending, of the credit of the State in aid of, or to any person, association or corporation, whether municipal or other, or to pledge the credit of the State in any manner whatsoever, for the payment of the liabilities, present or prospective, of any individual, association of individuals, municipal or other corporation whatsoever.

Section 50a. Repealed

Section 50b. Repealed

Section 50b-1. Repealed

Section 50b-2. Repealed

Section 50b-3. Repealed

Section 50b-4. Additional Student Loans

(a) The legislature by general law may authorize the Texas Higher Education Coordinating Board or its successor or successors to issue and sell general obligation bonds of the State of Texas in an amount authorized by constitutional amendment or by a debt proposition under Section 49 of this article to finance educational loans to students who have been admitted to attend an institution of higher education within the State of Texas, public or private, which is recognized or accredited under terms and conditions prescribed by the Legislature.

(b) The bonds shall be executed in the form, on the terms, and in the denominations, bear interest, and be issued in installments as prescribed by the Texas Higher Education Coordinating Board or its successor or successors.

(c) The maximum net effective interest rate to be borne by bonds issued under this section must be set by law.

(d) The legislature may provide for the investment of bond proceeds and may establish and provide for the investment of an interest and sinking fund to pay the bonds. Income from the investment shall be used for the purposes prescribed by the legislature.

(e) While any of the bonds issued under this section or interest on the bonds is outstanding and unpaid, there is appropriated out of the first money coming into the treasury in each fiscal year, not otherwise appropriated by this constitution, the amount sufficient to pay the principal of and interest on the bonds that mature or become due during the fiscal year, less any amount in an interest and sinking fund established under this section at the end of the preceding fiscal year that is pledged to the payment of the bonds or interest.

(f) Bonds issued under this section, after approval by the attorney general, registration by the comptroller of public accounts, and delivery to the purchasers, are incontestable.

Section 50b-5. Additional Student Loans

(a) The legislature by general law may authorize the Texas Higher Education Coordinating Board or its successor or successors to issue and sell general obligation bonds of the State of Texas in an amount not to exceed $400 million to finance educational loans to students. The bonds are in addition to those bonds issued under Sections 50b, 50b-1, 50b-2, 50b-3, and 50b-4 of this article.

(b) The bonds shall be executed in the form, on the terms, and in the denominations, bear interest, and be issued in installments as prescribed by the Texas Higher Education Coordinating Board or its successor or successors.

(c) The maximum net effective interest rate to be borne by bonds issued under this section may not exceed the maximum rate provided by law.

(d) The legislature may provide for the investment of bond proceeds and may establish and provide for the investment of an interest and sinking fund to pay the bonds. Income from the investment shall be used for the purposes prescribed by the legislature.

(e) While any of the bonds issued under this section or interest on the bonds is outstanding and unpaid, there is appropriated out of the first money coming into the treasury in each fiscal year, not otherwise appropriated by this constitution, the amount sufficient to pay the principal of and interest on the bonds that mature or become due during the fiscal year, less any amount in an interest and sinking fund established under this section at the end of the preceding fiscal year that is pledged to the payment of the bonds or interest.

(f) Bonds issued under this section, after approval by the attorney general, registration by the comptroller of public accounts, and delivery to the purchasers, are incontestable.

Section 50b-6. Additional Student Loans

(a) The legislature by general law may authorize the Texas Higher Education Coordinating Board or its successor or successors to issue and sell general obligation bonds of the State of Texas in an amount not to exceed $500 million in order to finance educational loans to students in the manner provided by law. The bonds are in addition to bonds issued under Sections 50b-4 and 50b-5 of this article and under any other provision or former provision of this constitution authorizing similar bonds.

(b) The bonds shall be executed in the form, on the terms, and in the denominations, bear interest, and be issued in installments as prescribed by the Texas Higher Education Coordinating Board or its successor or successors.

(c) The maximum net effective interest rate to be borne by bonds issued under this section may not exceed the maximum rate provided by law.

(d) The legislature may provide for the investment of bond proceeds and may establish and provide for the investment of an interest and sinking fund to pay the bonds. Income from the investment shall be used for the purposes prescribed by the legislature.

(e) Notwithstanding any other provision of this article, there is appropriated out of the first money coming into the treasury in each fiscal year, not otherwise appropriated by this constitution, the amount sufficient to pay the principal of and interest on any bonds issued under this section, under Sections 50b-4 and 50b-5 of this article, and under any other provision or former provision of this article authorizing similar bonds that mature or become due during the fiscal year, less any amount remaining in an interest and sinking fund established under this section, Section 50b-4 or 50b-5 of this article, or any other provision or former provision of this article authorizing similar bonds at the end of the preceding fiscal year that is pledged to the payment of the bonds or interest.

(f) Bonds issued under this section, after approval by the attorney general, registration by the comptroller of public accounts, and delivery to the purchasers, are incontestable.

Section 50b-6a. Bond Enhancement Agreements with Respect to Bonds Issued for Student Loans

The legislature by general law may provide for the Texas Higher Education Coordinating Board or its successor or successors to enter into bond enhancement agreements with appropriate entities with respect to any bonds issued under Section 50b-4, 50b-5, or 50b-6 of this article or under any other provision or former provision of this article authorizing similar bonds. Payments due from the coordinating board under a bond enhancement agreement with respect to the principal of or interest on the bonds shall be treated for purposes of this constitution as payments of the principal of and interest on the bonds, and money appropriated for the purpose of paying the principal of and interest on the bonds as they mature or become due may be used to make payments under bond enhancement agreements authorized by this section with respect to the bonds.

Section 50b-7. Continuing Authorization for Additional Bonds for Student Loans

(a) The legislature by general law may authorize the Texas Higher Education Coordinating Board or its successor or successors to issue and sell general obligation bonds of the State of Texas for the purpose of financing educational loans to students in the manner provided by law. The principal amount of outstanding bonds issued under this section must at all times be equal to or less than the aggregate principal amount of state general obligation bonds previously authorized for that purpose by any other provision or former provision of this constitution.

(b) The bonds shall be executed in the form, on the terms, and in the denominations, bear interest, and be issued in installments as prescribed by the Texas Higher Education Coordinating Board or its successor or successors.

(c) The maximum net effective interest rate to be borne by bonds issued under this section may not exceed the maximum rate provided by law.

(d) The legislature may provide for the investment of bond proceeds and may establish and provide for the investment of an interest and sinking fund to pay the bonds. Income from the investment shall be used for the purposes prescribed by the legislature.

(e) While any of the bonds issued under this section or interest on the bonds is outstanding and unpaid, there is appropriated out of the first money coming into the treasury in each fiscal year, not otherwise appropriated by this constitution, the amount sufficient to pay the principal of and interest on the bonds that mature or become due during the fiscal year, less any amount in an interest and sinking fund established under this section at the end of the preceding fiscal year that is pledged to the payment of the bonds or interest.

(f) Bonds issued under this section, after approval by the attorney general, registration by the comptroller of public accounts, and delivery to the purchasers, are incontestable.

Section 50c. Farm and Ranch Loan Security Fund

(a) The legislature may provide that the commissioner of agriculture shall have the authority to provide for, issue, and sell general obligation bonds of the State of Texas in an amount not to exceed $10 million. The bonds shall be called "Farm and Ranch Loan Security Bonds" and shall be executed in such form, denominations, and on such terms as may be prescribed by law. The bonds shall bear interest rates fixed by the Legislature of the State of Texas.

(b) All money received from the sale of Farm and Ranch Loan Security Bonds shall be deposited in a fund hereby created with the comptroller of public accounts to be known as the "Farm and Ranch Loan Security Fund." This fund shall be administered without further appropriation by the commissioner of agriculture in the manner prescribed by law.

(c) The Farm and Ranch Loan Security Fund shall be used by the commissioner of agriculture under provisions prescribed by the legislature for the purpose of guaranteeing loans used for the purchase of farm and ranch real estate, for acquiring real estate mortgages or deeds of trust on lands purchased with guaranteed loans, and to advance to the borrower a percentage of the principal and interest due on those loans; provided that the commissioner shall require at least six percent interest be paid by the borrower on any advance of principal and interest. The legislature may authorize the commissioner to sell at foreclosure any land acquired in this manner, and proceeds from that sale shall be deposited in the Farm and Ranch Loan Security Fund.

(d) The legislature may provide for the investment of money available in the Farm and Ranch Loan Security Fund and the interest and sinking fund established for the payment of bonds issued by the commissioner of agriculture. Income from the investment shall be used for purposes prescribed by the legislature.

(e) While any of the bonds authorized by this section or any interest on those bonds is outstanding and unpaid, there is hereby appropriated out of the first money coming into the treasury in each fiscal year not otherwise appropriated by this constitution an amount that is sufficient to pay the principal and interest on the bonds that mature or become due during the fiscal year less the amount in the interest and sinking fund at the close of the prior fiscal year.

Section 50-D. Agricultural Water Conservation Fund

(a) On a two-thirds vote of the members elected to each house of the legislature, the Texas Water Development Board may issue and sell Texas agricultural water conservation bonds in an amount not to exceed $200 million.

(b) The proceeds from the sale of Texas agricultural water conservation bonds shall be deposited in a fund created in the state treasury to be known as the agricultural water conservation fund.

(c) Texas agricultural water conservation bonds are general obligations of the State of Texas. During the time that Texas agricultural water conservation bonds or any interest on those bonds is outstanding or unpaid, there is appropriated out of the first money coming into the state treasury in each fiscal year, not otherwise appropriated by this constitution, an amount that is sufficient to pay the principal of and interest on those bonds that mature or become due during that fiscal year.

(d) The terms, conditions, provisions, and procedures for issuance and sale and management of proceeds of Texas agricultural water conservation bonds shall be provided by law.

(e) Repealed

Section 50-e. Guarantee of Texas Grain Warehouse Self-Insurance Fund

(a) For the purposes of providing surety for the Texas grain warehouse self-insurance fund, the legislature by general law may establish or provide for a guarantee of the fund not to exceed $5 million.

(b) At the beginning of the fiscal year after the fund reaches $5 million, as certified by the comptroller of public accounts, the guarantee of the fund shall cease and this provision shall expire.

(c) Should the legislature enact any enabling laws in anticipation of this amendment, no such law shall be void by reason of its anticipating nature.

(d) If the provisions of this section conflict with any other provisions of this constitution, the provisions of this section shall prevail.

Section 50-F. General Obligation Bonds for Construction and Repair Projects and for Purchase of Equipment

(a) The legislature by general law may authorize the Texas Public Finance Authority to provide for, issue, and sell general obligation bonds of the State of Texas in an amount not to exceed $850 million and to enter into related credit agreements.

The bonds shall be executed in the form, on the terms, and in the denominations, bear interest, and be issued in installments as prescribed by the Texas Public Finance Authority.

(b) Proceeds from the sale of the bonds shall be deposited in a separate fund or account within the state treasury created by the comptroller for this purpose. Money in the separate fund or account may be used only to pay for:

(1) construction and repair projects authorized by the legislature by general law or the General Appropriations Act and administered by or on behalf of the General Services Commission, the Texas Youth Commission, the Texas Department of Criminal Justice, the Texas Department of Mental Health and Mental Retardation, the Parks and Wildlife Department, the adjutant general's department, the Texas School for the Deaf, the Department of Agriculture, the Department of Public Safety of the State of Texas, the State Preservation Board, the Texas Department of Health, the Texas Historical Commission, or the Texas School for the Blind and Visually Impaired; or

(2) the purchase, as authorized by the legislature by general law or the General Appropriations Act, of needed equipment by or on behalf of a state agency listed in Subdivision (1) of this subsection.

(c) The maximum net effective interest rate to be borne by bonds issued under this section may be set by general law.

(d) While any of the bonds or interest on the bonds authorized by this section is outstanding and unpaid, from the first money coming into the state treasury in each fiscal year not otherwise appropriated by this constitution, an amount sufficient to pay the principal and interest on bonds that mature or become due during the fiscal year and to make payments that become due under a related credit agreement during the fiscal year is appropriated, less the amount in the sinking fund at the close of the previous fiscal year.

(e) Bonds issued under this section, after approval by the attorney general, registration by the comptroller of public accounts, and delivery to the purchasers, are incontestable and are general obligations of the State of Texas under this constitution.

Section 50-G. General Obligation Bonds for Maintenance, Improvement, Repair, or Construction Projects and for Purchase of Equipment

(a) The legislature by general law may authorize the Texas Public Finance Authority to provide for, issue, and sell general obligation bonds of the State of Texas in an amount not to exceed $1 billion and to enter into related credit agreements. The bonds shall be executed in the form, on the terms, and in the denominations, bear interest, and be issued in installments as prescribed by the Texas Public Finance Authority.

(b) Proceeds from the sale of the bonds shall be deposited in a separate fund or account within the state treasury created by the comptroller of public accounts for this purpose. Money in the separate fund or account may be used only to pay for:

(1) maintenance, improvement, repair, or construction projects authorized by the legislature by general law or the General Appropriations Act and administered by or on behalf of the Texas Building and Procurement Commission, the Parks and Wildlife Department, the adjutant general's department, the Department of State Health Services, the Department of Aging and Disability Services, the Texas School for the Blind and Visually Impaired, the Texas Youth Commission, the Texas Historical Commission, the Texas Department of Criminal Justice, the Texas School for the Deaf, or the Department of Public Safety of the State of Texas; or

(2) the purchase, as authorized by the legislature by general law or the General Appropriations Act, of needed equipment by or on behalf of a state agency listed in Subdivision (1) of this subsection.

(c) The maximum net effective interest rate to be borne by bonds issued under this section may be set by general law.

(d) While any of the bonds or interest on the bonds authorized by this section is outstanding and unpaid, from the first money coming into the state treasury in each fiscal year not otherwise appropriated by this constitution, an amount sufficient to pay the principal and interest on bonds that mature or become due during the fiscal year and to make payments that become due under a related credit agreement during the fiscal year is appropriated, less the amount in the sinking fund at the close of the previous fiscal year.

(e) Bonds issued under this section, after approval by the attorney general, registration by the comptroller of public accounts, and delivery to the purchasers, are incontestable and are general obligations of the State of Texas under this constitution.

Section 51. Grants of Public Money Prohibited

The Legislature shall have no power to make any grant or authorize the making of any grant of public moneys to any individual, association of individuals, municipal or other corporations whatsoever; provided that the provisions of this Section shall not be construed so as to prevent the grant of aid in cases of public calamity.

Section 51-A. Assistance Grants, Medical Care, and Certain Other Services for Needy Persons; Federal Matching Funds

(a) The Legislature shall have the power, by General Laws, to provide, subject to limitations herein contained, and such other limitations, restrictions and regulations as may by the Legislature be deemed expedient, for assistance grants to needy dependent children and the caretakers of such children, needy persons who are totally and permanently disabled because of a mental or physical handicap, needy aged persons and needy blind persons.

(b) The Legislature may provide by General Law for medical care, rehabilitation and other similar services for needy persons. The Legislature may prescribe such other eligibility requirements for participation in these programs as it deems appropriate and may make appropriations out of state funds for such purposes. The maximum amount paid out of state funds for assistance grants to or on behalf of needy dependent children and their caretakers shall not exceed one percent of the state budget. The Legislature by general statute shall provide for the means for determining the state budget amounts, including state and other funds appropriated by the Legislature, to be used in establishing the biennial limit.

(c) Provided further, that if the limitations and restrictions herein contained are found to be in conflict with the provisions of appropriate federal statutes, as they now are or as they may be amended to the extent that federal matching money is not available to the state for these purposes, then and in that event the Legislature is specifically authorized and empowered to prescribe such limitations and restrictions and enact such laws as may be necessary in order that such federal matching money will be available for assistance and/or medical care for or on behalf of needy persons.

(d) Nothing in this Section shall be construed to amend, modify or repeal Section 31 of Article XVI of this Constitution; provided further, however, that such medical care, services or assistance shall also include the employment of objective or subjective means, without the use of drugs, for the purpose of ascertaining and measuring the powers of vision of the human eye, and fitting lenses or prisms to correct or remedy any defect or abnormal condition of vision. Nothing herein shall be construed to permit optometrists to treat the eyes for any defect whatsoever in any manner nor to administer nor to prescribe any drug or physical treatment whatsoever, unless such optometrist is a regularly licensed physician or surgeon under the laws of this state.

Section 51-A-1. Financial Assistance to Local Fire Departments and Other Public Fire-Fighting Organizations

(a) The legislature by general law may authorize the use of public money to provide to local fire departments and other public fire-fighting organizations:

(1) loans or other financial assistance to purchase fire-fighting equipment and to aid in providing necessary equipment and facilities to comply with federal and state law; and

(2) scholarships and grants to educate and train the members of local fire departments and other public fire-fighting organizations.

(b) A portion of the money used under this section may be used for the administrative costs of the program. The legislature shall provide for the terms and conditions of scholarships, grants, loans, and other financial assistance to be provided under this section.

Section 51-b. Repealed

Section 51-C. Aid or Compensation to Persons Improperly Fined Or Imprisoned

The Legislature may grant aid and compensation to any person who has heretofore paid a fine or served a sentence in prison, or who may hereafter pay a fine or serve a sentence in prison, under the laws of this State for an offense for which he or she is not guilty, under such regulations and limitations as the Legislature may deem expedient.

Section 51-D. Assistance to Survivors of Public Servant Suffering Death in Performance of Hazardous Duty

The Legislature shall have the power, by general law, to provide for the payment of assistance by the State of Texas to the surviving spouse, minor children, and surviving dependent parents, brothers, and sisters of officers, employees, and agents, including members of organized volunteer fire departments and members of organized police reserve or auxiliary units with authority to make an arrest, of the state or of any city, county, district, or other political subdivision who, because of the hazardous nature of their duties, suffer death in the course of the performance of those official duties. Should the Legislature enact any enabling laws in anticipation of this amendment, no such law shall be void by reason of its anticipatory nature.

Section 51-e. Repealed

Section 51-f. Repealed

Section 51g. Social Security Coverage of Proprietary Employees of Political Subdivisions

The Legislature shall have the power to pass such laws as may be necessary to enable the State to enter into agreements with the Federal Government to obtain for proprietary employees of its political subdivisions coverage under the old-age and survivors insurance provisions of Title II of the Federal Social Security Act as amended. The Legislature shall have the power to make appropriations and authorize all obligations necessary to the establishment of such Social Security coverage program.

Section 52. Restrictions on Lending Credit or Making Grants by Political Corporations or Political Subdivisions; Authorized Bonds; Investment of Funds

(a) Except as otherwise provided by this section, the Legislature shall have no power to authorize any county, city, town or other political corporation or subdivision of the State to lend its credit or to grant public money or thing of value in aid of, or to any individual, association or corporation whatsoever, or to become a stockholder in such corporation, association or company. However, this section does not prohibit the use of public funds or credit for the payment of premiums on non-assessable property and casualty, life, health, or accident insurance policies and annuity contracts issued by a mutual insurance company authorized to do business in this State.

(b) Under Legislative provision, any county, political subdivision of a county, number of adjoining counties, political subdivision of the State, or defined district now or hereafter to be described and defined within the State of Texas, and which may or may not include, towns, villages or municipal corporations, upon a vote of two-thirds majority of the voting qualified voters of such district or territory to be affected thereby, may issue bonds or otherwise lend its credit in any amount not to exceed one-fourth of the assessed valuation of the real property of such district or territory, except that the total bonded indebtedness of any city or town shall never exceed the limits imposed by other provisions of this Constitution, and levy and collect taxes to pay the interest thereon and provide a sinking fund for the redemption thereof, as the Legislature may authorize, and in such manner as it may authorize the same, for the following purposes to wit:

(1) The improvement of rivers, creeks, and streams to prevent overflows, and to permit of navigation thereof, or irrigation thereof, or in aid of such purposes.

(2) The construction and maintenance of pools, lakes, reservoirs, dams, canals and waterways for the purposes of irrigation, drainage or navigation, or in aid thereof.

(3) The construction, maintenance and operation of macadamized, graveled or paved roads and turnpikes, or in aid thereof.

(c) Notwithstanding the provisions of Subsection (b) of this Section, bonds may be issued by any county in an amount not to exceed one-fourth of the assessed valuation of the real property in the county, for the construction, maintenance, and operation of macadamized, graveled, or paved roads and turnpikes, or in aid thereof, upon a vote of a majority of the voting qualified voters of the county, and without the necessity of further or amendatory legislation. The county may levy and collect taxes to pay the interest on the bonds as it becomes due and to provide a sinking fund for redemption of the bonds.

(d) Any defined district created under this section that is authorized to issue bonds or otherwise lend its credit for the purposes stated in Subdivisions (1) and (2) of Subsection (b) of this section may engage in fire-fighting activities and may issue bonds or otherwise lend its credit for fire-fighting purposes as provided by law and this constitution.

(e) A county, city, town, or other political corporation or subdivision of the state may invest its funds as authorized by law.

Section 52-A. Programs and Loans or Grants of Public Money for Economic Development

Notwithstanding any other provision of this constitution, the legislature may provide for the creation of programs and the making of loans and grants of public money, other than money otherwise dedicated by this constitution to use for a different purpose, for the public purposes of development and diversification of the economy of the state, the elimination of unemployment or underemployment in the state, the stimulation of agricultural innovation, the fostering of the growth of enterprises based on agriculture, or the development or expansion of transportation or commerce in the state. Any bonds or other obligations of a county, municipality, or other political subdivision of the state that are issued for the purpose of making loans or grants in connection with a program authorized by the legislature under this section and that are payable from ad valorem taxes must be approved by a vote of the majority of the registered voters of the county, municipality, or political subdivision voting on the issue. A program created or a loan or grant made as provided by this section that is not secured by a pledge of ad valorem taxes or financed by the issuance of any bonds or other obligations payable from ad valorem taxes of the political subdivision does not constitute or create a debt for the purpose of any provision of this constitution. An enabling law enacted by the legislature in anticipation of the adoption of this amendment is not void because of its anticipatory character.

Section 52-B. Loan of State's Credit, Grant of Public Money, or Assumption of Debt for Toll Road Purposes

The Legislature shall have no power or authority to in any manner lend the credit of the State or grant any public money to, or assume any indebtedness, present or future, bonded or otherwise, of any individual, person, firm, partnership, association, corporation, public corporation, public agency, or political subdivision of the State, or anyone else, which is now or hereafter authorized to construct, maintain or operate toll roads and turnpikes within this State except that the Legislature may authorize the Texas Department of Transportation to expend, grant, or loan money, from any source available, for the acquisition, construction, maintenance, or operation of turnpikes, toll roads, and toll bridges.

Section 52-c. Blank

Section 52d. County or Road District Tax for Road and Bridge Purposes in Harris County

(a) Upon the vote of a majority of the qualified voters so authorizing, a county or road district may collect an annual tax for a period not exceeding five (5) years to create a fund for constructing lasting and permanent roads and bridges or both.

No contract involving the expenditure of any of such fund shall be valid unless, when it is made, money shall be on hand in such fund.

(b) At such election, the Commissioners' Court shall submit for adoption a road plan and designate the amount of special tax to be levied; the number of years said tax is to be levied; the location, description, and character of the roads and bridges; and the estimated cost thereof. The funds raised by such taxes shall not be used for purposes other than those specified in the plan submitted to the voters. Elections may be held from time to time to extend or discontinue said plan or to increase or diminish said tax. The Legislature shall enact laws prescribing the procedure hereunder.

(c) The provisions of this section shall apply only to Harris County and road districts therein.

Section 52e. County Payment of Medical Expenses of Law Enforcement Officials

Each county in the State of Texas is hereby authorized to pay all medical expenses, all doctor bills and all hospital bills for Sheriffs, Deputy Sheriffs, Constables, Deputy Constables and other county and precinct law enforcement officials who are injured in the course of their official duties; providing that while said Sheriff, Deputy Sheriff, Constable, Deputy Constable or other county or precinct law enforcement official is hospitalized or incapacitated that the county shall continue to pay his maximum salary; providing, however, that said payment of salary shall cease on the expiration of the term of office to which such official was elected or appointed. Provided, however, that no provision contained herein shall be construed to amend, modify, repeal or nullify Article 16, Section 31, of the Constitution of the State of Texas.

Section 52f. Private Road Work by Counties with Population of 7,500 or Less

A county with a population of 7,500 or less, according to the most recent federal census, may construct and maintain private roads if it imposes a reasonable charge for the work. The Legislature by general law may limit this authority. Revenue received from private road work may be used only for the construction, including right-of-way acquisition, or maintenance of public roads.

Section 52g. Dallas County Bond Issues for Roads and Turnpikes

Bonds to be issued by Dallas County under Section 52(b)(3) of Article III of this Constitution may, without the necessity of further or amendatory legislation, be issued upon a vote of a majority of the voting qualified voters of said county, and bonds heretofore or hereafter issued under Subsections (a) and (b) of said Section 52 shall not be included in determining the debt limit prescribed in said Section.

Section 52h. Donations by Municipalities of Outdated or Surplus Fire Fighting Equipment to Underdeveloped Countries

A municipality may donate to an underdeveloped country outdated or surplus equipment, supplies, or other materials used in fighting fires.

Section 52i. Donations by Municipalities of Surplus Fire Fighting Equipment for Rural Fire Protection

(a) A municipality may donate surplus equipment, supplies, or other materials used in fighting fires to the Texas Forest Service or to a successor agency authorized to cooperate in the development of rural fire protection plans.

(b) The Texas Forest Service or the successor agency may, based on need, redistribute to rural volunteer fire departments the equipment, supplies, or materials donated under Subsection (a).

Section 52j. Sale of Real Property Acquired Through Eminent Domain

A governmental entity may sell real property acquired through eminent domain to the person who owned the real property interest immediately before the governmental entity acquired the property interest, or to the person's heirs, successors, or assigns, at the price the entity paid at the time of acquisition if:

(1) the public use for which the property was acquired through eminent domain is canceled;

(2) no actual progress is made toward the public use during a prescribed period of time; or

(3) the property is unnecessary for the public use.

Section 52k. County or Municipal Bonds or Notes to Acquire Land Adjacent to Military Installations

The legislature by general law may authorize a municipality or county to issue bonds or notes to finance the acquisition of buffer areas or open spaces adjacent to a military installation for the prevention of encroachment or for the construction of roadways, utilities, or other infrastructure to protect or promote the mission of the military installation. The municipality or county may pledge increases in ad valorem tax revenues imposed in the area by the municipality, county, or other political subdivisions for repayment of the bonds or notes.

Section 53. Payment of Extra Compensation or Unauthorized Claims Prohibited

The Legislature shall have no power to grant, or to authorize any county or municipal authority to grant, any extra compensation, fee or allowance to a public officer, agent, servant or contractor, after service has been rendered, or a contract has been entered into, and performed in whole or in part; nor pay, nor authorize the payment of, any claim created against any county or municipality of the State, under any agreement or contract, made without authority of law.

Section 54. Repealed

Section 55. Release or Extinguishment of Indebtedness to State, County, Subdivision, or Municipal Corporation

The Legislature shall have no power to release or extinguish, or to authorize the releasing or extinguishing, in whole or in part, the indebtedness, liability or obligation of any corporation or individual, to this State or to any county or defined subdivision thereof, or other municipal corporation therein, except delinquent taxes which have been due for a period of at least ten years.

Section 56. Prohibited Local and Special Laws

(a) The Legislature shall not, except as otherwise provided in this Constitution, pass any local or special law, authorizing:

(1) the creation, extension or impairing of liens;

(2) regulating the affairs of counties, cities, towns, wards or school districts;

(3) changing the names of persons or places;

(4) changing the venue in civil or criminal cases;

(5) authorizing the laying out, opening, altering or maintaining of roads, highways, streets or alleys;

(6) relating to ferries or bridges, or incorporating ferry or bridge companies, except for the erection of bridges crossing streams which form boundaries between this and any other State;

(7) vacating roads, town plats, streets or alleys;

(8) relating to cemeteries, grave-yards or public grounds not of the State;

(9) authorizing the adoption or legitimation of children;

(10) locating or changing county seats;

(11) incorporating cities, towns or villages, or changing their charters;

(12) for the opening and conducting of elections, or fixing or changing the places of voting;

(13) granting divorces;

(14) creating offices, or prescribing the powers and duties of officers, in counties, cities, towns, election or school districts;

(15) changing the law of descent or succession;

(16) regulating the practice or jurisdiction of, or changing the rules of evidence in any judicial proceeding or inquiry before courts, justices of the peace, sheriffs, commissioners, arbitrators or other tribunals, or providing or changing methods for the collection of debts, or the enforcing of judgments, or prescribing the effect of judicial sales of real estate;

(17) regulating the fees, or extending the powers and duties of aldermen, justices of the peace, magistrates or constables;

(18) regulating the management of public schools, the building or repairing of school houses, and the raising of money for such purposes;

(19) fixing the rate of interest;

(20) affecting the estates of minors, or persons under disability;

(21) remitting fines, penalties and forfeitures, and refunding moneys legally paid into the treasury;

(22) exempting property from taxation;

(23) regulating labor, trade, mining and manufacturing;

(24) declaring any named person of age;

(25) extending the time for the assessment or collection of taxes, or otherwise relieving any assessor or collector of taxes from the due performance of his official duties, or his securities from liability;

(26) giving effect to informal or invalid wills or deeds;

(27) summoning or empanelling grand or petit juries;

(28) for limitation of civil or criminal actions;

(29) for incorporating railroads or other works of internal improvements; or

(30) relieving or discharging any person or set of persons from the performance of any public duty or service imposed by general law.

(b) In addition to those laws described by Subsection (a) of this section in all other cases where a general law can be made applicable, no local or special law shall be enacted; provided, that nothing herein contained shall be construed to prohibit the Legislature from passing:

(1) special laws for the preservation of the game and fish of this State in certain localities; and

(2) fence laws applicable to any subdivision of this State or counties as may be needed to meet the wants of the people.

Section 57. Notice of Intention to Apply for Local or Special Law

No local or special law shall be passed, unless notice of the intention to apply therefor shall have been published in the locality where the matter or thing to be affected may be situated, which notice shall state the substance of the contemplated law, and shall be published at least thirty days prior to the introduction into the Legislature of such bill and in the manner to be provided by law. The evidence of such notice having been published, shall be exhibited in the Legislature, before such act shall be passed.

Section 58. Seat of Government

The Legislature shall hold its sessions at the City of Austin, which is hereby declared to be the seat of government.

Section 59. Workers Compensation Insurance for State Employees

The Legislature shall have power to pass such laws as may be necessary to provide for Workers' Compensation Insurance for such State employees, as in its judgment is necessary or required; and to provide for the payment of all costs, charges, and premiums on such policies of insurance; providing the State shall never be required to purchase insurance for any employee.

Section 60. Workers Compensation Insurance for Employees of Political Subdivisions

The Legislature shall have the power to pass such laws as may be necessary to enable all counties, cities, towns, villages, and other political subdivisions of this State to provide Workers' Compensation Insurance, including the right of a political subdivision to provide its own insurance risk, for all employees of the political subdivision as in its judgment is necessary or required; and the Legislature shall provide suitable laws for the administration of such insurance in the counties, cities, towns, villages, or other political subdivisions of this State and for the payment of the costs, charges and premiums on such policies of insurance and the benefits to be paid thereunder.

Section 61. Repealed

Section 61-A. Minimum Salaries of Certain State Officers

The Legislature shall not fix the salary of the Governor, Attorney General, Comptroller of Public Accounts, Commissioner of the General Land Office or Secretary of State at a sum less than that fixed for such officials in the Constitution on January 1, 1953.

Section 62. Continuity of State and Local Governmental Operations Following Enemy Attack

(a) The Legislature, in order to insure continuity of state and local governmental operations in periods of emergency resulting from disasters caused by enemy attack, shall have the power and the immediate duty to provide for prompt and temporary succession to the powers and duties of public offices, of whatever nature and whether filled by election or appointment, the incumbents of which may become unavailable for carrying on the powers and duties of such offices. Provided, however, that Article I of the Constitution of Texas, known as the "Bill of

Rights" shall not be in any manner affected, amended, impaired, suspended, repealed or suspended hereby.

(b) When such a period of emergency or the immediate threat of enemy attack exists, the Legislature may suspend procedural rules imposed by this Constitution that relate to:

(1) the order of business of the Legislature;

(2) the percentage of each house of the Legislature necessary to constitute a quorum;

(3) the requirement that a bill must be read on three days in each house before it has the force of law;

(4) the requirement that a bill must be referred to and reported from committee before its consideration; and

(5) the date on which laws passed by the Legislature take effect.

(c) When such a period of emergency or the immediate threat of enemy attack exists, the Governor, after consulting with the Lieutenant Governor and the Speaker of the House of Representatives, may suspend the constitutional requirement that the Legislature hold its sessions in Austin, the seat of government. When this requirement has been suspended, the Governor shall determine a place other than Austin at which the Legislature will hold its sessions during such period of emergency or immediate threat of enemy attack. The Governor shall notify the Lieutenant Governor and the Speaker of the House of Representatives of the place and time at which the Legislature will meet. The Governor may take security precautions, consistent with the state of emergency, in determining the extent to which that information may be released.

(d) To suspend the constitutional rules specified by Subsection (b) of this section, the Governor must issue a proclamation and the House of Representatives and the Senate must concur in the proclamation as provided by this section.

(e) The Governor's proclamation must declare that a period of emergency resulting from disasters caused by enemy attack exists, or that the immediate threat of enemy attack exists, and that suspension of constitutional rules relating to legislative procedure is necessary to assure continuity of state government. The proclamation must specify the period, not to exceed two years, during which the constitutional rules specified by Subsection (b) of this section are suspended.

(f) The House of Representatives and the Senate, by concurrent resolution approved by the majority of the members present, must concur in the Governor's proclamation. A resolution of the House of Representatives and the Senate concurring in the Governor's proclamation suspends the constitutional rules specified by Subsection (b) of this section for the period of time specified by the Governor's proclamation.

(g) The constitutional rules specified by Subsection (b) of this section may not be suspended for more than two years under a single proclamation. A suspension may be renewed, however, if the Governor issues another proclamation as provided by Subsection (e) of this section and the House of Representatives and the Senate, by concurrent resolution, concur in that proclamation.

Section 63. Repealed

Section 64. Consolidation of Offices and Functions of Political Subdivisions; Contracts Between Political Subdivisions

(a) The Legislature may by special statute provide for consolidation of governmental offices and functions of government of any one or more political subdivisions comprising or located within any county. Any such statute shall require an election to be held within the political subdivisions affected thereby with approval by a majority of the voters in each of these subdivisions, under such terms and conditions as the Legislature may require.

(b) The county government, or any political subdivision(s) comprising or located therein, may contract one with another for the performance of governmental functions required or authorized by this Constitution or the Laws of this State, under such terms and conditions as the Legislature may prescribe. No person acting under a contract made pursuant to this Subsection (b) shall be deemed to hold more than one office of honor, trust or profit or more than one civil office of emolument. The term "governmental functions," as it relates to counties, includes all duties, activities and operations of statewide importance in which the county acts for the State, as well as of local importance, whether required or authorized by this Constitution or the Laws of this State.

Section 65. Maximum Interest Rate on Public Bonds

(a) Wherever the Constitution authorizes an agency, instrumentality, or subdivision of the State to issue bonds and specifies the maximum rate of interest which may be paid on such bonds issued pursuant to such constitutional authority, such bonds may bear interest at rates not to exceed a weighted average annual interest rate of 12% unless otherwise provided by Subsection (b) of this section. All Constitutional provisions specifically setting rates in conflict with this provision are hereby repealed.

(b) Bonds issued by the Veterans' Land Board after the effective date of this subsection bear interest at a rate or rates determined by the board, but the rate or rates may not exceed a net effective interest rate of 10% per year unless otherwise provided by law. A statute that is in effect on the effective date of this subsection and that sets as a maximum interest rate payable on bonds issued by the Veterans' Land Board a rate different from the maximum rate provided by this subsection is ineffective unless reenacted by the legislature after that date.

Section 66. Limitation of Liability for Non-economic Damages

(a) In this section "economic damages" means compensatory damages for any pecuniary loss or damage. The term does not include any loss or damage, however characterized, for past, present, and future physical pain and suffering, mental anguish and suffering, loss of consortium, loss of companionship and society, disfigurement, or physical impairment.

(b) Notwithstanding any other provision of this constitution, the legislature by statute may determine the limit of liability for all damages and losses, however characterized, other than economic damages, of a provider of medical or health care with respect to treatment, lack of treatment, or other claimed departure from an accepted standard of medical or health care or safety, however characterized, that is or is claimed to be a cause of, or that contributes or is claimed to contribute to, disease, injury, or death of a person. This subsection applies without regard to whether the claim or cause of action arises under or is derived from common law, a statute, or other law, including any claim or cause of action based or sounding in tort, contract, or any other theory or any combination of theories of liability. The claim or cause of action includes a medical or health care liability claim as defined by the legislature.

(c) Notwithstanding any other provision of this constitution, after January 1, 2005, the legislature by statute may determine the limit of liability for all damages and losses, however characterized, other than economic damages, in a claim or cause of action not covered by Subsection (b) of this section. This subsection applies without regard to whether the claim or cause of action arises under or is derived from common law, a statute, or other law, including any claim or cause of action based or sounding in tort, contract, or any other theory or any combination of theories of liability.

(d) Except as provided by Subsection (c) of this section, this section applies to a law enacted by the 78th Legislature, Regular Session, 2003, and to all subsequent regular or special sessions of the legislature.

(e) A legislative exercise of authority under Subsection (c) of this section requires a three-fifths vote of all the members elected to each house and must include language citing this section.

Section 67. Cancer Prevention and Research Institute of Texas; Bonds

(a) The legislature shall establish the Cancer Prevention and Research Institute of Texas to:

(1) make grants to provide funds to public or private persons to implement the Texas Cancer Plan, and to institutions of learning and to advanced medical research facilities and collaborations in this state for:

(A) research into the causes of and cures for all forms of cancer in humans;

(B) facilities for use in research into the causes of and cures for cancer; and

(C) research, including translational research, to develop therapies, protocols, medical pharmaceuticals, or procedures for the cure or substantial mitigation of all types of cancer in humans;

(2) support institutions of learning and advanced medical research facilities and collaborations in this state in all stages in the process of finding the causes of all types of cancer in humans and developing cures, from laboratory research to clinical trials and including programs to address the problem of access to advanced cancer treatment; and

(3) establish the appropriate standards and oversight bodies to ensure the proper use of funds authorized under this provision for cancer research and facilities development.

(b) The members of the governing body and any other decision-making body of the Cancer Prevention and Research Institute of Texas may serve four-year terms.

(c) The legislature by general law may authorize the Texas Public Finance Authority to provide for, issue, and sell general obligation bonds of the State of Texas on behalf of the Cancer Prevention and Research Institute of Texas in an amount not to exceed $3 billion and to enter into related credit agreements. The Texas Public Finance Authority may not issue more than $300 million in bonds authorized by this subsection in a year. The bonds shall be executed in the form, on the terms, and in the denominations, bear interest, and be issued in installments as prescribed by the Texas Public Finance Authority.

(d) Proceeds from the sale of the bonds shall be deposited in separate funds or accounts, as provided by general law, within the state treasury to be used by the Cancer Prevention and Research Institute of Texas for the purposes of this section.

(e) Notwithstanding any other provision of this constitution, the Cancer Prevention and Research Institute of Texas, which is established in state government, may use the proceeds from bonds issued under Subsection (c) of this section and federal or private grants and gifts to pay for:

(1) grants for cancer research, for research facilities, and for research opportunities in this state to develop therapies, protocols, medical pharmaceuticals, or procedures for the cure or substantial mitigation of all types of cancer in humans;

(2) grants for cancer prevention and control programs in this state to mitigate the incidence of all types of cancer in humans;

(3) the purchase, subject to approval by the Cancer Prevention and Research Institute, of laboratory facilities by or on behalf of a state agency or grant recipient; and

(4) the operation of the Cancer Prevention and Research Institute of Texas.

(f) The bond proceeds may be used to pay the costs of issuing the bonds and any administrative expense related to the bonds.

(g) While any of the bonds or interest on the bonds authorized by this section is outstanding and unpaid, from the first money coming into the state treasury in each fiscal year not otherwise appropriated by this constitution, an amount sufficient to pay the principal of and interest on bonds that mature or become due during the fiscal year and to make payments that become due under a related credit agreement during the fiscal year is appropriated, less the amount in the sinking fund at the close of the previous fiscal year.

(h) Bonds issued under this section, after approval by the attorney general, registration by the comptroller of public accounts, and delivery to the purchasers, are incontestable and are general obligations of the State of Texas under this constitution.

(i) Before the Cancer Prevention and Research Institute of Texas may make a grant of any proceeds of the bonds issued under this section, the recipient of the grant must have an amount of funds equal to one-half the amount of the grant dedicated to the research that is the subject of the grant request.

(j) The Texas Public Finance Authority shall consider using a business whose principal place of business is located in the state to issue the bonds authorized by this section and shall include using a historically underutilized business as defined by general law.

ARTICLE 4. EXECUTIVE DEPARTMENT

Section 1. Officers Constituting Executive Department

The Executive Department of the State shall consist of a Governor, who shall be the Chief Executive Officer of the State, a Lieutenant Governor, Secretary of State, Comptroller of Public Accounts, Commissioner of the General Land Office, and Attorney General.

Section 2. Election of Officers of Executive Department

All the above officers of the Executive Department (except Secretary of State) shall be elected by the qualified voters of the State at the time and places of election for members of the Legislature.

Section 3. Returns of Election; Declaration of Election; Tie Votes; Contests

The returns of every election for said executive officers, until otherwise provided by law, shall be made out, sealed up, and transmitted by the returning officers prescribed by law, to the seat of Government, directed to the Secretary of State, who shall deliver the same to the Speaker of the House of Representatives, as soon as the Speaker shall be chosen, and the said Speaker shall, during the first week of the session of the Legislature, open and publish them in the presence of both Houses of the Legislature. The person, voted for at said election, having the highest number of votes for each of said offices respectively, and being constitutionally eligible, shall be declared by the Speaker, under sanction of the Legislature, to be elected to said office. But, if two or more persons shall have the highest and an equal number of votes for either of said offices, one of them shall be immediately chosen to such office by joint vote of both Houses of the Legislature. Contested elections for either of said offices, shall be determined by both Houses of the Legislature in joint session.

Section 3a. Death, Disability, or Failure to Qualify of Person Receiving Highest Vote for Governor

If, at the time the Legislature shall canvass the election returns for the offices of Governor and Lieutenant Governor, the person receiving the highest number of votes for the office of Governor, as declared by the Speaker, has died, fails to qualify, or for any other reason is unable to assume the office of Governor, then the person having the highest number of votes for the office of Lieutenant Governor shall become Governor for the full term to which the person was elected as Governor. By becoming the Governor, the person forfeits the office of Lieutenant Governor, and the resulting vacancy in the office of Lieutenant Governor shall be filled as provided by Section 9, Article III, of this Constitution. If the person with the highest number of votes for the office of Governor, as declared by the Speaker, becomes temporarily unable to take office, then the Lieutenant Governor shall act as Governor until the person with the highest number of votes for the office of Governor becomes able to assume the office of Governor. Any succession to the Governorship not otherwise provided for in this Constitution, may be provided for by law; provided, however, that any person succeeding to the office of Governor shall be qualified as otherwise provided in this Constitution, and shall, during the entire term to which he may succeed, be under all the restrictions and inhibitions imposed in this Constitution on the Governor.

Section 4. Installation of Governor; Term; Eligibility

The Governor elected at the general election in 1974, and thereafter, shall be installed on the first Tuesday after the organization of the Legislature, or as soon thereafter as practicable, and shall hold his office for the term of four years, or until his successor shall be duly installed. He shall be at least thirty years of age, a citizen of the United States, and shall have resided in this State at least five years immediately preceding his election.

Section 5. Compensation of Governor

The Governor shall, at stated times, receive as compensation for his services an annual salary in an amount to be fixed by the Legislature, and shall have the use and occupation of the Governor's Mansion, fixtures and furniture.

Section 6. Holding Other Office, Practice of Profession, and Receipt of Other Compensation by Governor Prohibited

During the time he holds the office of Governor, he shall not hold any other office: civil, military or corporate; nor shall he practice any profession, and receive compensation, reward, fee, or the promise thereof for the same; nor receive any salary, reward or compensation or the promise thereof from any person or corporation, for any service rendered or performed during the time he is Governor, or to be thereafter rendered or performed.

Section 7. Governor as Commander-in-Chief of Military Forces

He shall be Commander-in-Chief of the military forces of the State, except when they are called into actual service of the United States. He shall have power to call forth the militia to execute the laws of the State, to suppress insurrections, and to repel invasions.

Section 8. Convening Legislature on Extraordinary Occasions

(a) The Governor may, on extraordinary occasions, convene the Legislature at the seat of Government, or at a different place, in case that should be in possession of the public enemy or in case of the prevalence of disease threat. His proclamation therefor shall state specifically the purpose for which the Legislature is convened.

(b) The Governor shall convene the Legislature in special session to appoint presidential electors if the Governor determines that a reasonable likelihood exists that a final determination of the appointment of electors will not occur before the deadline prescribed by law to ascertain a conclusive determination of the appointment. The Legislature may not consider any subject other than the appointment of electors at that special session.

Section 9. Governor's Message and Recommendations; Accounting for Public Money; Estimates of Money Required

The Governor shall, at the commencement of each session of the Legislature, and at the close of his term of office, give to the Legislature information, by message, of the condition of the State; and he shall recommend to the Legislature such measures as he may deem expedient. He shall account to the Legislature for all public moneys received and paid out by him, from any funds subject to his order, with vouchers; and shall accompany his message with a statement of the same. And at the commencement of each regular session, he shall present estimates of the amount of money required to be raised by taxation for all purposes.

Section 10. Execution of Laws and Conduct of Business with other States and United States by Governor

He shall cause the laws to be faithfully executed and shall conduct, in person, or in such manner as shall be prescribed by law, all intercourse and business of the State with other States and with the United States.

Section 11. Board of Pardons and Paroles; Parole Laws; Reprieves, Commutations, and Pardons; Remission of Fines and Forfeitures

(a) The Legislature shall by law establish a Board of Pardons and Paroles and shall require it to keep record of its actions and the reasons for its actions. The Legislature shall have authority to enact parole laws and laws that require or permit courts to inform juries about the effect of good conduct time and eligibility for parole or mandatory supervision on the period of incarceration served by a defendant convicted of a criminal offense.

(b) In all criminal cases, except treason and impeachment, the Governor shall have power, after conviction or successful completion of a term of deferred adjudication community supervision, on the written signed recommendation and advice of the Board of Pardons and Paroles, or a majority thereof, to grant reprieves and commutations of punishment and pardons; and under such rules as the Legislature may prescribe, and upon the written recommendation and advice of a majority of the Board of Pardons and Paroles, he shall have the power to remit fines and forfeitures. The Governor shall have the power to grant one reprieve in any capital case for a period not to exceed thirty (30) days; and he shall have power to revoke conditional pardons. With the advice and consent of the Legislature, he may grant reprieves, commutations of punishment and pardons in cases of treason.

Section 11a. Suspension Of Sentence; Probation

The Courts of the State of Texas having original jurisdiction of criminal actions shall have the power, after conviction, to suspend the imposition or execution of sentence and to place the defendant upon probation and to reimpose such sentence, under such conditions as the Legislature may prescribe.
(Added Aug. 24, 1935.)

Section 11b. Criminal Justice Agencies

(a) The legislature by law may organize and combine into one or more agencies all agencies of the state that:

(1) have authority over the confinement or supervision of persons convicted of criminal offenses;

(2) set standards or distribute state funds to political subdivisions that have authority over the confinement or supervision of persons convicted of criminal offenses; or

(3) gather information about the administration of criminal justice.

(b) The legislature by law may authorize the appointment of members of more than one department of government to serve on the governing body.

Section 12. Vacancies in State or District Offices

(a) All vacancies in State or district offices, except members of the Legislature, shall be filled unless otherwise provided by law by appointment of the Governor.

(b) An appointment of the Governor made during a session of the Senate shall be with the advice and consent of two-thirds of the Senate present.

(c) In accordance with this section, the Senate may give its advice and consent on an appointment of the Governor made during a recess of the Senate. To be confirmed, the appointment must be with the advice and consent of two-thirds of the Senate present. If an appointment of the Governor is made during the recess of the Senate, the Governor shall nominate the appointee, or some other person to fill the vacancy, to the Senate during the first ten days of its next session following the appointment. If the Senate does not confirm a person under this subsection, the Governor shall nominate in accordance with this section the recess appointee or another person to fill the vacancy during the first ten days of each subsequent session of the Senate until a confirmation occurs. If the Governor does not nominate a person to the Senate during the first ten days of a session of the Senate as required by this subsection, the Senate at that session may consider the recess appointee as if the Governor had nominated the appointee.

(d) If the Senate, at any special session, does not take final action to confirm or reject a previously unconfirmed recess appointee or another person nominated to fill the vacancy for which the appointment was made:

(1) the Governor after the session may appoint another person to fill the vacancy; and

(2) the appointee, if otherwise qualified and if not removed as provided by law, is entitled to continue in office until the earlier of the following occurs:

(A) the Senate rejects the appointee at a subsequent session; or

(B) the Governor appoints another person to fill the vacancy under Subdivision (1) of this subsection.

(e) If the Senate, at a regular session, does not take final action to confirm or reject a previously unconfirmed recess appointee or another person nominated to fill the vacancy for which the appointment was made, the appointee or other person, as appropriate, is considered to be rejected by the Senate when the Senate session ends.

(f) If an appointee is rejected, the office shall immediately become vacant, and the Governor shall, without delay, make further nominations, until a confirmation takes place. If a person has been rejected by the Senate to fill a vacancy, the Governor may not appoint the person to fill the vacancy or, during the term of the vacancy for which the person was rejected, to fill another vacancy in the same office or on the same board, commission, or other body.

(g) Appointments to vacancies in offices elective by the people shall only continue until the next general election.

(h) The Legislature by general law may limit the term to be served by a person appointed by the Governor to fill a vacancy in a state or district office to a period that ends before the vacant term otherwise expires or, for an elective office, before the next election at which the vacancy is to be filled, if the appointment is made on or after November 1 preceding the general election for the succeeding term of the office of Governor and the Governor is not elected at that election to the succeeding term.

(i) For purposes of this section, the expiration of a term of office or the creation of a new office constitutes a vacancy.

(j) Expired

Section 13. Residence of Governor

During the session of the Legislature the Governor shall reside where its sessions are held, and at all other times at the seat of Government, except when by act of the Legislature, he may be required or authorized to reside elsewhere.

Section 14. Approval or Veto of Bills; Return and Reconsideration; Failure to Return; Veto of Items of Appropriation

Every bill which shall have passed both houses of the Legislature shall be presented to the Governor for his approval. If he approve he shall sign it; but if he disapprove it, he shall return it, with his objections, to the House in which it originated, which House shall enter the objections at large upon its journal, and proceed to reconsider it. If after such reconsideration, two-thirds of the members present agree to pass the bill, it shall be sent, with the objections, to the other House, by which likewise it shall be reconsidered; and, if approved by two-thirds of the members of that House, it shall become a law; but in such cases the votes of both Houses shall be determined by yeas and nays, and the names of the members voting for and against the bill shall be entered on the journal of each House respectively. If any bill shall not be returned by the Governor with his objections within ten days (Sundays excepted) after it shall have been presented to him, the same shall be a law, in like manner as if he had signed it, unless the Legislature, by its adjournment, prevent its return, in which case it shall be a law, unless he shall file the same, with his objections, in the office of the Secretary of State and give notice thereof by public proclamation within twenty days after such adjournment. If any bill presented to the Governor contains several items of appropriation he may object to one or more of such items, and approve the other portion of the bill. In such case he shall append to the bill, at the time of signing it, a statement of the items to which he objects, and no item so objected to shall take effect. If the Legislature be in session, he shall transmit to the House in which the bill originated a copy of such statement and the items objected to shall be separately considered. If, on reconsideration, one or more of such items be approved by two-thirds of the members present of each House, the same shall be part of the law, notwithstanding the objections of the Governor. If any such bill, containing several items of appropriation, not having been presented to the Governor ten days (Sundays excepted) prior to adjournment, be in the hands of the Governor at the time of adjournment, he shall have twenty days from such adjournment within which to file objections to any items thereof and make proclamation of the same, and such item or items shall not take effect.

Section 15. Approval or Veto of Orders, Resolutions, or Votes

Every order, resolution or vote to which the concurrence of both Houses of the Legislature may be necessary, except on questions of adjournment, shall be presented to the Governor, and, before it shall take effect, shall be approved by him; or, being disapproved, shall be repassed by both Houses, and all the rules, provisions and limitations shall apply thereto as prescribed in the last preceding section in the case of a bill.

Section 16. Lieutenant Governor

(a) There shall also be a Lieutenant Governor, who shall be chosen at every election for Governor by the same voters, in the same manner, continue in office for the same time, and possess the same qualifications. The voters shall distinguish for whom they vote as Governor and for whom as Lieutenant Governor.

(b) The Lieutenant Governor shall by virtue of his office be President of the Senate, and shall have, when in Committee of the Whole, a right to debate and vote on all questions; and when the Senate is equally divided to give the casting vote.

(c) In the case of the temporary inability or temporary disqualification of the Governor to serve, the impeachment of the Governor, or the absence of the Governor from the State, the Lieutenant Governor shall exercise the powers and authority appertaining to the office of Governor until the Governor becomes able or qualified to resume serving, is acquitted, or returns to the State.

(d) If the Governor refuses to serve or becomes permanently unable to serve, or if the office of Governor becomes vacant, the Lieutenant Governor becomes Governor for the remainder of the term being served by the Governor who refused or became unable to serve or vacated the office. On becoming Governor, the person vacates the office of Lieutenant Governor, and the resulting vacancy in the office of Lieutenant Governor shall be filled in the manner provided by Section 9, Article III, of this Constitution.

Section 17. President Pro Tempore of Senate Serving as Governor; Compensation of Lieutenant Governor and President Pro Tempore of Senate

(a) If, while exercising the powers and authority appertaining to the office of Governor under Section 16(c) of this article, the Lieutenant Governor becomes temporarily unable or disqualified to serve, is impeached, or is absent from the State, the President pro tempore of the Senate, for the time being, shall exercise the powers and authority appertaining to the office of Governor until the Governor or Lieutenant Governor reassumes those powers and duties.

(b) The Lieutenant Governor shall, while acting as President of the Senate, receive for his or her services the same compensation and mileage which shall be allowed to the members of the Senate, and no more unless the Texas Ethics Commission recommends and the voters approve a higher salary, in which case the salary is that amount; and during the time the Lieutenant Governor exercises the powers and authority appertaining to the office of Governor, the Lieutenant Governor shall receive in like manner the same compensation which the Governor would have received had the Governor been employed in the duties of that office, and no more. An increase in the emoluments of the office of Lieutenant Governor does not make a member of the Legislature ineligible to serve in the office of Lieutenant Governor.

(c) The President pro tempore of the Senate shall, during the time that officer exercises the powers and authority appertaining to the office of Governor, receive in like manner the same compensation which the Governor would have received had the Governor been employed in the duties of that office.

Section 18. Restrictions and Inhibitions Applicable to Lieutenant Governor or President Pro Tempore of Senate Serving as Governor

The Lieutenant Governor or President pro tempore of the Senate shall, during the time the Lieutenant Governor or President pro tempore exercises the powers and authority appertaining to the office of Governor, be under all the restrictions and inhibitions imposed in this Constitution on the Governor.

Section 19. Seal of State

There shall be a Seal of the State which shall be kept by the Secretary of State, and used by him officially under the direction of the Governor. The Seal of the State shall be a star of five points encircled by olive and live oak branches, and the words "The State of Texas."

Section 20. Commissions

All commissions shall be in the name and by the authority of the State of Texas, sealed with the State Seal, signed by the Governor and attested by the Secretary of State.

Section 21. Secretary of State

There shall be a Secretary of State, who shall be appointed by the Governor, by and with the advice and consent of the Senate, and who shall continue in office during the term of service of the Governor. He shall authenticate the publication of the laws, and keep a fair register of all official acts and proceedings of the Governor, and shall, when required, lay the same and all papers, minutes and vouchers relative thereto, before the Legislature, or either House thereof, and shall perform such other duties as may be required of him by law. He shall receive for his services an annual salary in an amount to be fixed by the Legislature.

Section 22. Attorney General

The Attorney General shall represent the State in all suits and pleas in the Supreme Court of the State in which the State may be a party, and shall especially inquire into the charter rights of all private corporations, and from time to time, in the name of the State, take such action in the courts as may be proper and necessary to prevent any private corporation from exercising any power or demanding or collecting any species of taxes, tolls, freight or wharfage not authorized by law. He shall, whenever sufficient cause exists, seek a judicial forfeiture of such charters, unless otherwise expressly directed by law, and give legal advice in writing to the Governor and other executive officers, when requested by them, and perform such other duties as may be required by law.

Section 23. Term and Salary of Elected State Officers; Fees, Costs, and Perquisites

The Comptroller of Public Accounts, the Commissioner of the General Land Office, the Attorney General, and any statutory State officer who is elected by the electorate of Texas at large, unless a term of office is otherwise specifically provided in this Constitution, shall each hold office for the term of four years. Each shall receive an annual salary in an amount to be fixed by the Legislature and perform such duties as are or may be required by law. They and the Secretary of State shall not receive to their own use any fees, costs or perquisites of office. All fees that may be payable by law for any service performed by any officer specified in this section or in the officer's office, shall be paid, when received, into the State Treasury.

Section 24. Accounts and Reports of Executive Officers to Governor; Perjury for False Report

An account shall be kept by the officers of the Executive Department, and by all officers and managers of State institutions, of all moneys and choses in action received and disbursed or otherwise disposed of by them, severally, from all sources, and for every service performed; and a semi-annual report thereof shall be made to the Governor under oath. The Governor may, at any time, require information in writing from any and all of said officers or managers, upon any subject relating to the duties, condition, management and expenses of their respective offices and institutions, which information shall be required by the Governor under oath, and the Governor may also inspect their books, accounts, vouchers and public funds;

and any officer or manager who, at any time, shall wilfully make a false report or give false information, shall be guilty of perjury, and so adjudged, and punished accordingly, and removed from office.

Section 25. Breaches of Trust and Duty by Custodians of Public Funds

The Legislature shall pass efficient laws facilitating the investigation of breaches of trust and duty by all custodians of public funds and providing for their suspension from office on reasonable cause shown, and for the appointment of temporary incumbents of their offices during such suspension.

Section 26. Notaries Public

(a) The Secretary of State shall appoint a convenient number of Notaries Public for the state who shall perform such duties as now are or may be prescribed by law. The qualifications of Notaries Public shall be prescribed by law.

(b) The terms of office of Notaries Public shall be not less than two years nor more than four years as provided by law.

ARTICLE 5. JUDICIAL DEPARTMENT

Section 1. Judicial Power Vested in Courts; Legislative Power Regarding Courts

The judicial power of this State shall be vested in one Supreme Court, in one Court of Criminal Appeals, in Courts of Appeals, in District Courts, in County Courts, in Commissioners Courts, in Courts of Justices of the Peace, and in such other courts as may be provided by law.

The Legislature may establish such other courts as it may deem necessary and prescribe the jurisdiction and organization thereof, and may conform the jurisdiction of the district and other inferior courts thereto.

Section 1-A. Retirement, Compensation, Discipline, and Removal of Justices and Judges; State Commission on Judicial Conduct

(1) Subject to the further provisions of this Section, the Legislature shall provide for the retirement and compensation of Justices and Judges of the Appellate Courts and District and Criminal District Courts on account of length of service, age and disability, and for their reassignment to active duty where and when needed. The office of every such Justice and Judge shall become vacant on the expiration of the term during which the incumbent reaches the age of seventy-five (75) years or such earlier age, not less than seventy (70) years, as the Legislature may prescribe, except that if a Justice or Judge elected to serve or fill the remainder of a six-year term reaches the age of seventy-five (75) years during the first four years of the term, the office of that Justice or Judge shall become vacant on December 31 of the fourth year of the term to which the Justice or Judge was elected.

(2) The State Commission on Judicial Conduct consists of thirteen (13) members, to wit: (i) one (1) Justice of a Court of Appeals; (ii) one (1) District Judge; (iii) two (2) members of the State Bar, who have respectively practiced as such for over ten (10) consecutive years next preceding their selection; (iv) five (5) citizens, at least thirty (30) years of age, not licensed to practice law nor holding any salaried public office or employment; (v) one (1) Justice of the Peace; (vi) one (1) Judge of a Municipal Court; (vii) one (1) Judge of a County Court at Law; and (viii) one (1) Judge of a Constitutional County Court; provided that no person shall be or remain a member of the Commission, who does not maintain physical residence within this State, or who shall have ceased to retain the qualifications above specified for that person's respective class of membership, and provided that a Commissioner of class (i), (ii), (iii), (vii), or (viii) may not reside or hold a judgeship in the same court of appeals district as another member of the Commission. Commissioners of classes (i), (ii), (vii), and (viii) above shall be chosen by the Supreme Court with advice and consent of the Senate, those of class (iii) by the Board of Directors of the State Bar under regulations to be prescribed by the Supreme Court with advice and consent of the Senate, those of class (iv) by appointment of the Governor with advice and consent of the Senate, and the commissioners of classes (v) and (vi) by appointment of the Supreme Court as provided by law, with the advice and consent of the Senate.

(3) The regular term of office of Commissioners shall be six (6) years; but the initial members of each of classes (i), (ii) and (iii) shall respectively be chosen for terms of four (4) and six (6) years, and the initial members of class (iiii) for respective terms of two (2), four (4) and six (6) years. Interim vacancies shall be filled in the same manner as vacancies due to expiration of a full term, but only for the unexpired portion of the term in question. Commissioners may succeed themselves in office only if having served less than three (3) consecutive years.

(4) Commissioners shall receive no compensation for their services as such. The Legislature shall provide for the payment of the necessary expense for the operation of the Commission.

(5) The Commission may hold its meetings, hearings and other proceedings at such times and places as it shall determine but shall meet at Austin at least once each year. It shall annually select one of its members as Chairman. A quorum shall consist of seven (7) members. Proceedings shall be by majority vote of those present, except that recommendations for retirement, censure, suspension, or removal of any person holding an office named in Paragraph A of Subsection (6) of this Section shall be by affirmative vote of at least seven (7) members.

(6) A. Any Justice or Judge of the courts established by this Constitution or created by the Legislature as provided in Section 1, Article V, of this Constitution, may, subject to the other provisions hereof, be removed from office for willful or persistent violation of rules promulgated by the Supreme Court of Texas, incompetence in performing the duties of the office, willful violation of the Code of Judicial Conduct, or willful or persistent conduct that is clearly inconsistent with the proper performance of his duties or casts public discredit upon the judiciary or administration of justice. Any person holding such office may be disciplined or censured, in lieu of removal from office, as provided by this section. Any person holding an office specified in this subsection may be suspended from office with or without pay by the Commission immediately on being indicted by a State or Federal grand jury for a felony offense or charged with a misdemeanor involving official misconduct. On the filing of a sworn complaint charging a person holding such office with willful or persistent violation of rules promulgated by the Supreme Court of Texas, incompetence in performing the duties of the office, willful violation of the Code of Judicial Conduct, or willful and persistent conduct that is clearly inconsistent with the proper performance of his duties or casts public discredit on the judiciary or on the administration of justice, the Commission, after giving the person notice and an opportunity to appear and be heard before the Commission, may recommend to the Supreme Court the suspension of such person from office. The Supreme Court, after considering the record of such appearance and the recommendation of the Commission, may suspend the person from office with or without pay, pending final disposition of the charge.

B. Any person holding an office named in Paragraph A of this subsection who is eligible for retirement benefits under the laws of this state providing for judicial retirement may be involuntarily retired, and any person holding an office named in that paragraph who is not eligible for retirement benefits under such laws may be removed from office, for disability seriously interfering with the performance of his duties, which is, or is likely to become, permanent in nature.

C. The law relating to the removal, discipline, suspension, or censure of a Justice or Judge of the courts established by this Constitution or created by the Legislature as provided in this Constitution applies to a master or magistrate appointed as provided by law to serve a trial court of this State and to a retired or former Judge who continues as a judicial officer subject to an assignment to sit on a court of this State. Under the law relating to the removal of an active Justice or Judge, the Commission and the review tribunal may prohibit a retired or former Judge from holding judicial office in the future or from sitting on a court of this State by assignment.

(7) The Commission shall keep itself informed as fully as may be of circumstances relating to the misconduct or disability of particular persons holding an office named in Paragraph A of Subsection (6) of this Section, receive complaints or reports, formal or informal, from any source in this behalf and make such preliminary investigations as it may determine. Its orders for the attendance or testimony of witnesses or for the production of documents at any hearing or investigation shall be enforceable by contempt proceedings in the District Court or by a Master.

(8) After such investigation as it deems necessary, the Commission may in its discretion issue a private or public admonition, warning, reprimand, or requirement that the person obtain additional training or education, or if the Commission determines that the situation merits such action, it may institute formal proceedings and order a formal hearing to be held before it concerning a person holding an office or position specified in Subsection (6) of this Section, or it may in its discretion request the Supreme Court to appoint an active or retired District Judge or Justice of a Court of Appeals, or retired Judge or Justice of the Court of Criminal Appeals or the Supreme Court, as a Master to hear and take evidence in the matter, and to report thereon to the Commission. The Master shall have all the power of a District Judge in the enforcement of orders pertaining to witnesses, evidence, and procedure. If, after formal hearing, or after considering the record and report of a Master, the Commission finds good cause therefor, it shall issue an order of public admonition, warning, reprimand, censure, or requirement that the person holding an office or position specified in Subsection (6) of this Section obtain additional training or education, or it shall recommend to a review tribunal the removal or retirement, as the case may be, of the person and shall thereupon file with the tribunal the entire record before the Commission.

(9) A tribunal to review the Commission's recommendation for the removal or retirement of a person holding an office or position specified in Subsection (6) of this Section is composed of seven (7) Justices or Judges of the Courts of Appeals who are selected by lot by the Chief Justice of the Supreme Court. Each Court of Appeals shall designate one of its members for inclusion in the list from which the selection is made. Service on the tribunal shall be considered part of the official duties of a judge, and no additional compensation may be paid for such service. The review tribunal shall review the record of the proceedings on the law and facts and in its discretion may, for good cause shown, permit the introduction of additional evidence. Within 90 days after the date on which the record is filed with the review tribunal, it shall order public censure, retirement or removal, as it finds just and proper, or wholly reject the recommendation. A Justice, Judge, Master, or Magistrate may appeal a decision of the review tribunal to the Supreme Court under the substantial evidence rule. Upon an order for involuntary retirement for disability or an order for removal, the office in question shall become vacant. The review tribunal, in an order for involuntary retirement for disability or an order for removal, may prohibit such person from holding judicial office in the future. The rights of an incumbent so retired to retirement benefits shall be the same as if his retirement had been voluntary.

(10) All papers filed with and proceedings before the Commission or a Master shall be confidential, unless otherwise provided by law, and the filing of papers with, and the giving of testimony before the Commission or a Master shall be privileged, unless otherwise provided by law. However, the Commission may issue a public statement through its executive director or its Chairman at any time during any of its proceedings under this Section when sources other than the Commission cause notoriety concerning a Judge or the Commission itself and the Commission determines that the best interests of a Judge or of the public will be served by issuing the statement.

(11) The Supreme Court shall by rule provide for the procedure before the Commission, Masters, review tribunal, and the Supreme Court. Such rule shall provide the right of discovery of evidence to a Justice, Judge, Master, or Magistrate after formal proceedings are instituted and shall afford to any person holding an office or position specified in Subsection (6) of this Section, against whom a proceeding is instituted to cause his retirement or removal, due process of law for the procedure before the Commission, Masters, review tribunal, and the Supreme Court in the same manner that any person whose property rights are in jeopardy in an adjudicatory proceeding is entitled to due process of law, regardless of whether or not the interest of the person holding an office or position specified in Subsection (6) of this Section in remaining in active status is considered to be a right or a privilege. Due process shall include the right to notice, counsel, hearing, confrontation of his accusers, and all such other incidents of due process as are ordinarily available in proceedings whether or not misfeasance is charged, upon proof of which a penalty may be imposed.

(12) No person holding an office specified in Subsection (6) of this Section shall sit as a member of the Commission in any proceeding involving his own suspension, discipline, censure, retirement or removal.

(13) This Section 1-a is alternative to and cumulative of, the methods of removal of persons holding an office named in Paragraph A of Subsection (6) of this Section provided elsewhere in this Constitution.

(14) The Legislature may promulgate laws in furtherance of this Section that are not inconsistent with its provisions.

Section 2. Supreme Court; Justices

(a) The Supreme Court shall consist of the Chief Justice and eight Justices, any five of whom shall constitute a quorum, and the concurrence of five shall be necessary to a decision of a case; provided, that when the business of the court may require, the court may sit in sections as designated by the court to hear argument of causes and to consider applications for writs of error or other preliminary matters.

(b) No person shall be eligible to serve in the office of Chief Justice or Justice of the Supreme Court unless the person is licensed to practice law in this state and is, at the time of election, a citizen of the United States and of this state, and has attained the age of thirty-five years, and has been a practicing lawyer, or a lawyer and judge of a court of record together at least ten years.

(c) Said Justices shall be elected (three of them each two years) by the qualified voters of the state at a general election; shall hold their offices six years; and shall each receive such compensation as shall be provided by law.

Section 3. Jurisdiction Of Supreme Court

(a) The Supreme Court shall exercise the judicial power of the state except as otherwise provided in this Constitution. Its jurisdiction shall be co-extensive with the limits of the State and its determinations shall be final except in criminal law matters. Its appellate jurisdiction shall be final and shall extend to all cases except in criminal law matters and as otherwise provided in this Constitution or by law. The Supreme Court and the Justices thereof shall have power to issue writs of habeas corpus, as may be prescribed by law, and under such regulations as may be prescribed by law, the said courts and the Justices thereof may issue the writs of mandamus, procedendo, certiorari and such other writs, as may be necessary to enforce its jurisdiction. The Legislature may confer original jurisdiction on the Supreme Court to issue writs of quo warranto and mandamus in such cases as may be specified, except as against the Governor of the State.

(b) The Supreme Court shall also have power, upon affidavit or otherwise as by the court may be determined, to ascertain such matters of fact as may be necessary to the proper exercise of its jurisdiction.

Section 3a. Repealed

Section 3-B. Direct Appeal From Order Granting or Denying Injunction

The Legislature shall have the power to provide by law, for an appeal direct to the Supreme Court of this State from an order of any trial court granting or denying an interlocutory or permanent injunction on the grounds of the constitutionality or unconstitutionality of any statute of this State, or on the validity or invalidity of any administrative order issued by any state agency under any statute of this State.

Section 3-C. Questions of State Law Certified from Federal Appellate Court

(a) The supreme court and the court of criminal appeals have jurisdiction to answer questions of state law certified from a federal appellate court.

(b) The supreme court and the court of criminal appeals shall promulgate rules of procedure relating to the review of those questions.

Section 4. Court of Criminal Appeals; Judges

(a) The Court of Criminal Appeals shall consist of eight Judges and one Presiding Judge. The Judges shall have the same qualifications and receive the same salaries as the Associate Justices of the Supreme Court, and the Presiding Judge shall have the same qualifications and receive the same salary as the Chief Justice of the Supreme Court. The Presiding Judge and the Judges shall be elected by the qualified voters of the state at a general election and shall hold their offices for a term of six years.

(b) For the purpose of hearing cases, the Court of Criminal Appeals may sit in panels of three Judges, the designation thereof to be under rules established by the court. In a panel of three Judges, two Judges shall constitute a quorum and the concurrence of two Judges shall be necessary for a decision. The Presiding Judge, under rules established by the court, shall convene the court en banc for the transaction of all other business and may convene the court en banc for the purpose of hearing cases. The court must sit en banc during proceedings involving capital punishment and other cases as required by law. When convened en banc, five Judges shall constitute a quorum and the concurrence of five Judges shall be necessary for a decision. The Court of Criminal Appeals may appoint Commissioners in aid of the Court of Criminal Appeals as provided by law.

Section 5. Jurisdiction of Court of Criminal Appeals

(a) The Court of Criminal Appeals shall have final appellate jurisdiction coextensive with the limits of the state, and its determinations shall be final, in all criminal cases of whatever grade, with such exceptions and under such regulations as may be provided in this Constitution or as prescribed by law.

(b) The appeal of all cases in which the death penalty has been assessed shall be to the Court of Criminal Appeals. The appeal of all other criminal cases shall be to the Courts of Appeal as prescribed by law. In addition, the Court of Criminal Appeals may, on its own motion, review a decision of a Court of Appeals in a criminal case as provided by law. Discretionary review by the Court of Criminal Appeals is not a matter of right, but of sound judicial discretion.

(c) Subject to such regulations as may be prescribed by law, the Court of Criminal Appeals and the Judges thereof shall have the power to issue the writ of habeas corpus, and, in criminal law matters, the writs of mandamus, procedendo, prohibition, and certiorari. The Court and the Judges thereof shall have the power to issue such other writs as may be necessary to protect its jurisdiction or enforce its judgments. The court shall have the power upon affidavit or otherwise to ascertain such matters of fact as may be necessary to the exercise of its jurisdiction.

Section 5a. Clerks of Appellate Courts

The Supreme Court, Court of Criminal Appeals, and each Court of Appeals shall each appoint a clerk of the court, who shall give bond in the manner required by law, may hold office for four years subject to removal by the appointing court for good cause entered of record on the minutes of the court, and shall receive such compensation as the legislature may provide.

Section 5b. Supreme Court and Court of Criminal Appeals: Location and Term

The Supreme Court and the Court of Criminal Appeals may sit at any time during the year at the seat of government or, at the court's discretion, at any other location in this state for the transaction of business, and each term of either court shall begin and end with each calendar year.

Section 6. Courts of Appeals; Justices; Jurisdiction

(a) The state shall be divided into courts of appeals districts, with each district having a Chief Justice, two or more other Justices, and such other officials as may be provided by law. The Justices shall have the qualifications prescribed for Justices of the Supreme Court. The Court of Appeals may sit in sections as authorized by law. The concurrence of a majority of the judges sitting in a section is necessary to decide a case. Said Court of Appeals shall have appellate jurisdiction co-extensive with the limits of their respective districts, which shall extend to all cases of which the District Courts or County Courts have original or appellate jurisdiction, under such restrictions and regulations as may be prescribed by law. Provided, that the decision of said courts shall be conclusive on all questions of fact brought before them on appeal or error. Said courts shall have such other jurisdiction, original and appellate, as may be prescribed by law.

(b) Each of said Courts of Appeals shall hold its sessions at a place in its district to be designated by the Legislature, and at such time as may be prescribed by law. Said Justices shall be elected by the qualified voters of their respective districts at a general election, for a term of six years and shall receive for their services the sum provided by law.

(c) All constitutional and statutory references to the Courts of Civil Appeals shall be construed to mean the Courts of Appeals.

Section 7. Judicial Districts; District Judges; Terms or Sessions; Absence, Disability, or Disqualification of District Judge

The State shall be divided into judicial districts, with each district having one or more Judges as may be provided by law or by this Constitution. Each district judge shall be elected by the qualified voters at a General Election and shall be a citizen of the United States and of this State, who is licensed to practice law in this State and has been a practicing lawyer or a Judge of a Court in this State, or both combined, for four (4) years next preceding his election, who has resided in the district in which he was elected for two (2) years next preceding his election, and who shall reside in his district during his term of office and hold his office for the period of four (4) years, and who shall receive for his services an annual salary to be fixed by the Legislature. The Court shall conduct its proceedings at the county seat of the county in which the case is pending, except as otherwise provided by law. He shall hold the regular terms of his Court at the County Seat of each County in his district in such manner as may be prescribed by law. The Legislature shall have power by General or Special Laws to make such provisions concerning the terms or sessions of each Court as it may deem necessary.
The Legislature shall also provide for the holding of District Court when the Judge thereof is absent, or is from any cause disabled or disqualified from presiding.

Section 7a. Judicial Districts Board; Reapportionment of Judicial Districts

(a) The Judicial Districts Board is created to reapportion the judicial districts authorized by Article V, Section 7, of this constitution.

(b) The membership of the board consists of the Chief Justice of the Texas Supreme Court who serves as chairman, the presiding judge of the Texas Court of Criminal Appeals, the presiding judge of each of the administrative judicial districts of the state, the president of the Texas Judicial Council, and one person who is licensed to practice law in this state appointed by the governor with the advice and consent of the senate for a term of four years. In the event of a vacancy in the appointed membership, the vacancy is filled for the unexpired term in the same manner as the original appointment.

(c) A majority of the total membership of the board constitutes a quorum for the transaction of business. The adoption of a reapportionment order requires a majority vote of the total membership of the board.

(d) The reapportionment powers of the board shall be exercised in the interims between regular sessions of the legislature, except that a reapportionment may not be ordered by the board during an interim immediately following a regular session of the legislature in which a valid and subsisting statewide apportionment of judicial districts is enacted by the legislature. The board has other powers and duties as provided by the legislature and shall exercise its powers under the policies, rules, standards, and conditions, not inconsistent with this section, that the legislature provides.

(e) Unless the legislature enacts a statewide reapportionment of the judicial districts following each federal decennial census, the board shall convene not later than the first Monday of June of the third year following the year in which the federal decennial census is taken to make a statewide reapportionment of the districts. The board shall complete its work on the reapportionment and file its order with the secretary of state not later than August 31 of the same year. If the Judicial Districts Board fails to make a statewide apportionment by that date, the Legislative Redistricting Board established by Article III, Section 28, of this constitution shall make a statewide reapportionment of the judicial districts not later than the 150th day after the final day for the Judicial Districts Board to make the reapportionment.

(f) In addition to the statewide reapportionment, the board may reapportion the judicial districts of the state as the necessity for reapportionment appears by re-designating, in one or more reapportionment orders, the county or counties that comprise the specific judicial districts affected by those reapportionment orders. In modifying any judicial district, no county having a population as large or larger than the population of the judicial district being reapportioned shall be added to the judicial district.

(g) Except as provided by Subsection (i) of this section, this section does not limit the power of the legislature to reapportion the judicial districts of the state, to increase the number of judicial districts, or to provide for consequent matters on reapportionment. The legislature may provide for the effect of a reapportionment made by the board on pending cases or the transfer of pending cases, for jurisdiction of a county court where county court jurisdiction has been vested by law in a district court affected by the reapportionment, for terms of the courts upon existing officers and their duties, and for all other matters affected by the reapportionment. The legislature may delegate any of these powers to the board. The legislature shall provide for the necessary expenses of the board.

(h) Any judicial reapportionment order adopted by the board must be approved by a record vote of the majority of the membership of both the senate and house of representatives before such order can become effective and binding.

(i) The legislature, the Judicial Districts Board, or the Legislative Redistricting Board may not redistrict the judicial districts to provide for any judicial district smaller in size than an entire county except as provided by this section. Judicial districts smaller in size than the entire county may be created subsequent to a general election where a majority of the persons voting on the proposition adopt the proposition "to allow the division of

_____ County into judicial districts composed of parts of _____ County." No redistricting plan may be proposed or adopted by the legislature, the Judicial Districts Board, or the Legislative Redistricting Board in anticipation of a future action by the voters of any county.

Section 8. Jurisdiction of District Courts

District Court jurisdiction consists of exclusive, appellate, and original jurisdiction of all actions, proceedings, and remedies, except in cases where exclusive, appellate, or original jurisdiction may be conferred by this Constitution or other law on some other court, tribunal, or administrative body. District Court judges shall have the power to issue writs necessary to enforce their jurisdiction.

The District Court shall have appellate jurisdiction and general supervisory control over the County Commissioners Court, with such exceptions and under such regulations as may be prescribed by law.

Section 9. Clerk of District Court

There shall be a Clerk for the District Court of each county, who shall be elected by the qualified voters and who shall hold his office for four years, subject to removal by information, or by indictment of a grand jury, and conviction of a petit jury. In case of vacancy, the Judge of the District Court shall have the power to appoint a Clerk, who shall hold until the office can be filled by election.

Section 10. Trial by Jury in Civil Cases

In the trial of all causes in the District Courts, the plaintiff or defendant shall, upon application made in open court, have the right of trial by jury; but no jury shall be empaneled in any civil case unless demanded by a party to the case, and a jury fee be paid by the party demanding a jury, for such sum, and with such exceptions as may be prescribed by the Legislature.

Section 11. Disqualification of Judges; Exchange of Districts; Holding Court for Other Judges

No judge shall sit in any case wherein the judge may be interested, or where either of the parties may be connected with the judge, either by affinity or consanguinity, within such a degree as may be prescribed by law, or when the judge shall have been counsel in the case. When the Supreme Court, the Court of Criminal Appeals, the Court of Appeals, or any member of any of those courts shall be thus disqualified to hear and determine any case or cases in said court, the same shall be certified to the Governor of the State, who shall immediately commission the requisite number of persons learned in the law for the trial and determination of such cause or causes. When a judge of the District Court is disqualified by any of the causes above stated, the parties may, by consent, appoint a proper person to try said case; or upon their failing to do so, a competent person may be appointed to try the same in the county where it is pending, in such manner as may be prescribed by law.

And the District Judges may exchange districts, or hold courts for each other when they may deem it expedient, and shall do so when required by law. This disqualification of judges of inferior tribunals shall be remedied and vacancies in their offices filled as may be prescribed by law.

Section 12. Judges to be Conservators of the Peace; Indictments and Information

(a) All judges of courts of this State, by virtue of their office, are conservators of the peace throughout the State.

(b) An indictment is a written instrument presented to a court by a grand jury charging a person with the commission of an offense. An information is a written instrument presented to a court by an attorney for the State charging a person with the commission of an offense. The practice and procedures relating to the use of indictments and informations, including their contents, amendment, sufficiency, and requisites, are as provided by law. The presentment of an indictment or information to a court invests the court with jurisdiction of the cause.

Section 13. Grand and Petit Juries in District Courts: Composition and Verdict

Grand and petit juries in the District Courts shall be composed of twelve persons, except that petit juries in a criminal case below the grade of felony shall be composed of six persons; but nine members of a grand jury shall be a quorum to transact business and present bills. In trials of civil cases in the District Courts, nine members of the jury, concurring, may render a verdict, but when the verdict shall be rendered by less than the whole number, it shall be signed by every member of the jury concurring in it. When, pending the trial of any case, one or more jurors not exceeding three, may die, or be disabled from sitting, the remainder of the jury shall have the power to render the verdict; provided, that the Legislature may change or modify the rule authorizing less than the whole number of the jury to render a verdict.

Section 14. Juror Qualifications

(a) The legislature shall prescribe by law the qualifications of grand jurors and petit jurors.

(b) The legislature shall enact laws to exclude from serving on juries persons who have been convicted of bribery, perjury, forgery, or other high crimes.

Section 15. County Court; County Judge

There shall be established in each county in this State a County Court, which shall be a court of record; and there shall be elected in each county, by the qualified voters, a County Judge, who shall be well informed in the law of the State; shall be a conservator of the peace, and shall hold his office for four years, and until his successor shall be elected and qualified. He shall receive as compensation for his services such fees and perquisites as may be prescribed by law.

Section 16. County Courts: Jurisdiction; County Judge Powers; Disqualification of County Judge

The County Court has jurisdiction as provided by law. The County Judge is the presiding officer of the County Court and has judicial functions as provided by law. County court judges shall have the power to issue writs necessary to enforce their jurisdiction.

County Courts in existence on the effective date of this amendment are continued unless otherwise provided by law. When the judge of the County Court is disqualified in any case pending in the County Court the parties interested may, by consent, appoint a proper person to try said case, or upon their failing to do so a competent person may be appointed to try the same in the county where it is pending in such manner as may be prescribed by law.

Section 16a. Repealed

Section 17. County Court: Terms, Prosecutions, and Juries

The County Court shall hold terms as provided by law. Prosecutions may be commenced in said court by information filed by the county attorney, or by affidavit, as may be provided by law. Grand juries empaneled in the District Courts shall inquire into misdemeanors, and all indictments therefor returned into the District Courts shall forthwith be certified to the County Courts or other inferior courts, having jurisdiction to try them for trial; and if such indictment be quashed in the County, or other inferior court, the person charged, shall not be discharged if there is probable cause of guilt, but may be held by such court or magistrate to answer an information or affidavit. A jury in the County Court shall consist of six persons; but no jury shall be empaneled to try a civil case unless demanded by one of the parties, who shall pay such jury fee therefor, in advance, as may be prescribed by law, unless the party makes affidavit that the party is unable to pay the jury fee.

Section 18. Division of Counties into Precincts; Justices of the Peace and Constables; County Commissioners and County Commissioners Court

(a) Each county in the State with a population of 50,000 or more, according to the most recent federal census, from time to time, for the convenience of the people, shall be divided into not less than four and not more than eight precincts. Each county in the State with a population of 18,000 or more but less than 50,000, according to the most recent federal census, from time to time, for the convenience of the people, shall be divided into not less than two and not more than eight precincts. Each county in the State with a population of less than 18,000, according to the most recent federal census, from time to time, for the convenience of the people, shall be designated as a single precinct or, if the Commissioners Court determines that the county needs more than one precinct, shall be divided into not more than four precincts. Notwithstanding the population requirements of this subsection, Chambers County and Randall County, from time to time, for the convenience of the people, shall be divided into not less than two and not more than six precincts. A division or designation under this subsection shall be made by the Commissioners Court provided for by this Constitution. Except as provided by this section, in each such precinct there shall be elected one Justice of the Peace and one Constable, each of whom shall hold his office for four years and until his successor shall be elected and qualified; provided that in a county with a population of less than 150,000, according to the most recent federal census, in any precinct in which there may be a city of 18,000 or more inhabitants, there shall be elected two Justices of the Peace, and in a county with a population of 150,000 or more, according to the most recent federal census, each precinct may contain more than one Justice of the Peace Court. Notwithstanding the population requirements of this subsection, any county that is divided into four or more precincts on November 2, 1999, shall continue to be divided into not less than four precincts.

(b) Each county shall, in the manner provided for justice of the peace and constable precincts, be divided into four commissioners precincts in each of which there shall be elected by the qualified voters thereof one County Commissioner, who shall hold his office for four years and until his successor shall be elected and qualified. The County Commissioners so chosen, with the County Judge as presiding officer, shall compose the County Commissioners Court, which shall exercise such powers and jurisdiction over all county business, as is conferred by this Constitution and the laws of the State, or as may be hereafter prescribed.

(c) When the boundaries of justice of the peace and constable precincts are changed, each Justice and Constable in office on the effective date of the change, or elected to a term of office beginning on or after the effective date of the change, shall serve in the precinct in which the person resides for the term to which each was elected or appointed, even though the change in boundaries places the person's residence outside the precinct for which he was elected or appointed, abolishes the precinct for which he was elected or appointed, or temporarily results in extra Justices or Constables serving in a precinct. When, as a result of a change of precinct boundaries, a vacancy occurs in the office of Justice of the Peace or Constable, the Commissioners Court shall fill the vacancy by appointment until the next general election.

(d) When the boundaries of commissioners precincts are changed, each commissioner in office on the effective date of the change, or elected to a term of office beginning on or after the effective date of the change, shall serve in the precinct to which each was elected or appointed for the entire term to which each was elected or appointed, even though the change in boundaries places the person's residence outside the precinct for which he was elected or appointed.

(e) The office of Constable is abolished in Mills County, Reagan County, and Roberts County. The powers, duties, and records of the office are transferred to the County Sheriff.

(f) The Legislature by general law may prescribe the qualifications of constables.

(g) Re-designated

(h) The commissioners court of a county may declare the office of constable in a precinct dormant if at least seven consecutive years have passed since the end of the term of the person who was last elected or appointed to the office and during that period of time no person was elected to fill that office, or during that period a person was elected to that office, but the person failed to meet the qualifications of that office or failed to assume the duties of that office. If an office of constable is declared dormant, the office may not be filled by election or appointment and the previous officeholder does not continue to hold the office under Subsection (a) of this section or Section 17, Article XVI, of this constitution. The records of an office of constable declared dormant are transferred to the county clerk of the county. The commissioners court may reinstate an office of constable declared dormant by vote of the commissioners court or by calling an election in the precinct to reinstate the office. The commissioners court shall call an election to reinstate the office if the commissioners court receives a petition signed by at least 10 percent of the qualified voters of the precinct. If an election is called under this subsection, the commissioners court shall order the ballot for the election to be printed to permit voting for or against the proposition: "Reinstating the office of Constable of Precinct No. ___ that was previously declared dormant." The office of constable is reinstated if a majority of the voters of the precinct voting on the question at the election approve the reinstatement.

Section 19. Jurisdiction of Justice of the Peace Courts; Ex Officio Notaries Public

Justice of the peace courts shall have original jurisdiction in criminal matters of misdemeanor cases punishable by fine only, exclusive jurisdiction in civil matters where the amount in controversy is two hundred dollars or less, and such other jurisdiction as may be provided by law. Justices of the peace shall be ex officio notaries public.

Section 20. County Clerk

There shall be elected for each county, by the qualified voters, a County Clerk, who shall hold his office for four years, who shall be clerk of the County and Commissioners Courts and recorder of the county, whose duties, perquisites and fees of office shall be prescribed by the Legislature, and a vacancy in whose office shall be filled by the Commissioners Court, until the next general election; provided, that in counties having a population of less than 8,000 persons there may be an election of a single Clerk, who shall perform the duties of District and County Clerks.

Section 21. County Attorneys; District Attorneys

A County Attorney, for counties in which there is not a resident Criminal District Attorney, shall be elected by the qualified voters of each county, who shall be commissioned by the Governor, and hold his office for the term of four years. In case of vacancy the Commissioners Court of the county shall have the power to appoint a County Attorney until the next general election. The County Attorneys shall represent the State in all cases in the District and inferior courts in their respective counties; but if any county shall be included in a district in which there shall be a District Attorney, the respective duties of District Attorneys and

County Attorneys shall in such counties be regulated by the Legislature. The Legislature may provide for the election of District Attorneys in such districts, as may be deemed necessary, and make provision for the compensation of District Attorneys and County Attorneys. District Attorneys shall hold office for a term of four years, and until their successors have qualified.

Section 22. Repealed

Section 23. Sheriffs

There shall be elected by the qualified voters of each county a Sheriff, who shall hold his office for the term of four years, whose duties, qualifications, perquisites, and fees of office, shall be prescribed by the Legislature, and vacancies in whose office shall be filled by the Commissioners Court until the next general election.

Section 24. Removal of County Officers

County Judges, county attorneys, clerks of the District and County Courts, justices of the peace, constables, and other county officers, may be removed by the Judges of the District Courts for incompetency, official misconduct, habitual drunkenness, or other causes defined by law, upon the cause therefor being set forth in writing and the finding of its truth by a jury.

Section 25. Repealed

Section 26. Appeal by State in Criminal Cases

The State is entitled to appeal in criminal cases, as authorized by general law.

Section 27. Repealed

Section 28. Vacancy in Judicial Office

(a) A vacancy in the office of Chief Justice, Justice, or Judge of the Supreme Court, the Court of Criminal Appeals, the Court of Appeals, or the District Courts shall be filled by the Governor until the next succeeding General Election for state officers, and at that election the voters shall fill the vacancy for the unexpired term.

(b) A vacancy in the office of County Judge or Justice of the Peace shall be filled by the Commissioners Court until the next succeeding General Election.

Section 29. County Courts: Terms of Court; Probate Business

The County Court shall hold at least four terms for both civil and criminal business annually, as may be provided by the Legislature, or by the Commissioners Court of the county under authority of law, and such other terms each year as may be fixed by the Commissioners Court; provided, the Commissioners Court of any county having fixed the times and number of terms of the County Court, shall not change the same again until the expiration of one year. Said court shall dispose of probate business either in term time or vacation, under such regulation as may be prescribed by law. Until otherwise provided, the terms of the County Court shall be held on the first Mondays in February, May, August and November, and may remain in session three weeks.

Section 30. Term of Office of Judges of County-Wide Courts and of Criminal District Attorneys

The Judges of all Courts of county-wide jurisdiction heretofore or hereafter created by the Legislature of this State, and all Criminal District Attorneys now or hereafter authorized by the laws of this State, shall be elected for a term of four years, and shall serve until their successors have qualified.

Section 31. Court Administration and Rules; Action on Motion for Rehearing by Supreme Court

(a) The Supreme Court is responsible for the efficient administration of the judicial branch and shall promulgate rules of administration not inconsistent with the laws of the state as may be necessary for the efficient and uniform administration of justice in the various courts.

(b) The Supreme Court shall promulgate rules of civil procedure for all courts not inconsistent with the laws of the state as may be necessary for the efficient and uniform administration of justice in the various courts.

(c) The legislature may delegate to the Supreme Court or Court of Criminal Appeals the power to promulgate such other rules as may be prescribed by law or this Constitution, subject to such limitations and procedures as may be provided by law.

(d) Notwithstanding Section 1, Article II, of this constitution and any other provision of this constitution, if the supreme court does not act on a motion for rehearing before the 180th day after the date on which the motion is filed, the motion is denied.

Section 32. Legal Challenges to Constitutionality of State Statutes

Notwithstanding Section 1, Article II, of this constitution, the legislature may:

(1) require a court in which a party to litigation files a petition, motion, or other pleading challenging the constitutionality of a statute of this state to provide notice to the attorney general of the challenge if the party raising the challenge notifies the court that the party is challenging the constitutionality of the statute; and

(2) prescribe a reasonable period, which may not exceed 45 days, after the provision of that notice during which the court may not enter a judgment holding the statute unconstitutional.

ARTICLE 6. SUFFRAGE

Section 1. Classes of Persons not Allowed to Vote

(a) The following classes of persons shall not be allowed to vote in this State:

(1) persons under 18 years of age;

(2) persons who have been determined mentally incompetent by a court, subject to such exceptions as the Legislature may make; and

(3) persons convicted of any felony, subject to such exceptions as the Legislature may make.

(b) The legislature shall enact laws to exclude from the right of suffrage persons who have been convicted of bribery, perjury, forgery, or other high crimes.

Section 2. Qualified Voter; Registration; Absentee Voting

(a) Every person subject to none of the disqualifications provided by Section 1 of this article or by a law enacted under that section who is a citizen of the United States and who is a resident of this State shall be deemed a qualified voter; provided, however, that before offering to vote at an election a voter shall have registered, but such requirement for registration shall not be considered a qualification of a voter within the meaning of the term "qualified voter" as used in any other Article of this Constitution in respect to any matter except qualification and eligibility to vote at an election.

(b) The Legislature may authorize absentee voting.

(c) The privilege of free suffrage shall be protected by laws regulating elections and prohibiting under adequate penalties all undue influence in elections from power, bribery, tumult, or other improper practice.

Section 2a. Voting for Presidential Electors and Statewide Offices and Propositions by Persons Qualified Except for Local Residence Requirements

(a) Notwithstanding any other provision of this Constitution, the Legislature may enact laws and provide a method of registration, including the time of such registration, permitting any person who is qualified to vote in this State except for the residence requirements within a county or district, as set forth in Section 2 of this Article, to vote for (1) electors for President and Vice President of the United States and (2) all offices, questions or propositions to be voted on by all voters throughout this State.

(b) Notwithstanding any other provision of this Constitution, the Legislature may enact laws and provide for a method of registration, including the time for such registration, permitting any person (1) who is qualified to vote in this State except for the residence requirements of Section 2 of this Article, and (2) who shall have resided anywhere within this State at least thirty (30) days next preceding a General Election in a presidential election year, and (3) who shall have been a qualified voter in another state immediately prior to his removal to this State or would have been eligible to vote in such other state had he remained there until such election, to vote for electors for President and Vice President of the United States in that election.

(c) Notwithstanding any other provision of this Constitution, the Legislature may enact laws and provide for a method of registration, including the time for such registration, permitting absentee voting for electors for President and Vice President of the United States in this State by former residents of this State:

(1) who have removed to another state, and

(2) who meet all qualifications, except residence requirements, for voting for electors for President and Vice President in this State at the time of the election, but the privileges of suffrage so granted shall be only for such period of time as would permit a former resident of this State to meet the residence requirements for voting in his new state of residence, and in no case for more than twenty-four (24) months.

Section 3. Qualifications of Voters in Municipal Elections

All qualified voters of the State, as herein described, who reside within the limits of any city or corporate town, shall have the right to vote for Mayor and all other elective officers.

Section 3a. Qualifications of Voters in Local Elections Regarding Public Debts or Expenditures

When an election is held by any county, or any number of counties, or any political sub-division of the State, or any political sub-division of a county, or any defined district now or hereafter to be described and defined within the State and which may or may not include towns, villages or municipal corporations, or any city, town or village, for the purpose of issuing bonds or otherwise lending credit, or expending money or assuming any debt, only qualified voters of the State, county, political sub-division, district, city, town or village where such election is held shall be qualified to vote.

Section 4. Elections by Ballot; Purity of Elections; Registration of Voters

In all elections by the people, the vote shall be by ballot, and the Legislature shall provide for the numbering of tickets and make such other regulations as may be necessary to detect and punish fraud and preserve the purity of the ballot box; and the Legislature shall provide by law for the registration of all voters.

Section 5. Voters Privileged From Arrest

Voters shall, in all cases, except treason, felony or breach of the peace, be privileged from arrest during their attendance at elections, and in going to and returning therefrom.

ARTICLE 7. EDUCATION

Section 1. Support and Maintenance of System of Public Free Schools

A general diffusion of knowledge being essential to the preservation of the liberties and rights of the people, it shall be the duty of the Legislature of the State to establish and make suitable provision for the support and maintenance of an efficient system of public free schools.

Section 2. Permanent School Fund

All funds, lands and other property heretofore set apart and appropriated for the support of public schools; all the alternate sections of land reserved by the State out of grants heretofore made or that may hereafter be made to railroads or other corporations of any nature whatsoever; one half of the public domain of the State; and all sums of money that may come to the State from the sale of any portion of the same, shall constitute a permanent school fund.

Section 2a. Release of State Claim to Certain Lands and Minerals Within Shelby, Frazier, and Mccormick League and in Bastrop County

(a) The State of Texas hereby relinquishes and releases any claim of sovereign ownership or title to an undivided one-third interest in and to the lands and minerals within the Shelby, Frazier, and McCormick League (now located in Fort Bend and Austin counties) arising out of the interest in that league originally granted under the Mexican Colonization Law of 1823 to John McCormick on or about July 24, 1824, and subsequently voided by the governing body of Austin's Original Colony on or about December 15, 1830.

(b) The State of Texas relinquishes and releases any claim of sovereign ownership or title to an interest in and to the lands, excluding the minerals, in Tracts 2-5, 13, 15-17, 19-20, 23-26, 29-32, and 34-37, in the A. P. Nance Survey, Bastrop County, as said tracts are:

(1) shown on Bastrop County Rolled Sketch No. 4, recorded in the General Land Office on December 15, 1999; and

(2) further described by the field notes prepared by a licensed state land surveyor of Travis County in September through November 1999 and May 2000.

(c) Title to such interest in the lands and minerals described by Subsection (a) is confirmed to the owners of the remaining interests in such lands and minerals. Title to the lands, excluding the minerals, described by Subsection (b) is confirmed to the holder of record title to each tract. Any outstanding land award or land payment obligation owed to the state for lands described by Subsection (b) is canceled, and any funds previously paid related to an outstanding land award or land payment obligation may not be refunded.

(d) The General Land Office shall issue a patent to the holder of record title to each tract described by Subsection (b). The patent shall be issued in the same manner as other patents except that no filing fee or patent fee may be required.

(e) A patent issued under Subsection (d) shall include a provision reserving all mineral interest in the land to the state.

(f) This section is self-executing.

Section 2b. Authority to Release State's Interest in Certain Permanent School Fund Land Held by Person Under Color of Title

(a) The legislature by law may provide for the release of all or part of the state's interest in land, excluding mineral rights, if:

(1) the land is surveyed, unsold, permanent school fund land according to the records of the General Land Office;

(2) the land is not patentable under the law in effect before January 1, 2002; and

(3) the person claiming title to the land:

(A) holds the land under color of title;

(B) holds the land under a chain of title that originated on or before January 1, 1952;

(C) acquired the land without actual knowledge that title to the land was vested in the State of Texas;

(D) has a deed to the land recorded in the appropriate county; and

(E) has paid all taxes assessed on the land and any interest and penalties associated with any period of tax delinquency.

(b) This section does not apply to:

(1) beach land, submerged or filled land, or islands; or

(2) land that has been determined to be state-owned by judicial decree.

(c) This section may not be used to:

(1) resolve boundary disputes; or

(2) change the mineral reservation in an existing patent.

Section 2C. RELEASE OF STATE CLAIM TO CERTAIN LANDS IN UPSHUR AND SMITH COUNTIES

(a) Except as provided by Subsection (b) of this section, the State of Texas relinquishes and releases any claim of sovereign ownership or title to an interest in and to the tracts of land, including mineral rights, described as follows:

Tract 1:

The first tract of land is situated in Upshur County, Texas, about 14 miles South 30 degrees east from Gilmer, the county seat, and is bounded as follows: Bound on the North by the J. Manning Survey, A-314 the S.W. Beasley Survey A-66 and the David Meredith Survey A-315 and bound on the East by the M. Mann Survey, A-302 and by the M. Chandler Survey, A-84 and bound on the South by the G. W. Hooper Survey, A-657 and by the D. Ferguson Survey, A-158 and bound on the West by the J. R. Wadkins Survey, A-562 and the H. Alsup Survey, A-20, and by the W. Bratton Survey, A-57 and the G. H. Burroughs Survey, A-30 and the M. Tidwell Survey, A-498 of Upshur County, Texas.

Tract 2:

The second tract of land is situated in Smith County, Texas, north of Tyler and is bounded as follows: on the north and west by the S. Leeper A-559, the Frost Thorn Four League Grant A-3, A-9, A-7, A-19, and the H. Jacobs A-504 and on the south and east by the following surveys: John Carver A-247, A. Loverly A-609, J. Gimble A-408, R. Conner A-239, N.J. Blythe A-88, N.J. Blythe A-89, J. Choate A-195, Daniel Minor A-644, William Keys A-527, James H. Thomas A-971, Seaborn Smith A-899, and Samuel Leeper A-559.

(b) This section does not apply to:

(1) any public right-of-way, including a public road right-of-way, or related interest owned by a governmental entity;

(2) any navigable waterway or related interest owned by a governmental entity; or

(3) any land owned by a governmental entity and reserved for public use, including a park, recreation area, wildlife area, scientific area, or historic site.

(c) This section is self-executing.
(Added Nov. 8, 2005.)

Section 3. Taxes for Benefit of Schools; Provision of Free Text Books; School Districts

(a) One-fourth of the revenue derived from the State occupation taxes shall be set apart annually for the benefit of the public free schools.

(b) It shall be the duty of the State Board of Education to set aside a sufficient amount of available funds to provide free text books for the use of children attending the public free schools of this State.

(c) Should the taxation herein named be insufficient the deficit may be met by appropriation from the general funds of the State.

(d) The Legislature may provide for the formation of school districts by general laws, and all such school districts may embrace parts of two or more counties.

(e) The Legislature shall be authorized to pass laws for the assessment and collection of taxes in all school districts and for the management and control of the public school or schools of such districts, whether such districts are composed of territory wholly within a county or in parts of two or more counties, and the Legislature may authorize an additional ad valorem tax to be levied and collected within all school districts for the further maintenance of public free schools, and for the erection and equipment of school buildings therein; provided that a majority of the qualified voters of the district voting at an election to be held for that purpose, shall approve the tax.

Section 3a. Repealed

Section 3-B. Independent School District and Junior College District Taxes and Bonds not Affected by Changes in Boundaries

No tax for the maintenance of public free schools voted in any independent school district and no tax for the maintenance of a junior college voted by a junior college district, nor any bonds voted in any such district, but unissued, shall be abrogated, canceled or invalidated by change of any kind in the boundaries thereof. After any change in boundaries, the governing body of any such district, without the necessity of an additional election, shall have the power to assess, levy and collect ad valorem taxes on all taxable property within the boundaries of the district as changed, for the purposes of the maintenance of public free schools or the maintenance of a junior college, as the case may be, and the payment of principal of and interest on all bonded indebtedness outstanding against, or attributable, adjusted or allocated to, such district or any territory therein, in the amount, at the rate, or not to exceed the rate, and in the manner authorized in the district prior to the change in its boundaries, and further in accordance with the laws under which all such bonds, respectively, were voted; and such governing body also shall have the power, without the necessity of an additional election, to sell and deliver any unissued bonds voted in the district prior to any such change in boundaries, and to assess, levy and collect ad valorem taxes on all taxable property in the district as changed, for the payment of principal of and interest on such bonds in the manner permitted by the laws under which such bonds were voted. In those instances where the boundaries of any such independent school district are changed by the annexation of, or consolidation with, one or more whole school districts, the taxes to be levied for the purposes hereinabove authorized may be in the amount or at not to exceed the rate theretofore voted in the district having at the time of such change the greatest scholastic population according to the latest scholastic census and only the unissued bonds of such district voted prior to such change, may be subsequently sold and delivered and any voted, but unissued, bonds of other school districts involved in such annexation or consolidation shall not thereafter be issued.

Section 4. Sale of Permanent School Fund Lands; Investment of Proceeds

The lands herein set apart to the Permanent School fund, shall be sold under such regulations, at such times, and on such terms as may be prescribed by law; and the Legislature shall not have power to grant any relief to purchasers thereof. The proceeds of such sales must be used to acquire other land for the Permanent School fund as provided by law or the proceeds shall be invested by the comptroller of public accounts, as may be directed by the Board of Education herein provided for, in the bonds of the United States, the State of Texas, or counties in said State, or in such other securities, and under such restrictions as may be prescribed by law; and the State shall be responsible for all investments.

Section 4A. Repealed

Section 4b. Donation of Real Property by Independent School District for Historical Preservation

(a) The legislature by general law may authorize the board of trustees of an independent school district to donate district real property and improvements formerly used as a school campus for the purpose of preserving the improvements.

(b) A law enacted under this section must provide that before the board of trustees may make the donation, the board must determine that:

(1) the improvements have historical significance;

(2) the transfer will further the preservation of the improvements; and

(3) at the time of the transfer, the district does not need the real property or improvements for educational purposes.

Section 5. Permanent School Fund and Available School Fund: Composition, Management, Use, and Distribution

(a) The permanent school fund consists of all land appropriated for public schools by this constitution or the other laws of this state, other properties belonging to the permanent school fund, and all revenue derived from the land or other properties. The available school fund consists of the distributions made to it from the total return on all investment assets of the permanent school fund, the taxes authorized by this constitution or general law to be part of the available school fund, and appropriations made to the available school fund by the legislature. The total amount distributed from the permanent school fund to the available school fund:

(1) in each year of a state fiscal biennium must be an amount that is not more than six percent of the average of the market value of the permanent school fund, excluding real property belonging to the fund that is managed, sold, or acquired under Section 4 of this article, but including discretionary real assets investments and cash in the state treasury derived from property belonging to the fund, on the last day of each of the 16 state fiscal quarters preceding the regular session of the legislature that begins before that state fiscal biennium, in accordance with the rate adopted by:

(A) a vote of two-thirds of the total membership of the State Board of Education, taken before the regular session of the legislature convenes; or

(B) the legislature by general law or appropriation, if the State Board of Education does not adopt a rate as provided by Paragraph (A) of this subdivision; and

(2) over the 10-year period consisting of the current state fiscal year and the nine preceding state fiscal years may not exceed the total return on all investment assets of the permanent school fund over the same 10-year period.

(b) The expenses of managing permanent school fund land and investments shall be paid by appropriation from the permanent school fund.

(c) The available school fund shall be applied annually to the support of the public free schools. Except as provided by this section, the legislature may not enact a law appropriating any part of the permanent school fund or available school fund to any other purpose. The permanent school fund and the available school fund may not be appropriated to or used for the support of any sectarian school. The available school fund shall be distributed to the several counties according to their scholastic population and applied in the manner provided by law.

(d) The legislature by law may provide for using the permanent school fund to guarantee bonds issued by school districts or by the state for the purpose of making loans to or purchasing the bonds of school districts for the purpose of acquisition, construction, or improvement of instructional facilities including all furnishings thereto. If any payment is required to be made by the permanent school fund as a result of its guarantee of bonds issued by the state, an amount equal to this payment shall be immediately paid by the state from the treasury to the permanent school fund. An amount owed by the state to the permanent school fund under this section shall be a general obligation of the state until paid. The amount of bonds authorized hereunder shall not exceed $750 million or a higher amount authorized by a two-thirds record vote of both houses of the legislature. If the proceeds of bonds issued by the state are used to provide a loan to a school district and the district becomes delinquent on the loan payments, the amount of the delinquent payments shall be offset against state aid to which the district is otherwise entitled.

(e) The legislature may appropriate part of the available school fund for administration of a bond guarantee program established under this section.

(f) Notwithstanding any other provision of this constitution, in managing the assets of the permanent school fund, the State Board of Education may acquire, exchange, sell, supervise, manage, or retain, through procedures and subject to restrictions it establishes and in amounts it considers appropriate, any kind of investment, including investments in the Texas growth fund created by Article XVI, Section 70, of this constitution, that persons of ordinary prudence, discretion, and intelligence, exercising the judgment and care under the circumstances then prevailing, acquire or retain for their own account in the management of their affairs, not in regard to speculation but in regard to the permanent disposition of their funds, considering the probable income as well as the probable safety of their capital.

(g) Notwithstanding any other provision of this constitution or of a statute, the General Land Office or an entity other than the State Board of Education that has responsibility for the management of permanent school fund land or other properties may in its sole discretion distribute to the available school fund each year revenue derived during that year from the land or properties, not to exceed $300 million each year.

(h) Expired

Section 6. County School Lands and Proceeds of Sales Held as School Trust

All lands heretofore, or hereafter granted to the several counties of this State for educational purposes, are of right the property of said counties respectively, to which they were granted, and title thereto is vested in said counties, and no adverse possession or limitation shall ever be available against the title of any county. Each county may sell or dispose of its lands in whole or in part, in manner to be provided by the Commissioners Court of the county. Said lands, and the proceeds thereof, when sold, shall be held by said counties alone as a trust for the benefit of public schools therein; said proceeds to be invested in bonds of the United States, the State of Texas, or counties in said State, or in such other securities, and under such restrictions as may be prescribed by law; and the counties shall be responsible for all investments; the interest thereon, and other revenue, except the principal shall be available fund.

Section 6a. County Agricultural or Grazing School Land Subject to Tax

All agriculture or grazing school land mentioned in Section 6 of this article owned by any county shall be subject to taxation except for State purposes to the same extent as lands privately owned.

Section 6b. County Permanent School Fund: Reduction and Distribution

Notwithstanding the provisions of Section 6, Article VII, Constitution of the State of Texas, any county, acting through the commissioners court, may reduce the county permanent school fund of that county and may distribute the amount of the reduction to the independent and common school districts of the county on a per scholastic basis to be used solely for the purpose of reducing bonded indebtedness of those districts or for making permanent improvements. The commissioners court shall,

however, retain a sufficient amount of the corpus of the county permanent school fund to pay ad valorem taxes on school lands or royalty interests owned at the time of the distribution.
Nothing in this Section affects financial aid to any school district by the state.

Section 7. Repealed

Section 8. State Board of Education

The Legislature shall provide by law for a State Board of Education, whose members shall be appointed or elected in such manner and by such authority and shall serve for such terms as the Legislature shall prescribe not to exceed six years. The said board shall perform such duties as may be prescribed by law.

Section 9. Repealed

Section 9-a. Expired

Section 10. Establishment of University of Texas; Agricultural and Mechanical Department

The legislature shall as soon as practicable establish, organize and provide for the maintenance, support and direction of a University of the first class, to be located by a vote of the people of this State, and styled, "The University of Texas," for the promotion of literature, and the arts and sciences, including an Agricultural, and Mechanical department.

Section 11. Establishment of Permanent University Fund; Investment in Government Bonds

In order to enable the Legislature to perform the duties set forth in the foregoing Section, it is hereby declared all lands and other property heretofore set apart and appropriated for the establishment and maintenance of the University of Texas, together with all the proceeds of sales of the same, heretofore made or hereafter to be made, and all grants, donations and appropriations that may hereafter be made by the State of Texas, or from any other source, except donations limited to specific purposes, shall constitute and become a Permanent University Fund. And the same as realized and received into the Treasury of the State (together with such sums belonging to the Fund, as may now be in the Treasury), shall be invested in bonds of the United States, the State of Texas, or counties of said State, or in School Bonds or municipalities, or in bonds of any city of this State, or in bonds issued under and by virtue of the Federal Farm Loan Act approved by the President of the United States, July 17, 1916, and amendments thereto; and the interest accruing thereon shall be subject to appropriation by the Legislature to accomplish the purpose declared in the foregoing Section; provided, that the one-tenth of the alternate Section of the lands granted to railroads, reserved by the State, which were set apart and appropriated to the establishment of the University of Texas, by an Act of the Legislature of February 11, 1858, entitled, "An Act to establish the University of Texas," shall not be included in, or constitute a part of, the Permanent University Fund.

Section 11a. Investment of Permanent University Fund

In addition to the bonds enumerated in Section 11 of Article VII of the Constitution of the State of Texas, the Board of Regents of The University of Texas may invest the Permanent University Fund in securities, bonds or other obligations issued, insured, or guaranteed in any manner by the United States Government, or any of its agencies, and in such bonds, debentures, or obligations, and preferred and common stocks issued by corporations, associations, or other institutions as the Board of Regents of The University of Texas System may deem to be proper investments for said funds; provided, however, that not more than one per cent (1%) of said fund shall be invested in the securities of any one (1) corporation, nor shall more than five per cent (5%) of the voting stock of any one (1) corporation be owned: provided, further, that stocks eligible for purchase shall be restricted to stocks of companies incorporated within the United States which have paid dividends for five (5) consecutive years or longer immediately prior to the date of purchase and which, except for bank stocks and insurance stocks, are listed upon an exchange registered with the Securities and Exchange Commission or its successors.

In making each and all of such investments said Board of Regents shall exercise the judgment and care under the circumstances then prevailing which men of ordinary prudence, discretion, and intelligence exercise in the management of their own affairs, not in regard to speculation but in regard to the permanent disposition of their funds, considering the probable income therefrom as well as the probable safety of their capital. The interest, dividends and other income accruing from the investments of the Permanent University Fund, except the portion thereof which is appropriated by the operation of Section 18 of Article VII for the payment of principal and interest on bonds or notes issued thereunder, shall be subject to appropriation by the Legislature to accomplish the purposes declared in Section 10 of Article VII of this Constitution. This amendment shall be self-enacting, and shall become effective upon its adoption, provided, however, that the Legislature shall provide by law for full disclosure of all details concerning the investments in corporate stocks and bonds and other investments authorized herein.

Section 11b. Expanded Investment Authority for Permanent University Fund

Notwithstanding any other provision of this constitution, in managing the assets of the permanent university fund, the Board of Regents of The University of Texas System may acquire, exchange, sell, supervise, manage, or retain, through procedures and subject to restrictions it establishes and in amounts it considers appropriate, any kind of investment, including investments in the Texas growth fund created by Article XVI, Section 70, of this constitution, that prudent investors, exercising reasonable care, skill, and caution, would acquire or retain in light of the purposes, terms, distribution requirements, and other circumstances of the fund then prevailing, taking into consideration the investment of all the assets of the fund rather than a single investment.

Section 12. Sale of Permanent University Fund Lands

The land herein set apart to the University fund shall be sold under such regulations, at such times, and on such terms as may be provided by law; and the Legislature shall provide for the prompt collection, at maturity, of all debts due on account of University lands, heretofore sold, or that may hereafter be sold, and shall in neither event have the power to grant relief to the purchasers.

Section 13. Agricultural and Mechanical College

The Agricultural and Mechanical College of Texas, established by an Act of the Legislature passed April 17th, 1871, located in the county of Brazos, is hereby made, and constituted a Branch of the University of Texas, for instruction in Agriculture, the Mechanic Arts, and the Natural Sciences connected therewith. And the Legislature shall at its next session, make an appropriation, not to exceed forty thousand dollars, for the construction and completion of the buildings and improvements, and for providing the furniture necessary to put said College in immediate and successful operation.

Section 14. Prairie View A&M University

Prairie View A&M University in Waller County is an institution of the first class under the direction of the same governing board as Texas A&M University referred to in Article VII, Section 13, of this constitution as the Agricultural and Mechanical College of Texas.

Section 15. Grant of Additional Lands to University of Texas

In addition to the lands heretofore granted to the University of Texas, there is hereby set apart, and appropriated, for the endowment maintenance, and support of said University and its branches, one million acres of the unappropriated public domain of the State, to be designated, and surveyed as may be provided by law; and said lands shall be sold under the same regulations, and the proceeds invested in the same manner, as is provided for the sale and investment of the permanent University fund; and the Legislature shall not have power to grant any relief to the purchasers of said lands.

Section 16. County Taxation of Certain University of Texas Lands

All land mentioned in Sections 11, 12, and 15 of Article VII, of the Constitution of the State of Texas, now belonging to the University of Texas shall be subject to the taxation for county purposes to the same extent as lands privately owned; provided they shall be rendered for taxation upon values fixed by the State Tax Board; and providing that the State shall remit annually to each of the counties in which said lands are located an amount equal to the tax imposed upon said land for county purposes.

Section 16-A. Terms of Office of Educational Officers

The Legislature shall fix by law the terms of all offices of the public school system and of the State institutions of higher education, inclusive, and the terms of members of the respective boards, not to exceed six years.

Section 17. Funding to Support Agencies and Institutions of Higher Education not Supported by Available University Fund

(a) In the fiscal year beginning September 1, 1985, and each fiscal year thereafter, there is hereby appropriated out of the first money coming into the state treasury not otherwise appropriated by the constitution $100 million to be used by eligible agencies and institutions of higher education for the purpose of acquiring land either with or without permanent improvements, constructing and equipping buildings or other permanent improvements, major repair or rehabilitation of buildings or other permanent improvements, acquisition of capital equipment, library books and library materials, and paying for acquiring, constructing, or equipping or for major repair or rehabilitation of buildings, facilities, other permanent improvements, or capital equipment used jointly for educational and general activities and for auxiliary enterprises to the extent of their use for educational and general activities. For the five-year period that begins on September 1, 2000, and for each five-year period that begins after that period, the legislature, during a regular session that is nearest, but preceding, a five-year period, may by two-thirds vote of the membership of each house increase the amount of the constitutional appropriation for the five-year period but may not adjust the appropriation in such a way as to impair any obligation created by the issuance of bonds or notes in accordance with this section.

(b) The funds appropriated under Subsection (a) of this section shall be for the use of the following eligible agencies and institutions of higher education (even though their names may be changed):

(1) East Texas State University including East Texas State University at Texarkana;

(2) Lamar University including Lamar University at Orange and Lamar University at Port Arthur;

(3) Midwestern State University;

(4) University of North Texas;

(5) The University of Texas-Pan American including The University of Texas at Brownsville;

(6) Stephen F. Austin State University;

(7) Texas College of Osteopathic Medicine;

(8) Texas State University System Administration and the following component institutions:

(9) Sam Houston State University;

(10) Southwest Texas State University;

(11) Sul Ross State University including Uvalde Study Center;

(12) Texas Southern University;

(13) Texas Tech University;

(14) Texas Tech University Health Sciences Center;

(15) Angelo State University;

(16) Texas Woman's University;

(17) University of Houston System Administration and the following component institutions:

(18) University of Houston;

(19) University of Houston-Victoria;

(20) University of Houston-Clear Lake;

(21) University of Houston-Downtown;

(22) Texas A&M University-Corpus Christi;

(23) Texas A&M International University;

(24) Texas A&M University-Kingsville;

(25) West Texas A&M University; and

(26) Texas State Technical College System and its campuses, but not its extension centers or programs.

(c) Pursuant to a two-thirds vote of the membership of each house of the legislature, institutions of higher education may be created at a later date by general law, and, when created, such an institution shall be entitled to participate in the funding provided by this section if it is not created as a part of The University of Texas System or The Texas A&M University System. An institution that is entitled to participate in dedicated funding provided by Article VII, Section 18, of this constitution may not be entitled to participate in the funding provided by this section.

(d) In the year 1985 and every 10 years thereafter, the legislature or an agency designated by the legislature no later than August 31 of such year shall allocate by equitable formula the annual appropriations made under Subsection (a) of this section to the governing boards of eligible agencies and institutions of higher education. The legislature shall review, or provide for a review, of the allocation formula at the end of the fifth year of each 10-year allocation period. At that time adjustments may be made in the allocation formula, but no adjustment that will prevent the payment of outstanding bonds and notes, both principal and interest, may be made.

(d-1) Notwithstanding Subsection (d) of this section, the allocation of the annual appropriation to Texas State Technical College System and its campuses may not exceed 2.2 percent of the total appropriation each fiscal year.

(e) Each governing board authorized to participate in the distribution of money under this section is authorized to expend all money distributed to it for any of the purposes enumerated in Subsection (a). In addition, such governing board may issue bonds and notes for the purposes of refunding bonds or notes issued under this section or prior law, acquiring land either with or without permanent improvements, constructing and equipping buildings or other permanent improvements, acquiring capital equipment, library books, and library materials, paying for acquiring, constructing, or equipping or for major repair or rehabilitation of buildings, facilities, other permanent improvements, or capital equipment used jointly for educational and general activities and for auxiliary enterprises to the extent of their use for educational and general activities, and for major repair and rehabilitation of buildings or other permanent improvements, and may pledge up to 50 percent of the money allocated to such governing board pursuant to this section to secure the payment of the principal and interest of such bonds or notes. Proceeds from the issuance of bonds or notes under this subsection shall be maintained in a local depository selected by the governing board issuing the bonds or notes. The bonds and notes issued under this subsection shall be payable solely out of the money appropriated by this section and shall mature serially or otherwise in not more than 10 years from their respective dates. All bonds issued under this section shall be sold only through competitive bidding and are subject to approval by the attorney general. Bonds approved by the attorney general shall be incontestable. The permanent university fund may be invested in the bonds and notes issued under this section.

(f) The funds appropriated by this section may not be used for the purpose of constructing, equipping, repairing, or rehabilitating buildings or other permanent improvements that are to be used only for student housing, intercollegiate athletics, or auxiliary enterprises.

(g) The comptroller of public accounts shall make annual transfers of the funds allocated pursuant to Subsection (d) directly to the governing boards of the eligible institutions.

(h) To assure efficient use of construction funds and the orderly development of physical plants to accommodate the state's real need, the legislature may provide for the approval or disapproval of all new construction projects at the eligible agencies and institutions entitled to participate in the funding provided by this section.

(i) Repealed

(j) The state systems and institutions of higher education designated in this section may not receive any additional funds from the general revenue of the state for acquiring land with or without permanent improvements, for constructing or equipping buildings or other permanent improvements, or for major repair and rehabilitation of buildings or other permanent improvements except that:

(1) in the case of fire or natural disaster the legislature may appropriate from the general revenue an amount sufficient to replace the uninsured loss of any building or other permanent improvement; and

(2) the legislature, by two-thirds vote of each house, may, in cases of demonstrated need, which need must be clearly expressed in the body of the act, appropriate additional general revenue funds for acquiring land with or without permanent improvements, for constructing or equipping buildings or other permanent improvements, or for major repair and rehabilitation of buildings or other permanent improvements.
This subsection does not apply to legislative appropriations made prior to the adoption of this amendment.

(k) Without the prior approval of the legislature, appropriations under this section may not be expended for acquiring land with or without permanent improvements, or for constructing and equipping buildings or other permanent improvements, for a branch campus or educational center that is not a separate degree-granting institution created by general law.

(l) This section is self-enacting upon the issuance of the governor's proclamation declaring the adoption of the amendment, and the state comptroller of public accounts shall do all things necessary to effectuate this section. This section does not impair any obligation created by the issuance of any bonds and notes in accordance with prior law, and all outstanding bonds and notes shall be paid in full, both principal and interest, in accordance with their terms. If the provisions of this section conflict with any other provisions of this constitution, then the provisions of this section shall prevail, notwithstanding all such conflicting provisions.

Section 18. Funding to Support Texas A&M University System and University of Texas System; Available University Fund

(a) The Board of Regents of The Texas A&M University System may issue bonds and notes not to exceed a total amount of 10 percent of the cost value of the investments and other assets of the permanent university fund (exclusive of real estate) at the time of the issuance thereof, and may pledge all or any part of its one-third interest in the available university fund to secure the payment of the principal and interest of those bonds and notes, for the purpose of acquiring land either with or without permanent improvements, constructing and equipping buildings or other permanent improvements, major repair and rehabilitation of buildings and other permanent improvements, acquiring capital equipment and library books and library materials, and refunding bonds or notes issued under this Section or prior law, at or for The Texas A&M University System administration and the following component institutions of the system:

(1) Texas A&M University, including its medical college which the legislature may authorize as a separate medical institution;

(2) Prairie View A&M University, including its nursing school in Houston;

(3) Tarleton State University;

(4) Texas A&M University at Galveston;

(5) Texas Forest Service;

(6) Texas Agricultural Experiment Stations;

(7) Texas Agricultural Extension Service;

(8) Texas Engineering Experiment Stations;

(9) Texas Transportation Institute; and

(10) Texas Engineering Extension Service.

(b) The Board of Regents of The University of Texas System may issue bonds and notes not to exceed a total amount of 20 percent of the cost value of investments and other assets of the permanent university fund (exclusive of real estate) at the time of issuance thereof, and may pledge all or any part of its two-thirds interest in the available university fund to secure the payment of the principal and interest of those bonds and notes, for the purpose of acquiring land either with or without permanent improvements, constructing and equipping buildings or other permanent improvements, major repair and rehabilitation of buildings and other permanent improvements, acquiring capital equipment and library books and library materials, and refunding bonds or notes issued under this section or prior law, at or for The University of Texas System administration and the following component institutions of the system:

(1) The University of Texas at Arlington;

(2) The University of Texas at Austin;

(3) The University of Texas at Dallas;

(4) The University of Texas at El Paso;

(5) The University of Texas of the Permian Basin;

(6) The University of Texas at San Antonio;

(7) The University of Texas at Tyler;

(8) The University of Texas Health Science Center at Dallas;

(9) The University of Texas Medical Branch at Galveston;

(10) The University of Texas Health Science Center at Houston;

(11) The University of Texas Health Science Center at San Antonio;

(12) The University of Texas System Cancer Center;

(13) The University of Texas Health Center at Tyler; and

(14) The University of Texas Institute of Texan Cultures at San Antonio.

(c) Pursuant to a two-thirds vote of the membership of each house of the legislature, institutions of higher education may be created at a later date as a part of The University of Texas System or The Texas A&M University System by general law, and, when created, such an institution shall be entitled to participate in the funding provided by this section for the system in which it is created. An institution that is entitled to participate in dedicated funding provided by Article VII, Section 17, of this constitution may not be entitled to participate in the funding provided by this section.

(d) The proceeds of the bonds or notes issued under Subsection (a) or (b) of this section may not be used for the purpose of constructing, equipping, repairing, or rehabilitating buildings or other permanent improvements that are to be used for student housing, intercollegiate athletics, or auxiliary enterprises.

(e) The available university fund consists of the distributions made to it from the total return on all investment assets of the permanent university fund, including the net income attributable to the surface of permanent university fund land. The amount of any distributions to the available university fund shall be determined by the board of regents of The University of Texas System in a manner intended to provide the available university fund with a stable and predictable stream of annual distributions and to maintain over time the purchasing power of permanent university fund investments and annual distributions to the available university fund. The amount distributed to the available university fund in a fiscal year must be not less than the amount needed to pay the principal and interest due and owing in that fiscal year on bonds and notes issued under this section. If the purchasing power of permanent university fund investments for any rolling 10-year period is not preserved, the board may not increase annual distributions to the available university fund until the purchasing power of the permanent university fund investments is restored, except as necessary to pay the principal and interest due and owing on bonds and notes issued under this section. An annual distribution made by the board to the available university fund during any fiscal year may not exceed an amount equal to seven percent of the average net fair market value of permanent university fund investment assets as determined by the board, except as necessary to pay any principal and interest due and owing on bonds issued under this section. The expenses of managing permanent university fund land and investments shall be paid by the permanent university fund.

(f) Out of one-third of the annual distribution from the permanent university fund to the available university fund, there shall be appropriated an annual sum sufficient to pay the principal and interest due on the bonds and notes issued by the Board of Regents of The Texas A&M University System under this section and prior law, and the remainder of that one-third of the annual distribution to the available university fund shall be appropriated to the Board of Regents of The Texas A&M University System which shall have the authority and duty in turn to appropriate an equitable portion of the same for the support and maintenance of The Texas A&M University System administration, Texas A&M University, and Prairie View A&M University. The Board of Regents of The Texas A&M University System, in making just and equitable appropriations to Texas A&M University and Prairie View A&M University, shall exercise its discretion with due regard to such criteria as the board may deem appropriate from year to year. Out of the other two-thirds of the annual distribution from the permanent university fund to the available university fund there shall be appropriated an annual sum sufficient to pay the principal and interest due on the bonds and notes issued by the Board of Regents of The University of Texas System under this section and prior law, and the remainder of such two-thirds of the annual distribution to the available university fund, shall be appropriated for the support and maintenance of The University of Texas at Austin and The University of Texas System administration.

(g) The bonds and notes issued under this section shall be payable solely out of the available university fund, mature serially or otherwise in not more than 30 years from their respective dates, and, except for refunding bonds, be sold only through competitive bidding. All of these bonds and notes are subject to approval by the attorney general and when so approved are incontestable. The permanent university fund may be invested in these bonds and notes.

(h) To assure efficient use of construction funds and the orderly development of physical plants to accommodate the state's real need, the legislature may provide for the approval or disapproval of all new construction projects at the eligible agencies and institutions entitled to participate in the funding provided by this section except The University of Texas at Austin, Texas A&M University in College Station, and Prairie View A&M University.

(i) The state systems and institutions of higher education designated in this section may not receive any funds from the general revenue of the state for acquiring land with or without permanent improvements, for constructing or equipping buildings or other permanent improvements, or for major repair and rehabilitation of buildings or other permanent improvements except that:

(1) in the case of fire or natural disaster the legislature may appropriate from the general revenue an amount sufficient to replace the uninsured loss of any building or other permanent improvement; and

(2) the legislature, by two-thirds vote of each house, may, in cases of demonstrated need, which need must be clearly expressed in the body of the act, appropriate general revenue funds for acquiring land with or without permanent improvements, for constructing or equipping buildings or other permanent improvements, or for major repair and rehabilitation of buildings or other permanent improvements.
This subsection does not apply to legislative appropriations made prior to the adoption of this amendment.

(j) This section is self-enacting on the issuance of the governor's proclamation declaring the adoption of this amendment, and the state comptroller of public accounts shall do all things necessary to effectuate this section. This section does not impair any obligation created by the issuance of bonds or notes in accordance with prior law, and all outstanding bonds and notes shall be paid in full, both principal and interest, in accordance with their terms, and the changes herein made in the allocation of the available university fund shall not affect the pledges thereof made in connection with such bonds or notes heretofore issued. If the provisions of this section conflict with any other provision of this constitution, then the provisions of this section shall prevail, notwithstanding any such conflicting provisions.

Section 19. Texas Tomorrow Fund

(a) The Texas tomorrow fund is created as a trust fund dedicated to the prepayment of tuition and fees for higher education as provided by the general laws of this state for the prepaid higher education tuition program. The assets of the fund are held in trust for the benefit of participants and beneficiaries and may not be diverted. The state shall hold the assets of the fund for the exclusive purposes of providing benefits to participants and beneficiaries and defraying reasonable expenses of administering the program.

(b) Financing of benefits must be based on sound actuarial principles. The amount contributed by a person participating in the prepaid higher education program shall be as provided by the general laws of this state, but may not be less than the amount anticipated for tuition and required fees based on sound actuarial principles. If in any fiscal year there is not enough money in the Texas tomorrow fund to pay the tuition and required fees of an institution of higher education in which a beneficiary enrolls or the appropriate portion of the tuition and required fees of a private or independent institution of higher education in which a beneficiary enrolls as provided by a prepaid tuition contract, there is appropriated out of the first money coming into the state treasury in each fiscal year not otherwise appropriated by the constitution the amount that is sufficient to pay the applicable amount of tuition and required fees of the institution.
(c) Assets of the fund may be invested by an entity designated by general law in securities considered prudent investments. Investments shall be made in the exercise of judgment and care

under the circumstances that a person of ordinary prudence, discretion, and intelligence exercises in the management of the person's affairs, not for speculation, but for the permanent disposition of funds, considering the probable income from the disposition as well as the probable safety of capital.

(d) The state comptroller of public accounts shall take the actions necessary to implement this section.

(e) To the extent this section conflicts with any other provision of this constitution, this section controls.

Section 20. National Research University Fund

(a) There is established the national research university fund for the purpose of providing a dedicated, independent, and equitable source of funding to enable emerging research universities in this state to achieve national prominence as major research universities.

(b) The fund consists of money transferred or deposited to the credit of the fund and any interest or other return on the investment assets of the fund. The legislature may dedicate state revenue to the credit of the fund.

(c) The legislature shall provide for administration of the fund, which shall be invested in the manner and according to the standards provided for investment of the permanent university fund. The expenses of managing the investments of the fund shall be paid from the fund.

(d) In each state fiscal biennium, the legislature may appropriate as provided by Subsection (f) of this section all or a portion of the total return on all investment assets of the fund to carry out the purposes for which the fund is established.

(e) The legislature biennially shall allocate the amounts appropriated under this section, or shall provide for a biennial allocation of those amounts, to eligible state universities to carry out the purposes of the fund. The money shall be allocated based on an equitable formula established by the legislature or an agency designated by the legislature. The legislature shall review and as appropriate adjust, or provide for a review and adjustment, of the allocation formula at the end of each state fiscal biennium.

(f) The portion of the total return on investment assets of the fund that is available for appropriation in a state fiscal biennium under this section is the portion determined by the legislature, or an agency designated by the legislature, as necessary to provide as nearly as practicable a stable and predictable stream of annual distributions to eligible state universities and to maintain over time the purchasing power of fund investment assets. If the purchasing power of fund investment assets for any rolling 10-year period is not preserved, the distributions may not be increased until the purchasing power of the fund investment assets is restored. The amount appropriated from the fund in any fiscal year may not exceed an amount equal to seven percent of the average net fair market value of the investment assets of the fund, as determined by law. Until the fund has been invested for a period of time sufficient to determine the purchasing power over a 10-year period, the legislature may provide by law for means of preserving the purchasing power of the fund.

(g) The legislature shall establish criteria by which a state university may become eligible to receive a portion of the distributions from the fund. A state university that becomes eligible to receive a portion of the distributions from the fund in a state fiscal biennium remains eligible to receive additional distributions from the fund in any subsequent state fiscal biennium. The University of Texas at Austin and Texas A&M University are not eligible to receive money from the fund.

An eligible state university may use distributions from the fund only for the support and maintenance of educational and general activities that promote increased research capacity at the university.

ARTICLE 8. TAXATION AND REVENUE

Section 1. Equality and Uniformity of Taxation; Taxation of Property in Proportion to Value; Occupation and Income Taxes; Exemption of Certain Tangible Personal Property and Small Mineral Interests from Ad Valorem Taxation; Valuation of Residence Homesteads for Tax Purposes

(a) Taxation shall be equal and uniform.

(b) All real property and tangible personal property in this State, unless exempt as required or permitted by this Constitution, whether owned by natural persons or corporations, other than municipal, shall be taxed in proportion to its value, which shall be ascertained as may be provided by law.

(c) The Legislature may provide for the taxation of intangible property and may also impose occupation taxes, both upon natural persons and upon corporations, other than municipal, doing any business in this State. Subject to the restrictions of Section 24 of this article, it may also tax incomes of both natural persons and corporations other than municipal. Persons engaged in mechanical and agricultural pursuits shall never be required to pay an occupation tax.

(d) The Legislature by general law shall exempt from ad valorem taxation household goods not held or used for the production of income and personal effects not held or used for the production of income. The Legislature by general law may exempt from ad valorem taxation:

(1) all or part of the personal property homestead of a family or single adult, "personal property homestead" meaning that personal property exempt by law from forced sale for debt;

(2) subject to Subsections (e) and (g) of this section, all other tangible personal property, except structures which are substantially affixed to real estate and are used or occupied as residential dwellings and except property held or used for the production of income;

(3) subject to Subsection (e) of this section, a leased motor vehicle that is not held primarily for the production of income by the lessee and that otherwise qualifies under general law for exemption; and

(4) one motor vehicle, as defined by general law, owned by an individual that is used in the course of the individual's occupation or profession and is also used for personal activities of the owner that do not involve the production of income.

(e) The governing body of a political subdivision may provide for the taxation of all property exempt under a law adopted under Subdivision (2) or (3) of Subsection (d) of this section and not exempt from ad valorem taxation by any other law. The Legislature by general law may provide limitations to the application of this subsection to the taxation of vehicles exempted under the authority of Subdivision (3) of Subsection (d) of this section.

(f) The occupation tax levied by any county, city or town for any year on persons or corporations pursuing any profession or business, shall not exceed one half of the tax levied by the State for the same period on such profession or business.

(g) The Legislature may exempt from ad valorem taxation tangible personal property that is held or used for the production of income and has a taxable value of less than the minimum amount sufficient to recover the costs of the administration of the taxes on the property, as determined by or under the general law granting the exemption.

(h) The Legislature may exempt from ad valorem taxation a mineral interest that has a taxable value of less than the minimum amount sufficient to recover the costs of the administration of the taxes on the interest, as determined by or under the general law granting the exemption.

(i) Notwithstanding Subsections (a) and (b) of this section, the Legislature by general law may limit the maximum appraised value of a residence homestead for ad valorem tax purposes in a tax year to the lesser of the most recent market value of the residence homestead as determined by the appraisal entity or 110 percent, or a greater percentage, of the appraised value of the residence homestead for the preceding tax year. A limitation on appraised values authorized by this subsection:

(1) takes effect as to a residence homestead on the later of the effective date of the law imposing the limitation or January 1 of the tax year following the first tax year the owner qualifies the property for an exemption under Section 1-b of this article; and

(2) expires on January 1 of the first tax year that neither the owner of the property when the limitation took effect nor the owner's spouse or surviving spouse qualifies for an exemption under Section 1-b of this article.

(j) The Legislature by general law may provide for the taxation of real property that is the residence homestead of the property owner solely on the basis of the property's value as a residence homestead, regardless of whether the residential use of the property by the owner is considered to be the highest and best use of the property.

Section 1-A. County Tax Levy for Roads and Flood Control

The several counties of the State are authorized to levy ad valorem taxes upon all property within their respective boundaries for county purposes, except the first Three Thousand Dollars ($3,000) value of residential homesteads of married or unmarried adults, including those living alone, not to exceed thirty cents (30¢) on each One Hundred Dollars ($100) valuation, in addition to all other ad valorem taxes authorized by the Constitution of this State, provided the revenue derived therefrom shall be used for construction and maintenance of Farm to Market Roads or for Flood Control, except as herein otherwise provided.

Section 1-b. Residence Homestead Tax Exemptions and Limitations

(a) Three Thousand Dollars ($3,000) of the assessed taxable value of all residence homesteads of married or unmarried adults, male or female, including those living alone, shall be exempt from all taxation for all State purposes.

(b) The governing body of any county, city, town, school district, or other political subdivision of the State may exempt by its own action not less than Three Thousand Dollars ($3,000) of the market value of residence homesteads of persons, married or unmarried, including those living alone, who are under a disability for purposes of payment of disability insurance benefits under Federal Old-Age, Survivors, and Disability Insurance or its successor or of married or unmarried persons sixty-five (65) years of age or older, including those living alone, from all ad valorem taxes thereafter levied by the political subdivision. As an alternative, upon receipt of a petition signed by twenty percent (20%) of the voters who voted in the last preceding election held by the political subdivision, the governing body of the subdivision shall call an election to determine by majority vote whether an amount not less than Three Thousand Dollars ($3,000) as provided in the petition, of the market value of residence homesteads of disabled persons or of persons sixty-five (65) years of age or over shall be exempt from ad valorem taxes thereafter levied by the political subdivision. An eligible disabled person who is sixty-five (65) years of age or older may not receive both exemptions from the same political subdivision in the same year but may choose either if the subdivision has adopted both. Where any ad valorem tax has theretofore been pledged for the payment of any debt, the taxing officers of the political subdivision shall have authority to continue to levy and collect the tax against the homestead property at the same rate as the tax so pledged until the debt is discharged, if the cessation of the levy would impair the obligation of the contract by which the debt was created.

(c) The amount of $25,000 of the market value of the residence homestead of a married or unmarried adult, including one living alone, is exempt from ad valorem taxation for general elementary and secondary public school purposes. The legislature by general law may provide that all or part of the exemption does not apply to a district or political subdivision that imposes ad valorem taxes for public education purposes but is not the principal school district providing general elementary and secondary public education throughout its territory. In addition to this exemption, the legislature by general law may exempt an amount not to exceed $10,000 of the market value of the residence homestead of a person who is disabled as defined in Subsection (b) of this section and of a person 65 years of age or older from ad valorem taxation for general elementary and secondary public school purposes. The legislature by general law may base the amount of and condition eligibility for the additional exemption authorized by this subsection for disabled persons and for persons 65 years of age or older on economic need. An eligible disabled person who is 65 years of age or older may not receive both exemptions from a school district but may choose either. An eligible person is entitled to receive both the exemption required by this subsection for all residence homesteads and any exemption adopted pursuant to Subsection (b) of this section, but the legislature shall provide by general law whether an eligible disabled or elderly person may receive both the additional exemption for the elderly and disabled authorized by this subsection and any exemption for the elderly or disabled adopted pursuant to Subsection (b) of this section. Where ad valorem tax has previously been pledged for the payment of debt, the taxing officers of a school district may continue to levy and collect the tax against the value of homesteads exempted under this subsection until the debt is discharged if the cessation of the levy would impair the obligation of the contract by which the debt was created. The legislature shall provide for formulas to protect school districts against all or part of the revenue loss incurred by the implementation of this subsection, Subsection (d) of this section, and Section 1-d-1 of this article. The legislature by general law may define residence homestead for purposes of this section.

(d) Except as otherwise provided by this subsection, if a person receives a residence homestead exemption prescribed by Subsection (c) of this section for homesteads of persons who are 65 years of age or older or who are disabled, the total amount of ad valorem taxes imposed on that homestead for general elementary and secondary public school purposes may not be increased while it remains the residence homestead of that person or that person's spouse who receives the exemption. If a person 65 years of age or older dies in a year in which the person received the exemption, the total amount of ad valorem taxes imposed on the homestead for general elementary and secondary public school purposes may not be increased while it remains the residence homestead of that person's surviving spouse if the spouse is 55 years of age or older at the time of the person's death, subject to any exceptions provided by general law. The legislature, by general law, may provide for the transfer of all or a proportionate amount of a limitation provided by this subsection for a person who qualifies for the limitation and establishes a different residence homestead. However, taxes otherwise limited by this subsection may be increased to the extent the value of the homestead is increased by improvements other than repairs or improvements made to comply with governmental requirements and except as may be consistent with the transfer of a limitation under this subsection. For a residence homestead subject to the limitation provided by this subsection in the 1996 tax year or an earlier tax year, the legislature shall provide for a reduction in the amount of the limitation for the 1997 tax year and subsequent tax years in an amount equal to $10,000 multiplied by the 1997 tax rate for general elementary and secondary public school purposes applicable to the residence homestead. For a residence homestead subject to the limitation provided by this subsection

in the 2014 tax year or an earlier tax year, the legislature shall
provide for a reduction in the amount of the limitation for the
2015 tax year and subsequent tax years in an amount equal to
$10,000 multiplied by the 2015 tax rate for general elementary
and secondary public school purposes applicable to the residence
homestead.

(d-1) Notwithstanding Subsection (d) of this section, the
legislature by general law may provide for the reduction of the
amount of a limitation provided by that subsection and applicable
to a residence homestead for the 2007 tax year to reflect any
reduction from the 2006 tax year in the tax rate for general
elementary and secondary public school purposes applicable to
the homestead. A general law enacted under this subsection
may also take into account any reduction in the tax rate for those
purposes from the 2005 tax year to the 2006 tax year if the
homestead was subject to the limitation in the 2006 tax year. A
general law enacted under this subsection may provide that,
except as otherwise provided by Subsection (d) of this section, a
limitation provided by that subsection that is reduced under the
general law continues to apply to the residence homestead in
subsequent tax years until the limitation expires.

(e) The governing body of a political subdivision, other than a
county education district, may exempt from ad valorem taxation
a percentage of the market value of the residence homestead of
a married or unmarried adult, including one living alone. In the
manner provided by law, the voters of a county education district
at an election held for that purpose may exempt from ad valorem
taxation a percentage of the market value of the residence
homestead of a married or unmarried adult, including one living
alone. The percentage may not exceed twenty percent.
However, the amount of an exemption authorized pursuant to
this subsection may not be less than $5,000 unless the
legislature by general law prescribes other monetary restrictions
on the amount of the exemption. The legislature by general law
may prohibit the governing body of a political subdivision that
adopts an exemption under this subsection from reducing the

amount of or repealing the exemption. An eligible adult is entitled to receive other applicable exemptions provided by law. Where ad valorem tax has previously been pledged for the payment of debt, the governing body of a political subdivision may continue to levy and collect the tax against the value of the homesteads exempted under this subsection until the debt is discharged if the cessation of the levy would impair the obligation of the contract by which the debt was created. The legislature by general law may prescribe procedures for the administration of residence homestead exemptions.

(f) The surviving spouse of a person who received an exemption under Subsection (b) of this section for the residence homestead of a person sixty-five (65) years of age or older is entitled to an exemption for the same property from the same political subdivision in an amount equal to that of the exemption received by the deceased spouse if the deceased spouse died in a year in which the deceased spouse received the exemption, the surviving spouse was fifty-five (55) years of age or older when the deceased spouse died, and the property was the residence homestead of the surviving spouse when the deceased spouse died and remains the residence homestead of the surviving spouse. A person who receives an exemption under Subsection (b) of this section is not entitled to an exemption under this subsection. The legislature by general law may prescribe procedures for the administration of this subsection.

(g) If the legislature provides for the transfer of all or a proportionate amount of a tax limitation provided by Subsection (d) of this section for a person who qualifies for the limitation and subsequently establishes a different residence homestead, the legislature by general law may authorize the governing body of a school district to elect to apply the law providing for the transfer of the tax limitation to a change of a person's residence homestead that occurred before that law took effect, subject to any restrictions provided by general law. The transfer of the limitation may apply only to taxes imposed in a tax year that begins after the tax year in which the election is made.

(h) The governing body of a county, a city or town, or a junior college district by official action may provide that if a person who is disabled or is sixty-five (65) years of age or older receives a residence homestead exemption prescribed or authorized by this section, the total amount of ad valorem taxes imposed on that homestead by the county, the city or town, or the junior college district may not be increased while it remains the residence homestead of that person or that person's spouse who is disabled or sixty-five (65) years of age or older and receives a residence homestead exemption on the homestead. As an alternative, on receipt of a petition signed by five percent (5%) of the registered voters of the county, the city or town, or the junior college district, the governing body of the county, the city or town, or the junior college district shall call an election to determine by majority vote whether to establish a tax limitation provided by this subsection. If a county, a city or town, or a junior college district establishes a tax limitation provided by this subsection and a disabled person or a person sixty-five (65) years of age or older dies in a year in which the person received a residence homestead exemption, the total amount of ad valorem taxes imposed on the homestead by the county, the city or town, or the junior college district may not be increased while it remains the residence homestead of that person's surviving spouse if the spouse is fifty-five (55) years of age or older at the time of the person's death, subject to any exceptions provided by general law. The legislature, by general law, may provide for the transfer of all or a proportionate amount of a tax limitation provided by this subsection for a person who qualifies for the limitation and establishes a different residence homestead within the same county, within the same city or town, or within the same junior college district. A county, a city or town, or a junior college district that establishes a tax limitation under this subsection must comply with a law providing for the transfer of the limitation, even if the legislature enacts the law subsequent to the county's, the city's or town's, or the junior college district's establishment of the limitation. Taxes otherwise limited by a county, a city or town, or a junior college district under this subsection may be increased to the extent the value of the homestead is increased by improvements other than repairs and other than improvements made to comply with governmental requirements and except as may be consistent with the transfer of a tax limitation under a law authorized by this subsection. The governing body of a county, a city or town, or a junior college district may not repeal or rescind a tax limitation established under this subsection.

(i) The legislature by general law may exempt from ad valorem taxation all or part of the market value of the residence homestead of a disabled veteran who is certified as having a service-connected disability with a disability rating of 100 percent or totally disabled and may provide additional eligibility requirements for the exemption. For purposes of this subsection, "disabled veteran" means a disabled veteran as described by Section 2(b) of this article.

(j) The legislature by general law may provide that the surviving spouse of a disabled veteran who qualified for an exemption in accordance with Subsection (i) or (l) of this section from ad valorem taxation of all or part of the market value of the disabled veteran's residence homestead when the disabled veteran died is entitled to an exemption from ad valorem taxation of the same portion of the market value of the same property to which the disabled veteran's exemption applied if:

(1) the surviving spouse has not remarried since the death of the disabled veteran; and

(2) the property:

(A) was the residence homestead of the surviving spouse when the disabled veteran died; and

(B) remains the residence homestead of the surviving spouse.

(j-1) The legislature by general law may provide that the surviving spouse of a disabled veteran who would have qualified for an exemption from ad valorem taxation of all or part of the market value of the disabled veteran's residence homestead under Subsection (i) of this section if that subsection had been in effect on the date the disabled veteran died is entitled to an exemption from ad valorem taxation of the same portion of the market value of the same property to which the disabled veteran's exemption would have applied if the surviving spouse otherwise meets the requirements of Subsection (j) of this section.

(k) The legislature by general law may provide that if a surviving spouse who qualifies for an exemption in accordance with Subsection (j) or (j-1) of this section subsequently qualifies a different property as the surviving spouse's residence homestead, the surviving spouse is entitled to an exemption from ad valorem taxation of the subsequently qualified homestead in an amount equal to the dollar amount of the exemption from ad valorem taxation of the former homestead in accordance with Subsection (j) or (j-1) of this section in the last year in which the surviving spouse received an exemption in accordance with the applicable subsection for that homestead if the surviving spouse has not remarried since the death of the disabled veteran.

(l) The legislature by general law may provide that a partially disabled veteran is entitled to an exemption from ad valorem taxation of a percentage of the market value of the disabled veteran's residence homestead that is equal to the percentage of disability of the disabled veteran if the residence homestead was donated to the disabled veteran by a charitable organization for less than the market value of the residence homestead, including at no cost to the disabled veteran. The legislature by general law may provide additional eligibility requirements for the exemption. For purposes of this subsection, "partially disabled veteran" means a disabled veteran as described by Section 2(b) of this article who is certified as having a disability rating of less than 100 percent. A limitation or restriction on a disabled veteran's entitlement to an exemption under Section 2(b) of this article, or on the amount of an exemption under Section 2(b), does not apply to an exemption under this subsection.

(m) The legislature by general law may provide that the surviving spouse of a member of the armed services of the United States who is killed in action is entitled to an exemption from ad valorem taxation of all or part of the market value of the surviving spouse's residence homestead if the surviving spouse has not remarried since the death of the member of the armed services.

(n) The legislature by general law may provide that a surviving spouse who qualifies for and receives an exemption in accordance with Subsection (m) of this section and who subsequently qualifies a different property as the surviving spouse's residence homestead is entitled to an exemption from ad valorem taxation of the subsequently qualified homestead in an amount equal to the dollar amount of the exemption from ad valorem taxation of the first homestead for which the exemption was received in accordance with Subsection (m) of this section in the last year in which the surviving spouse received the exemption in accordance with that subsection for that homestead if the surviving spouse has not remarried since the death of the member of the armed services.

(o) The legislature by general law may provide that the surviving spouse of a first responder who is killed or fatally injured in the line of duty is entitled to an exemption from ad valorem taxation of all or part of the market value of the surviving spouse's residence homestead if the surviving spouse has not remarried since the death of the first responder. The legislature by general law may define "first responder" for purposes of this subsection and may prescribe additional eligibility requirements for the exemption authorized by this subsection.

(p) The legislature by general law may provide that a surviving spouse who qualifies for and receives an exemption in accordance with Subsection (o) of this section and who subsequently qualifies a different property as the surviving spouse's residence homestead is entitled to an exemption from ad valorem taxation of the subsequently qualified homestead in an amount equal to the dollar amount of the exemption from ad valorem taxation of the first homestead for which the exemption was received in accordance with Subsection (o) of this section in the last year in which the surviving spouse received the exemption in accordance with that subsection for that homestead if the surviving spouse has not remarried since the death of the first responder.

Section 1-b-1. Repealed

Section 1-c. Repealed

Section 1-D. Assessment for Tax Purposes of Lands Designated for Agricultural Use

(a) All land owned by natural persons which is designated for agricultural use in accordance with the provisions of this Section shall be assessed for all tax purposes on the consideration of only those factors relative to such agricultural use. "Agricultural use" means the raising of livestock or growing of crops, fruit, flowers, and other products of the soil under natural conditions as a business venture for profit, which business is the primary occupation and source of income of the owner.

(b) For each assessment year the owner wishes to qualify his land under provisions of this Section as designated for agricultural use he shall file with the local tax assessor a sworn statement in writing describing the use to which the land is devoted.

(c) Upon receipt of the sworn statement in writing the local tax assessor shall determine whether or not such land qualifies for the designation as to agricultural use as defined herein and in the event it so qualifies he shall designate such land as being for agricultural use and assess the land accordingly.

(d) Such local tax assessor may inspect the land and require such evidence of use and source of income as may be necessary or useful in determining whether or not the agricultural use provision of this article applies.

(e) No land may qualify for the designation provided for in this Act unless for at least three (3) successive years immediately preceding the assessment date the land has been devoted exclusively for agricultural use, or unless the land has been continuously developed for agriculture during such time.

(f) Each year during which the land is designated for agricultural use, the local tax assessor shall note on his records the valuation which would have been made had the land not qualified for such designation under this Section. If designated land is subsequently diverted to a purpose other than that of agricultural use, or is sold, the land shall be subject to an additional tax. The additional tax shall equal the difference between taxes paid or payable, hereunder, and the amount of tax payable for the preceding three years had the land been otherwise assessed. Until paid there shall be a lien for additional taxes and interest on land assessed under the provisions of this Section.

(g) The valuation and assessment of any minerals or subsurface rights to minerals shall not come within the provisions of this Section.

Section 1-d-1. Taxation of Certain Open-Space Land

(a) To promote the preservation of open-space land, the legislature shall provide by general law for taxation of open-space land devoted to farm, ranch, or wildlife management purposes on the basis of its productive capacity and may provide by general law for taxation of open-space land devoted to timber production on the basis of its productive capacity. The legislature by general law may provide eligibility limitations under this section and may impose sanctions in furtherance of the taxation policy of this section.

(b) If a property owner qualifies his land for designation for agricultural use under Section 1-d of this article, the land is subject to the provisions of Section 1-d for the year in which the designation is effective and is not subject to a law enacted under this Section 1-d-1 in that year.

Section 1-e. State Ad Valorem Taxes Prohibited

No State ad valorem taxes shall be levied upon any property within this State.

Section 1-f. Ad Valorem Tax Relief

The legislature by law may provide for the preservation of cultural, historical, or natural history resources by:

(1) granting exemptions or other relief from state ad valorem taxes on appropriate property so designated in the manner prescribed by law; and

(2) authorizing political subdivisions to grant exemptions or other relief from ad valorem taxes on appropriate property so designated by the political subdivision in the manner prescribed by general law.

Section 1-g. Development or Redevelopment of Property; Ad Valorem Tax Relief and Issuance of Bonds and Notes

(a) The legislature by general law may authorize cities, towns, and other taxing units to grant exemptions or other relief from ad valorem taxes on property located in a reinvestment zone for the purpose of encouraging development or redevelopment and improvement of the property.

(b) The legislature by general law may authorize an incorporated city or town to issue bonds or notes to finance the development or redevelopment of an unproductive, underdeveloped, or blighted area within the city or town and to pledge for repayment of those bonds or notes increases in ad valorem tax revenues imposed on property in the area by the city or town and other political subdivisions.

Section 1-h. Validation Of Assessment Ratio

Section 26.03, Tax Code, is validated as of January 1, 1980.

Section 1-i. Mobile Marine Drilling Equipment; Ad Valorem Tax Relief

The legislature by general law may provide ad valorem tax relief for mobile marine drilling equipment designed for offshore drilling of oil or gas wells that is being stored while not in use in a county bordering on the Gulf of Mexico or on a bay or other body of water immediately adjacent to the Gulf of Mexico. (Added Nov. 3, 1987.)

Section 1-j. Exemption From Ad Valorem Taxation of Certain Tangible Personal Property Temporarily Located in this State

(a) To promote economic development in the State, goods, wares, merchandise, other tangible personal property, and ores, other than oil, natural gas, and other petroleum products, are exempt from ad valorem taxation by a political subdivision of this State if:

(1) the property is acquired in or imported into this State to be forwarded outside this State, whether or not the intention to forward the property outside this State is formed or the destination to which the property is forwarded is specified when the property is acquired in or imported into this State;

(2) the property is detained in this State for assembling, storing, manufacturing, processing, or fabricating purposes by the person who acquired or imported the property; and

(3) the property is transported outside of this State not later than:

(A) 175 days after the date the person acquired or imported the property in this State; or

(B) if applicable, a later date established by the governing body of the political subdivision under Subsection (d) of this section.
(b) The governing body of a county, common, or independent school district, junior college district, or municipality that, acting under previous constitutional authority, taxes property otherwise exempt by Subsection (a) of this section may subsequently exempt the property from taxation by rescinding its action to tax the property. The exemption applies to each tax year that begins after the date the action is taken and applies to the tax year in which the action is taken if the governing body so provides. A governing body that rescinds its action to tax the property may not take action to tax such property after the rescission.

(c) For purposes of this section:

(1) tangible personal property shall include aircraft and aircraft parts;

(2) property imported into this State shall include property brought into this State;

(3) property forwarded outside this State shall include property transported outside this State or to be affixed to an aircraft to be transported outside this State; and

(4) property detained in this State for assembling, storing, manufacturing, processing, or fabricating purposes shall include property, aircraft, or aircraft parts brought into this State or acquired in this State and used by the person who acquired the property, aircraft, or aircraft parts in or who brought the property, aircraft, or aircraft parts into this State for the purpose of repair or maintenance of aircraft operated by a certificated air carrier.

(d) The governing body of a political subdivision, in the manner provided by law for official action, may extend the date by which aircraft parts exempted from ad valorem taxation under this section must be transported outside the State to a date not later than the 730th day after the date the person acquired or imported the aircraft parts in this State. An extension adopted by official action under this subsection applies only to the exemption from ad valorem taxation by the political subdivision adopting the extension. The legislature by general law may provide the manner by which the governing body may extend the period of time as authorized by this subsection.

Section 1-k. Exemption From Ad Valorem Taxation of Property Owned by Nonprofit Corporations Supplying Water or Providing Wastewater Services

The legislature by general law may exempt from ad valorem taxation property owned by a nonprofit corporation organized to supply water or provide wastewater service that provides in the bylaws of the corporation that on dissolution of the corporation, the assets of the corporation remaining after discharge of the corporation's indebtedness shall be transferred to an entity that provides a water supply or wastewater service, or both, that is exempt from ad valorem taxation, if the property is reasonably necessary for and used in the acquisition, treatment, storage, transportation, sale, or distribution of water or the provision of wastewater service.

Section 1-l. Exemption From Ad Valorem Taxation of Property Used for Control of Air, Water, or Land Pollution

(a) The legislature by general law may exempt from ad valorem taxation all or part of real and personal property used, constructed, acquired, or installed wholly or partly to meet or exceed rules or regulations adopted by any environmental protection agency of the United States, this state, or a political subdivision of this state for the prevention, monitoring, control, or reduction of air, water, or land pollution.

(b) This section applies to real and personal property used as a facility, device, or method for the control of air, water, or land pollution that would otherwise be taxable for the first time on or after January 1, 1994.

(c) This section does not authorize the exemption from ad valorem taxation of real or personal property that was subject to a tax abatement agreement executed before January 1, 1994.

Section 1-m. Property on Which Water Conservation Initiative has been Implemented; Ad Valorem Tax Relief

The legislature by general law may authorize a taxing unit to grant an exemption or other relief from ad valorem taxes on property on which a water conservation initiative has been implemented.

Section 1-n. Exemption From Ad Valorem Taxation of Raw Cocoa and Green Coffee

(a) The legislature by general law may exempt from ad valorem taxation raw cocoa and green coffee that is held in Harris County.

(b) The legislature may impose additional requirements for qualification for an exemption under this section.

Section 1-n. Exemption From Ad Valorem Taxation of Tangible Personal Property Held Temporarily for Certain Commercial Purposes

(a) To promote economic development in this state, the legislature by general law may exempt from ad valorem taxation goods, wares, merchandise, other tangible personal property, and ores, other than oil, natural gas, and other petroleum products, if:

(1) the property is acquired in or imported into this state to be forwarded to another location in this state or outside this state, whether or not the intention to forward the property to another location in this state or outside this state is formed or the destination to which the property is forwarded is specified when the property is acquired in or imported into this state;

(2) the property is detained at a location in this state that is not owned or under the control of the property owner for assembling, storing, manufacturing, processing, or fabricating purposes by the person who acquired or imported the property; and

(3) the property is transported to another location in this state or outside this state not later than 270 days after the date the person acquired the property in or imported the property into this state.

(b) For purposes of this section:

(1) tangible personal property includes aircraft and aircraft parts;

(2) property imported into this state includes property brought into this state;

(3) property forwarded to another location in this state or outside this state includes property transported to another location in this state or outside this state or to be affixed to an aircraft to be transported to another location in this state or outside this state; and

(4) property detained at a location in this state for assembling, storing, manufacturing, processing, or fabricating purposes includes property, aircraft, or aircraft parts brought into this state or acquired in this state and used by the person who acquired the property, aircraft, or aircraft parts in this state or who brought the property, aircraft, or aircraft parts into this state for the purpose of repair or maintenance of aircraft operated by a certificated air carrier.

(c) A property owner who is eligible to receive the exemption authorized by Section 1-j of this article may apply for the exemption authorized by the legislature under this section in the manner provided by general law, subject to the provisions of Subsection (d) of this section. A property owner who receives the exemption authorized by the legislature under this section is not entitled to receive the exemption authorized by Section 1-j of this article for the same property.

(d) The governing body of a political subdivision that imposes ad valorem taxes may provide for the taxation of property exempt under a law adopted under Subsection (a) of this section and not exempt from ad valorem taxation by any other law. Before acting to tax the exempt property, the governing body of the political subdivision must conduct a public hearing at which members of the public are permitted to speak for or against the taxation of the property.

Section 1-o. Rural Economic Development; Limitation on Ad Valorem Tax Increase

To aid in the elimination of slum and blighted conditions in less populated communities in this state, to promote rural economic development in this state, and to improve the economy of this state, the legislature by general law may authorize the governing body of a municipality having a population of less than 10,000, in the manner required by law, to call an election to permit the voters to determine by majority vote whether to authorize the governing body of the municipality to enter into an agreement with an owner of real property that is located in or adjacent to a designated area of the municipality that has been approved for funding under the Downtown Revitalization Program or the Main Street Improvements Program administered by the Department of Agriculture, or a successor program administered by that agency, under which the parties agree that the ad valorem taxes imposed by any political subdivision on the owner's real property may not be increased for the first five tax years after the tax year in which the agreement is entered into, subject to the terms and conditions provided by the agreement. A general law enacted under this section must provide that, if authorized by the voters, an agreement to limit ad valorem tax increases authorized by this section:

(1) must be entered into by the governing body of the municipality and a property owner before December 31 of the tax year in which the election was held;

(2) takes effect as to a parcel of real property on January 1 of the tax year following the tax year in which the governing body and the property owner enter into the agreement;

(3) applies to ad valorem taxes imposed by any political subdivision on the real property covered by the agreement; and

(4) expires on the earlier of:

(A) January 1 of the sixth tax year following the tax year in which the governing body and the property owner enter into the agreement; or

(B) January 1 of the first tax year in which the owner of the property when the agreement was entered into ceases to own the property.

Section 2. Equality and Uniformity of Occupation Taxes; Additional Exemptions from Ad Valorem Taxation

(a) All occupation taxes shall be equal and uniform upon the same class of subjects within the limits of the authority levying the tax; but the legislature may, by general laws, exempt from taxation public property used for public purposes; actual places of religious worship, also any property owned by a church or by a strictly religious society for the exclusive use as a dwelling place for the ministry of such church or religious society, and which yields no revenue whatever to such church or religious society; provided that such exemption shall not extend to more property than is reasonably necessary for a dwelling place and in no event more than one acre of land; any property owned by a church or by a strictly religious society that owns an actual place of religious worship if the property is owned for the purpose of expansion of the place of religious worship or construction of a new place of religious worship and the property yields no revenue whatever to the church or religious society, provided that the legislature by general law may provide eligibility limitations for the exemption and may impose sanctions related to the exemption in furtherance of the taxation policy of this subsection; any property that is owned by a church or by a strictly religious society and is leased by that church or strictly religious society to a person for use as a school, as defined by Section 11.21, Tax Code, or a successor statute, for educational purposes; places of burial not held for private or corporate profit; solar or wind-powered energy devices; all buildings used exclusively and owned by persons or associations of persons for school purposes and the necessary furniture of all schools and property used exclusively and reasonably necessary in conducting any association engaged in promoting the religious, educational and physical development of boys, girls, young men or young women operating under a State or National organization of like character; also the endowment funds of such institutions of learning and religion not used with a view to profit; and when the same are invested in bonds or mortgages, or in land or other property which has been and shall hereafter be bought in by such institutions under foreclosure sales made to satisfy or protect such bonds or mortgages, that such exemption of such land and property shall continue only for two years after the purchase of the same at such sale by such institutions and no longer, and institutions engaged primarily in public charitable functions, which may conduct auxiliary activities to support those charitable functions; and all laws exempting property from taxation other than the property mentioned in this Section shall be null and void.

(b) The Legislature may, by general law, exempt property owned by a disabled veteran or by the surviving spouse and surviving minor children of a disabled veteran. A disabled veteran is a veteran of the armed services of the United States who is classified as disabled by the Veterans' Administration or by a successor to that agency or by the military service in which the veteran served. A veteran who is certified as having a disability of less than 10 percent is not entitled to an exemption. A veteran having a disability rating of not less than 10 percent but less than 30 percent may be granted an exemption from taxation for property valued at up to $5,000. A veteran having a disability rating of not less than 30 percent but less than 50 percent may be granted an exemption from taxation for property valued at up to $7,500. A veteran having a disability rating of not less than 50 percent but less than 70 percent may be granted an exemption from taxation for property valued at up to $10,000. A veteran who has a disability rating of 70 percent or more, or a veteran who has a disability rating of not less than 10 percent and has attained the age of 65, or a disabled veteran whose disability consists of the loss or loss of use of one or more limbs, total blindness in one or both eyes, or paraplegia, may be granted an exemption from taxation for property valued at up to $12,000. The spouse and children of any member of the United States Armed Forces who dies while on active duty may be granted an exemption from taxation for property valued at up to $5,000. A deceased disabled veteran's surviving spouse and children may be granted an exemption which in the aggregate is equal to the exemption to which the veteran was entitled when the veteran died.

(c) The Legislature by general law may exempt from ad valorem taxation property that is owned by a nonprofit organization composed primarily of members or former members of the armed forces of the United States or its allies and chartered or incorporated by the United States Congress.

(d) Unless otherwise provided by general law enacted after January 1, 1995, the amounts of the exemptions from ad valorem taxation to which a person is entitled under Section 11.22, Tax Code, for a tax year that begins on or after the date this subsection takes effect are the maximum amounts permitted under Subsection (b) of this section instead of the amounts specified by Section 11.22, Tax Code. This subsection may be repealed by the Legislature by general law.

Section 3. Taxation by General Law for Public Purposes

Taxes shall be levied and collected by general laws and for public purposes only.

Section 4. Surrender or Suspension of Taxing Power Prohibited

The power to tax corporations and corporate property shall not be surrendered or suspended by act of the Legislature, by any contract or grant to which the State shall be a party.

Section 5. Repealed

Section 6. Withdrawal of Money from Treasury; Duration of Appropriation

No money shall be drawn from the Treasury but in pursuance of specific appropriations made by law; nor shall any appropriation of money be made for a longer term than two years.

Section 7. Borrowing, Withholding, or Diverting Special Funds Prohibited

The Legislature shall not have power to borrow, or in any manner divert from its purpose, any special fund that may, or ought to, come into the Treasury; and shall make it penal for any person or persons to borrow, withhold or in any manner to divert from its purpose any special fund, or any part thereof.

Section 7-a. Use of Revenues from Motor Vehicle Registration Fees and Taxes on Motor Fuels and Lubricants

Subject to legislative appropriation, allocation and direction, all net revenues remaining after payment of all refunds allowed by law and expenses of collection derived from motor vehicle registration fees, and all taxes, except gross production and ad valorem taxes, on motor fuels and lubricants used to propel motor vehicles over public roadways, shall be used for the sole purpose of acquiring rights-of-way, constructing, maintaining, and policing such public roadways, and for the administration of such laws as may be prescribed by the Legislature pertaining to the supervision of traffic and safety on such roads; and for the payment of the principal and interest on county and road district bonds or warrants voted or issued prior to January 2, 1939, and declared eligible prior to January 2, 1945, for payment out of the County and Road District Highway Fund under existing law; provided, however, that one-fourth (1/4) of such net revenue from the motor fuel tax shall be allocated to the Available School Fund; and, provided, however, that the net revenue derived by counties from motor vehicle registration fees shall never be less than the maximum amounts allowed to be retained by each

County and the percentage allowed to be retained by each
County under the laws in effect on January 1, 1945. Nothing
contained herein shall be construed as authorizing the pledging
of the State's credit for any purpose.

Section 7-b. Use of Revenues from Federal Reimbursement

All revenues received from the federal government as
reimbursement for state expenditures of funds that are
themselves dedicated for acquiring rights-of-way and
constructing, maintaining, and policing public roadways are also
constitutionally dedicated and shall be used only for those
purposes.

Section 7-c. Dedication of Revenue from State Sales and Use
Tax and Taxes Imposed on Sale, Use, or Rental of Motor Vehicle
to State Highway Fund

(a) Subject to Subsections (d) and (e) of this section, in each
state fiscal year, the comptroller of public accounts shall deposit
to the credit of the state highway fund $2.5 billion of the net
revenue derived from the imposition of the state sales and use
tax on the sale, storage, use, or other consumption in this state
of taxable items under Chapter 151, Tax Code, or its successor,
that exceeds the first $28 billion of that revenue coming into the
treasury in that state fiscal year.

(b) Subject to Subsections (d) and (e) of this section, in each
state fiscal year, the comptroller of public accounts shall deposit
to the credit of the state highway fund an amount equal to 35
percent of the net revenue derived from the tax authorized by
Chapter 152, Tax Code, or its successor, and imposed on the
sale, use, or rental of a motor vehicle that exceeds the first $5
billion of that revenue coming into the treasury in that state fiscal
year.

(c) Money deposited to the credit of the state highway fund under this section may be appropriated only to:

(1) construct, maintain, or acquire rights-of-way for public roadways other than toll roads; or

(2) repay the principal of and interest on general obligation bonds issued as authorized by Section 49-p, Article III, of this constitution.

(d) The legislature by adoption of a resolution approved by a record vote of two-thirds of the members of each house of the legislature may direct the comptroller of public accounts to reduce the amount of money deposited to the credit of the state highway fund under Subsection (a) or (b) of this section. The comptroller may be directed to make that reduction only:

(1) in the state fiscal year in which the resolution is adopted, or in either of the following two state fiscal years; and

(2) by an amount or percentage that does not result in a reduction of more than 50 percent of the amount that would otherwise be deposited to the fund in the affected state fiscal year under the applicable subsection of this section.

(e) Subject to Subsection (f) of this section, the duty of the comptroller of public accounts to make a deposit under this section expires:

(1) August 31, 2032, for a deposit required by Subsection (a) of this section; and

(2) August 31, 2029, for a deposit required by Subsection (b) of this section.

(f) The legislature by adoption of a resolution approved by a record vote of a majority of the members of each house of the legislature may extend, in 10-year increments, the duty of the comptroller of public accounts to make a deposit under Subsection (a) or (b) of this section beyond the applicable date prescribed by Subsection (e) of this section.

Section 8. Assessment and Collection of Taxes on Property of Railroad Companies

All property of railroad companies shall be assessed, and the taxes collected in the several counties in which said property is situated, including so much of the roadbed and fixtures as shall be in each county. The rolling stock may be assessed in gross in the county where the principal office of the company is located, and the county tax paid upon it shall be apportioned as provided by general law in proportion to the distance such road may run through any such county, among the several counties through which the road passes, as a part of their tax assets.

Section 9. Maximum County, City, and Town Tax Rates; County Funds; Local Road Laws

(a) No county, city or town shall levy a tax rate in excess of Eighty Cents ($ .80) on the One Hundred Dollars ($100) valuation in any one (1) year for general fund, permanent improvement fund, road and bridge fund and jury fund purposes.

(b) At the time the Commissioners Court meets to levy the annual tax rate for each county it shall levy whatever tax rate may be needed for the four (4) constitutional purposes; namely, general fund, permanent improvement fund, road and bridge fund and jury fund so long as the Court does not impair any outstanding bonds or other obligations and so long as the total of the foregoing tax levies does not exceed Eighty Cents ($ .80) on the One Hundred Dollars ($100) valuation in any one (1) year. Once the Court has levied the annual tax rate, the same shall remain in force and effect during that taxable year.

(c) The Legislature may authorize an additional annual ad valorem tax to be levied and collected for the further maintenance of the public roads; provided, that a majority of the qualified voters of the county voting at an election to be held for that purpose shall approve the tax, not to exceed Fifteen Cents ($ .15) on the One Hundred Dollars ($100) valuation of the property subject to taxation in such county.

(d) Any county may put all tax money collected by the county into one general fund, without regard to the purpose or source of each tax.

(e) The Legislature may pass local laws for the maintenance of the public roads and highways, without the local notice required for special or local laws.

(f) This Section shall not be construed as a limitation of powers delegated to counties, cities or towns by any other Section or Sections of this Constitution.

Section 10. Release from Payment of Taxes Restricted

The Legislature shall have no power to release the inhabitants of, or property in, any county, city or town from the payment of taxes levied for State or county purposes, unless in case of great public calamity in any such county, city or town, when such release may be made by a vote of two-thirds of each House of the Legislature.

Section 11. Place of Assessment of Property for Taxation; Value of Property not Rendered by Owner for Taxation

All property, whether owned by persons or corporations shall be assessed for taxation, and the taxes paid in the county where situated, but the Legislature may, by a two-thirds vote, authorize the payment of taxes of non-residents of counties to be made at the office of the Comptroller of Public Accounts. And all lands and other property not rendered for taxation by the owner thereof shall be assessed at its fair value by the proper officer.

Section 12. Repealed

Section 13. Sales of Lands and Other Property for Unpaid Taxes; Redemption

(a) Provision shall be made by the Legislature for the sale of a sufficient portion of all lands and other property for the taxes due thereon that have not been paid.

(b) The deed of conveyance to the purchaser for all lands and other property thus sold shall be held to vest a good and perfect title in the purchaser thereof, subject only to redemption as provided by this section or impeachment for actual fraud.

(c) The former owner of a residence homestead, land designated for agricultural use, or a mineral interest sold for unpaid taxes shall within two years from date of the filing for record of the Purchaser's Deed have the right to redeem the property on the following basis:

(1) Within the first year of the redemption period, upon the payment of the amount of money paid for the property, including the Tax Deed Recording Fee and all taxes, penalties, interest, and costs paid plus an amount not exceeding 25 percent of the aggregate total; and

(2) Within the last year of the redemption period, upon the payment of the amount of money paid for the property, including the Tax Deed Recording Fee and all taxes, penalties, interest, and costs paid plus an amount not exceeding 50 percent of the aggregate total.

(d) If the residence homestead or land designated for agricultural use is sold pursuant to a suit to enforce the collection of the unpaid taxes, the Legislature may limit the application of Subsection (c) of this section to property used as a residence homestead when the suit was filed and to land designated for agricultural use when the suit was filed.

(e) The former owner of real property not covered by Subsection (c) of this section sold for unpaid taxes shall within six months from the date of filing for record of the Purchaser's Deed have the right to redeem the property upon the payment of the amount of money paid for the property, including the Tax Deed Recording Fee and all taxes, penalties, interest, and costs paid plus an amount not exceeding 25 percent of the aggregate total.

Section 14. Assessor and Collector of Taxes

(a) The qualified voters of each county shall elect an assessor-collector of taxes for the county, except as otherwise provided by this section.

(b) In any county having a population of less than 10,000 inhabitants, as determined by the most recent decennial census of the United States, the sheriff of the county, in addition to that officer's other duties, shall be the assessor-collector of taxes, except that the commissioners court of such a county may submit to the qualified voters of the county at an election the question of electing an assessor-collector of taxes as a county officer separate from the office of sheriff. If a majority of the voters voting in such an election approve of electing an assessor-collector of taxes for the county, then such official shall be elected at the next general election for the constitutional term of office as is provided for other tax assessor-collectors in this state.

(c) An assessor-collector of taxes shall hold office for four years; and shall perform all the duties with respect to assessing property for the purpose of taxation and of collecting taxes, as may be prescribed by the Legislature.

Section 15. Lien of Assessment; Seizure and Sale of Property of Delinquent Taxpayer

The annual assessment made upon landed property shall be a special lien thereon; and all property, both real and personal, belonging to any delinquent taxpayer shall be liable to seizure and sale for the payment of all the taxes and penalties due by such delinquent; and such property may be sold for the payment of the taxes and penalties due by such delinquent, under such regulations as the Legislature may provide.

Section 16. Repealed

Section 16a. Repealed

Section 17. Specification of Subjects not Limitation of Legislature's Power of Taxation

The specification of the objects and subjects of taxation shall not deprive the Legislature of the power to require other subjects or objects to be taxed in such manner as may be consistent with the principles of taxation fixed in this Constitution.

Section 18. Equalization of Property Valuations for Taxation; Single Appraisal and Single Board of Equalization

(a) The Legislature shall provide for equalizing, as near as may be, the valuation of all property subject to or rendered for taxation, and may also provide for the classification of all lands with reference to their value in the several counties.

(b) A single appraisal within each county of all property subject to ad valorem taxation by the county and all other taxing units located therein shall be provided by general law. The Legislature, by general law, may authorize appraisals outside a county when political subdivisions are situated in more than one county or when two or more counties elect to consolidate appraisal services.

(c) The Legislature, by general law, shall provide for a single board of equalization for each appraisal entity consisting of qualified persons residing within the territory appraised by that entity. The Legislature, by general law, may authorize a single board of equalization for two or more adjoining appraisal entities that elect to provide for consolidated equalizations. Members of a board of equalization may not be elected officials of a county or of the governing body of a taxing unit.

(d) The Legislature shall prescribe by general law the methods, timing, and administrative process for implementing the requirements of this section.

Section 19. Exemption from Taxation of Farm Products, Livestock, Poultry, and Family Supplies

Farm products, livestock, and poultry in the hands of the producer, and family supplies for home and farm use, are exempt from all taxation until otherwise directed by a two-thirds vote of all the members elect to both houses of the Legislature.

Section 19a. Exemption from Ad Valorem Taxation of Implements of Husbandry

Implements of husbandry that are used in the production of farm or ranch products are exempt from ad valorem taxation.

Section 20. Ad Valorem Taxation of Property at Value Exceeding Fair Cash Market Value Prohibited; Discounts for Advance Payment

No property of any kind in this State shall ever be assessed for ad valorem taxes at a greater value than its fair cash market value nor shall any Board of Equalization of any governmental or political subdivision or taxing district within this State fix the value of any property for tax purposes at more than its fair cash market value; provided that in order to encourage the prompt payment of taxes, the Legislature shall have the power to provide that the taxpayer shall be allowed by the State and all governmental and political subdivisions and taxing districts of the State a three per cent (3%) discount on ad valorem taxes due the State or due any governmental or political subdivision or taxing district of the State if such taxes are paid ninety (90) days before the date when they would otherwise become delinquent; and the taxpayer shall be allowed a two per cent (2%) discount on said taxes if paid sixty (60) days before said taxes would become delinquent; and the taxpayer shall be allowed a one per cent (1%) discount if said taxes are paid thirty (30) days before they would otherwise become delinquent. The Legislature shall pass necessary laws for the proper administration of this Section.

Section 21. Increase in Total Amount of Property Taxes Imposed Prohibited Without Notice and Hearing; Calculation and Notice to Property Owners

(a) Subject to any exceptions prescribed by general law, the total amount of property taxes imposed by a political subdivision in any year may not exceed the total amount of property taxes imposed by that subdivision in the preceding year unless the governing body of the subdivision gives notice of its intent to consider an increase in taxes and holds a public hearing on the proposed increase before it increases those total taxes. The legislature shall prescribe by law the form, content, timing, and methods of giving the notice and the rules for the conduct of the hearing.

(b) In calculating the total amount of taxes imposed in the current year for the purposes of Subsection (a) of this section, the taxes on property in territory added to the political subdivision since the preceding year and on new improvements that were not taxable in the preceding year are excluded. In calculating the total amount of taxes imposed in the preceding year for the purposes of Subsection (a) of this section, the taxes imposed on real property that is not taxable by the subdivision in the current year are excluded.

(c) The legislature by general law shall require that, subject to reasonable exceptions, a property owner be given notice of a revaluation of his property and a reasonable estimate of the amount of taxes that would be imposed on his property if the total amount of property taxes for the subdivision were not increased according to any law enacted pursuant to Subsection (a) of this section. The notice must be given before the procedures required in Subsection (a) are instituted.

Section 22. Restriction on Rate of Growth of Appropriations

(a) In no biennium shall the rate of growth of appropriations from state tax revenues not dedicated by this constitution exceed the estimated rate of growth of the state's economy. The legislature shall provide by general law procedures to implement this subsection.

(b) If the legislature by adoption of a resolution approved by a record vote of a majority of the members of each house finds that an emergency exists and identifies the nature of the emergency, the legislature may provide for appropriations in excess of the amount authorized by Subsection (a) of this section. The excess authorized under this subsection may not exceed the amount specified in the resolution.

(c) In no case shall appropriations exceed revenues as provided in Article III, Section 49a, of this constitution. Nothing in this section shall be construed to alter, amend, or repeal Article III, Section 49a, of this constitution.

Section 23. Statewide Appraisal of Real Property for Ad Valorem Tax Purposes Prohibited; Enforcement of Appraisal Standards and Procedures

(a) There shall be no statewide appraisal of real property for ad valorem tax purposes; however, this shall not preclude formula distribution of tax revenues to political subdivisions of the state.

(b) Administrative and judicial enforcement of uniform standards and procedures for appraisal of property for ad valorem tax purposes shall be prescribed by general law.

Section 24. Personal Income Tax; Dedication of Proceeds

(a) A general law enacted by the legislature that imposes a tax on the net incomes of natural persons, including a person's share of partnership and unincorporated association income, must provide that the portion of the law imposing the tax not take effect until approved by a majority of the registered voters voting in a statewide referendum held on the question of imposing the tax. The referendum must specify the rate of the tax that will apply to taxable income as defined by law.

(b) A general law enacted by the legislature that increases the rate of the tax, or changes the tax, in a manner that results in an increase in the combined income tax liability of all persons subject to the tax may not take effect until approved by a majority of the registered voters voting in a statewide referendum held on the question of increasing the income tax. A determination of whether a bill proposing a change in the tax would increase the combined income tax liability of all persons subject to the tax must be made by comparing the provisions of the proposed change in law with the provisions of the law for the most recent year in which actual tax collections have been made. A referendum held under this subsection must specify the manner in which the proposed law would increase the combined income tax liability of all persons subject to the tax.

(c) Except as provided by Subsection (b) of this section, the legislature may amend or repeal a tax approved by the voters under this section without submitting the amendment or the repeal to the voters as provided by Subsection (a) of this section.

(d) If the legislature repeals a tax approved by the voters under this section, the legislature may reenact the tax without submitting the reenactment to the voters as provided by

Subsection (a) of this section only if the effective date of the reenactment of the tax is before the first anniversary of the effective date of the repeal.

(e) The legislature may provide for the taxation of income in a manner which is consistent with federal law.

(f) In the first year in which a tax described by Subsection (a) is imposed and during the first year of any increase in the tax that is subject to Subsection (b) of this section, not less than two-thirds of all net revenues remaining after payment of all refunds allowed by law and expenses of collection from the tax shall be used to reduce the rate of ad valorem maintenance and operation taxes levied for the support of primary and secondary public education. In subsequent years, not less than two-thirds of all net revenues from the tax shall be used to continue such ad valorem tax relief.

(g) The net revenues remaining after the dedication of money from the tax under Subsection (f) of this section shall be used for support of education, subject to legislative appropriation, allocation, and direction.

(h) The maximum rate at which a school district may impose ad valorem maintenance and operation taxes is reduced by an amount equal to one cent per $100 valuation for each one cent per $100 valuation that the school district's ad valorem maintenance and operation tax is reduced by the minimum amount of money dedicated under Subsection (f) of this section, provided that a school district may subsequently increase the maximum ad valorem maintenance and operation tax rate if the increased maximum rate is approved by a majority of the voters of the school district voting at an election called and held for that purpose. The legislature by general law shall provide for the tax relief that is required by Subsection (f) and this subsection.

(i) Subsections (f) and (h) of this section apply to ad valorem maintenance and operation taxes levied by a school district on or after the first January 1 after the date on which a tax on the net incomes of natural persons, including a person's share of partnership and unincorporated association income, begins to apply to that income, except that if the income tax begins to apply on a January 1, Subsections (f) and (h) of this section apply to ad valorem maintenance and operation taxes levied on or after that date.

(j) A provision of this section prevails over a conflicting provision of Article VII, Section 3, of this Constitution to the extent of the conflict

Section 29. Transfer Tax on Transaction Conveying Fee Simple Title to Real Property Prohibited

(a) After January 1, 2016, no law may be enacted that imposes a transfer tax on a transaction that conveys fee simple title to real property.

(b) This section does not prohibit:

(1) the imposition of a general business tax measured by business activity;

(2) the imposition of a tax on the production of minerals;

(3) the imposition of a tax on the issuance of title insurance; or

(4) the change of a rate of a tax in existence on January 1, 2016.

ARTICLE 9. COUNTIES

Section 1. Creation and Modification of Counties

The Legislature shall have power to create counties for the convenience of the people subject to the following provisions:

(1) Within the territory of any county or counties, no new county shall be created with a less area than seven hundred square miles, nor shall any such county now existing be reduced to a less area than seven hundred square miles. No new counties shall be created so as to approach nearer than twelve miles of the county seat of any county from which it may in whole or in part be taken. Counties of a less area than nine hundred, but of seven hundred or more square miles, within counties now existing, may be created by a two-thirds vote of each House of the Legislature, taken by yeas and nays and entered on the journals. Any county now existing may be reduced to an area of not less than seven hundred square miles by a like two-thirds vote. When any part of a county is stricken off and attached to, or created into another county, the part stricken off shall be holden for and obliged to pay its proportion of all the liabilities then existing, of the county from which it was taken, in such manner as may be prescribed by law.

(2) No part of any existing county shall be detached from it and attached to another existing county until the proposition for such change shall have been submitted, in such manner as may be provided by law, to a vote of the voters of both counties, and shall have received a majority of those voting on the question in each.

Section 1-A. Authority of Coastal Counties to Regulate Motor Vehicles and Littering on Beaches

The Legislature may authorize the governing body of any county bordering on the Gulf of Mexico or the tidewater limits thereof to regulate and restrict the speed, parking and travel of motor vehicles on beaches available to the public by virtue of public right and the littering of such beaches.

Nothing in this amendment shall increase the rights of any riparian or littoral landowner with regard to beaches available to the public by virtue of public right or submerged lands.
The Legislature may enact any laws not inconsistent with this Section which it may deem necessary to permit said counties to implement, enforce and administer the provisions contained herein.

Should the Legislature enact legislation in anticipation of the adoption of this amendment, such legislation shall not be invalid by reason of its anticipatory character.

Section 2. Removal of County Seats

The Legislature shall pass laws regulating the manner of removing county seats, but no county seat situated within five miles of the geographical centre of the county shall be removed, except by a vote of two-thirds of all the voters voting on the subject. A majority of such voters, however, voting at such election, may remove a county seat from a point more than five miles from the geographical centre of the county to a point within five miles of such centre, in either case the centre to be determined by a certificate from the Commissioner of the General Land Office.

Section 3. Repealed

Section 4. County-Wide Hospital Districts in Certain Large Counties

The Legislature may by law authorize the creation of county-wide Hospital Districts in counties having a population in excess of 190,000 and in Galveston County, with power to issue bonds for the purchase, acquisition, construction, maintenance and operation of any county owned hospital, or where the hospital system is jointly operated by a county and city within the county, and to provide for the transfer to the county-wide Hospital District of the title to any land, buildings or equipment, jointly or separately owned, and for the assumption by the district of any outstanding bonded indebtedness theretofore issued by any county or city for the establishment of hospitals or hospital facilities; to levy a tax not to exceed seventy-five ($ .75) cents on the One Hundred ($100.00) Dollars valuation of all taxable property within such district, provided, however, that such district shall be approved at an election held for that purpose, and that only qualified voters in such county shall vote therein; provided further, that such Hospital District shall assume full responsibility for providing medical and hospital care to needy inhabitants of the county, and thereafter such county and cities therein shall not levy any other tax for hospital purposes; and provided further that should such Hospital District construct, maintain and support a hospital or hospital system, that the same shall never become a charge against the State of Texas, nor shall any direct appropriation ever be made by the Legislature for the construction, maintenance or improvement of the said hospital or hospitals.

Section 5. Creation and Funding of Hospital Districts in City of Amarillo, Wichita County, and Jefferson County

(a) The Legislature may by law authorize the creation of two hospital districts, one to be coextensive with and have the same boundaries as the incorporated City of Amarillo, as such boundaries now exist or as they may hereafter be lawfully extended, and the other to be coextensive with Wichita County. If such district or districts are created, they may be authorized to levy a tax not to exceed Seventy-five Cents (75¢) on the One Hundred Dollars ($100.00) valuation of taxable property within the district; provided, however, no tax may be levied until approved by a majority vote of the participating resident qualified voters. The maximum rate of tax may be changed at subsequent elections so long as obligations are not impaired, and not to exceed the maximum limit of Seventy-five Cents (75¢) per

One Hundred Dollars ($100.00) valuation, and no election shall be required by subsequent changes in the boundaries of the City of Amarillo.

If such tax is authorized, no political subdivision or municipality within or having the same boundaries as the district may levy a tax for medical or hospital care for needy individuals, nor shall they maintain or erect hospital facilities, but the district shall by resolution assume all such responsibilities and shall assume all of the liabilities and obligations (including bonds and warrants) of such subdivisions or municipalities or both. The maximum tax rate submitted shall be sufficient to discharge such obligations, liabilities, and responsibilities, and to maintain and operate the hospital system, and the Legislature may authorize the district to issue tax bonds for the purpose of the purchase, construction, acquisition, repair or renovation of improvements and initially equipping the same, and such bonds shall be payable from said Seventy-five Cents (75¢) tax. The Legislature shall provide for transfer of title to properties to the district.

(b) The Legislature may by law permit the County of Potter (in which the City of Amarillo is partially located) to render financial aid to that district by paying a part of the expenses of operating and maintaining the system and paying a part of the debts of the district (whether assumed or created by the district) and may authorize the levy of a tax not to exceed Ten Cents (10¢) per One Hundred Dollars ($100.00) valuation (in addition to other taxes permitted by this Constitution) upon all property within the county but without the City of Amarillo at the time such levy is made for such purposes. If such tax is authorized, the district shall by resolution assume the responsibilities, obligations, and liabilities of the county in the manner and to the extent hereinabove provided for political subdivisions having boundaries coextensive with the district, and the county shall not thereafter levy taxes (other than herein provided) for hospital purposes nor for providing hospital care for needy individuals of the county.

(c) The Legislature may by law authorize the creation of a hospital district within Jefferson County, the boundaries of which shall include only the area comprising the Jefferson County Drainage District No. 7 and the Port Arthur Independent School District, as such boundaries existed on the first day of January, 1957, with the power to issue bonds for the sole purpose of purchasing a site for, and the construction and initial equipping of, a hospital system, and with the power to levy a tax of not to exceed Seventy-five Cents (75¢) on the One Hundred Dollars ($100.00) valuation of property therein for the purpose of paying the principal and interest on such bonds.

The bonds may not be issued or such tax be levied until approved by such voters.

The district shall not have the power to levy any tax for maintenance or operation of the hospital or facilities, but shall contract with other political subdivisions of the state or private individuals, associations, or corporations for such purposes. If the district hereinabove authorized is finally created, no other hospital district may be created embracing any part of the territory within its boundaries, but the Legislature by law may authorize the creation of a hospital district incorporating therein the remainder of Jefferson County, having the powers and duties and with the limitations presently provided by Article IX, Section 4, of the Constitution of Texas. A majority of those participating in the election voting in favor of the district shall be necessary for bonds to be issued.

(d) Should the Legislature enact enabling laws in anticipation of the adoption of this amendment, such Acts shall not be invalid because of their anticipatory character.

(e) The legislature by law may authorize Randall County to render financial assistance to the Amarillo Hospital District by paying part of the district's operating and maintenance expenses and the debts assumed or created by the district and to levy a tax for that purpose in an amount not to exceed seventy-five cents (75¢) on the One Hundred Dollars ($100.00) valuation on all property in Randall County that is not within the boundaries of the City of Amarillo or the South Randall County Hospital District. This tax is in addition to any other tax authorized by this constitution. If the tax is authorized by the legislature and approved by the voters of the area to be taxed, the Amarillo Hospital District shall, by resolution, assume the responsibilities, obligations, and liabilities of Randall County in accordance with Subsection (a) of this section and, except as provided by this subsection, Randall County may not levy taxes or issue bonds for hospital purposes or for providing hospital care for needy inhabitants of the county.

(f) Notwithstanding the provisions of Article IX of this constitution, if a hospital district was created or authorized under a constitutional provision that includes a description of the district's boundaries or jurisdiction, the legislature by law may authorize the district to change its boundaries or jurisdiction. The change must be approved by a majority of the qualified voters of the district voting at an election called and held for that purpose.

Section 6. Repealed

Section 7. Repealed

Section 8. Creation and Funding of Hospital District in County Commissioners Precinct No. 4 of Comanche County

(a) The Legislature may by law authorize the creation of a Hospital District to be co-extensive with the limits of County Commissioners Precinct No. 4 of Comanche County, Texas. If such District is created, it may be authorized to levy a tax not to exceed seventy-five cents (75¢) on the One Hundred Dollar ($100) valuation of taxable property within the District; provided, however, no tax may be levied until approved by a majority vote of the participating resident qualified voters. The maximum rate of tax may be changed at subsequent elections so long as obligations are not impaired, and not to exceed the maximum limit of seventy-five cents (75¢) per One Hundred Dollar ($100) valuation, and no election shall be required by subsequent changes in the boundaries of the Commissioners Precinct No. 4 of Comanche County.

If such tax is authorized, no political subdivision or municipality within or having the same boundaries as the District may levy a tax for medical or hospital care for needy individuals, nor shall they maintain or erect hospital facilities, but the District shall by resolution assume all such responsibilities and shall assume all of the liabilities and obligations (including bonds and warrants) of such subdivisions or municipalities or both. The maximum tax rate submitted shall be sufficient to discharge such obligations, liabilities, and responsibilities, and to maintain and operate the hospital system, and the Legislature may authorize the District to issue tax bonds for the purpose of the purchase, construction, acquisition, repair or renovation of improvements and initially equipping the same, and such bonds shall be payable from said seventy-five cent (75¢) tax. The Legislature shall provide for transfer of title to properties to the District.

(b) The Legislature may by law permit the County of Comanche to render financial aid to that District by paying a part of the expenses of operating and maintaining the system and paying a part of the debts of the District (whether assumed or created by the District) and may authorize the levy of a tax not to exceed ten cents (10¢) per One Hundred Dollar ($100) valuation (in addition to other taxes permitted by this Constitution) upon all property within the County but without the County Commissioners Precinct No. 4 of Comanche County at the time such levy is made for such purposes. If such tax is authorized, the District shall by resolution assume the responsibilities, obligations, and liabilities of the County in the manner and to the extent hereinabove provided for political subdivisions having boundaries co-extensive with the District, and the County shall not thereafter levy taxes (other than herein provided) for hospital purposes nor for providing hospital care for needy individuals of the County.

(c) Should the Legislature enact enabling laws in anticipation of the adoption of this amendment, such Acts shall not be invalid because of their anticipatory character.

Section 9. Creation, Operation, and Dissolution of Hospital Districts

The Legislature may by general or special law provide for the creation, establishment, maintenance and operation of hospital districts composed of one or more counties or all or any part of one or more counties with power to issue bonds for the purchase, construction, acquisition, repair or renovation of buildings and improvements and equipping same, for hospital purposes; providing for the transfer to the hospital district of the title to any land, buildings, improvements and equipment located wholly within the district which may be jointly or separately owned by any city, town or county, providing that any district so created shall assume full responsibility for providing medical and hospital care for its needy inhabitants and assume the outstanding indebtedness incurred by cities, towns and counties for hospital purposes prior to the creation of the district, if same are located wholly within its boundaries, and a pro rata portion of such indebtedness based upon the then last approved tax assessment rolls of the included cities, towns and counties if less than all the territory thereof is included within the district boundaries; providing that after its creation no other municipality or political subdivision shall have the power to levy taxes or issue bonds or other obligations for hospital purposes or for providing medical care within the boundaries of the district; providing for the levy of annual taxes at a rate not to exceed seventy-five cents ($ .75) on the One Hundred Dollar valuation of all taxable property within such district for the purpose of meeting the requirements of the district's bonds, the indebtedness assumed by it and its maintenance and operating expenses, providing that such district shall not be created or such tax authorized unless approved by a majority of the qualified voters thereof voting at an election called for the purpose; and providing further that the support and maintenance of the district's hospital system shall never become a charge against or obligation of the State of Texas nor shall any direct appropriation be made by the Legislature for the construction, maintenance or improvement of any of the facilities of such district.

Provided, however, that no district shall be created by special law except after thirty (30) days' public notice to the district affected, and in no event may the Legislature provide for a district to be created without the affirmative vote of a majority of the qualified voters in the district concerned.

The Legislature may also provide for the dissolution of hospital districts provided that a process is afforded by statute for:

(1) determining the desire of a majority of the qualified voters within the district to dissolve it;

(2) disposing of or transferring the assets, if any, of the district; and

(3) satisfying the debts and bond obligations, if any, of the district, in such manner as to protect the interests of the citizens within the district, including their collective property rights in the assets and property of the district, provided, however, that any grant from federal funds, however dispensed, shall be considered an obligation to be repaid in satisfaction and provided that no election to dissolve shall be held more often than once each year. In such connection, the statute shall provide against disposal or transfer of the assets of the district except for due compensation unless such assets are transferred to another governmental agency, such as a county, embracing such district and using such transferred assets in such a way as to benefit citizens formerly within the district.

Section 9A. Hospital Districts: Regulation of Health Care Services

The legislature by law may determine the health care services a hospital district is required to provide, the requirements a resident must meet to qualify for services, and any other relevant provisions necessary to regulate the provision of health care to residents.

Section 9B. Hospital Districts in Counties with Population of 75,000 or Less

The legislature by general or special law may provide for the creation, establishment, maintenance, and operation of hospital districts located wholly in a county with a population of 75,000 or less, according to the most recent federal decennial census, and may authorize the commissioners court to levy a tax on the ad valorem property located in the district for the support and maintenance of the district. A district may not be created or a tax levied unless the creation and tax are approved by a majority of the registered voters who reside in the district. The legislature shall set the maximum tax rate a district may levy. The legislature may provide that the county in which the district is located may issue general obligation bonds for the district and provide other services to the district. The district may provide hospital care, medical care, and other services authorized by the legislature.

Section 10. Blank

Section 11. Creation and Funding of Hospital Districts in Ochiltree, Castro, Hansford, and Hopkins Counties

(a) The Legislature may by law authorize the creation of hospital districts in Ochiltree, Castro, Hansford and Hopkins Counties, each district to be coextensive with the limits of such county.

(b) If any such district is created, it may be authorized to levy a tax not to exceed Seventy-five Cents (75¢) on the One Hundred Dollar ($100) valuation of taxable property within the district; provided, however, no tax may be levied until approved by a majority vote of the participating resident qualified voters. The maximum rate of tax may be changed at subsequent elections so long as obligations are not impaired, and not to exceed the maximum limit of Seventy-five Cents (75¢) per One Hundred Dollar ($100) valuation.

(c) If such tax is authorized, no political subdivision or municipality within or having the same boundaries as the district may levy a tax for medical or hospital care for needy individuals, nor shall they maintain or erect hospital facilities, but the district shall by resolution assume all such responsibilities and shall assume all of the liabilities and obligations (including bonds and warrants) of such subdivisions or municipalities or both. The maximum tax rate submitted shall be sufficient to discharge obligations, liabilities, and responsibilities, and to maintain and operate the hospital system, and the Legislature may authorize the district to issue tax bonds for the purpose of the purchase, construction, acquisition, repair or renovation of improvements and initially equipping the same, and such bonds shall be payable from said Seventy-five Cent (75¢) tax. The Legislature shall provide for transfer of title to properties to the district.

Section 12. Airport Authorities

(a) The Legislature may by law provide for the creation, establishment, maintenance and operation of Airport Authorities composed of one or more counties, with power to issue general obligation bonds, revenue bonds, either or both of them, for the purchase, acquisition by the exercise of the power of eminent domain or otherwise, construction, reconstruction, repair or renovation of any airport or airports, landing fields and runways, airport buildings, hangars, facilities, equipment, fixtures, and any and all property, real or personal, necessary to operate, equip and maintain an airport.

(b) The Legislature shall provide for the option by the governing body of the city or cities whose airport facilities are served by certificated airlines and whose facility or some interest therein, is proposed to be or has been acquired by the Authority, to either appoint or elect a Board of Directors of said Authority. If the Directors are appointed such appointment shall be made by the County Commissioners Court after consultation with and consent of the governing body or bodies of such city or cities. If the Board of Directors is elected they shall be elected by the qualified voters of the county which chooses to elect the Directors to represent that county. Directors shall serve without compensation for a term fixed by the Legislature not to exceed six (6) years, shall be selected on the basis of the proportionate population of each county based upon the last preceding Federal Census, and shall be residents of such county. No county shall have less than one (1) member on the Board of Directors.

(c) The Legislature shall provide for the holding of an election in each county proposing the creation of an Authority to be called by the Commissioners Court or Commissioners Courts, as the case may be, upon petition of five per cent (5%) of the qualified voters within the county or counties. The elections must be held on the same day if more than one county is included. No more than one (1) such election may be called in a county until after the expiration of one (1) year in the event such an election has failed, and thereafter only upon a petition of ten per cent (10%) of the qualified voters being presented to the Commissioners Court or Commissioners Courts of the county or counties in which such an election has failed. In the event that two or more counties vote on the proposition of the creation of an Authority therein, the proposition shall not be deemed to carry unless the majority of the qualified voters in each county voting thereon vote in favor thereof. An Airport Authority may be created and be composed of the county or counties that vote in favor of its creation if separate propositions are submitted to the voters of each county so that they may vote for a two or more county Authority or a single county Authority.

(d) The Legislature shall provide for the appointment by the Board of Directors of an Assessor and Collector of Taxes in the Authority, whether constituted of one or more counties, whose duty it shall be to assess all taxable property, both real and personal, and collect the taxes thereon, based upon the tax rolls approved by the Board of Directors, the tax to be levied not to exceed Seventy-Five Cents ($.75) per One Hundred Dollars ($100) assessed valuation of the property. The property of state regulated common carriers required by law to pay a tax upon intangible assets shall not be subject to taxation by the Authority. The taxable property shall be assessed on a valuation not to exceed the market value and shall be equal and uniform throughout the Authority as is otherwise provided by the Constitution.

(e) The Legislature shall authorize the purchase or acquisition by the Authority of any existing airport facility publicly owned and financed and served by certificated airlines, in fee or of any interest therein, or to enter into any lease agreement therefor, upon such terms and conditions as may be mutually agreeable to the Authority and the owner of such facilities, or authorize the acquisition of same through the exercise of the power of eminent domain. In the event of such acquisition, if there are any general obligation bonds that the owner of the publicly owned airport facility has outstanding, the same shall be fully assumed by the Authority and sufficient taxes levied by the Authority to discharge said outstanding indebtedness. If any city or owner has outstanding revenue bonds where the revenues of the airport have been pledged or said bonds constitute a lien against the airport facilities, the Authority shall assume and discharge all the obligations of the city under the ordinances and bond indentures under which said revenue bonds have been issued and sold.

(f) Any city which owns airport facilities not serving certificated airlines which are not purchased or acquired or taken over as herein provided by such Authority shall have the power to operate the same under the existing laws or as the same may hereafter be amended.

(g) Any such Authority when created may be granted the power and authority to promulgate, adopt and enforce appropriate zoning regulations to protect the airport from hazards and obstructions which would interfere with the use of the airport and its facilities for landing and take-off.

(h) An additional county or counties may be added to an existing Authority if a petition of five per cent (5%) of the qualified voters is filed with and an election is called by the Commissioners Court of the county or counties seeking admission to an Authority. If the vote is favorable, then admission may be granted to such county or counties by the Board of Directors of the then existing Authority upon such terms and conditions as they may agree upon and evidenced by a resolution approved by two-thirds (2/3rds) of the then existing Board of Directors. The county or counties that may be so added to the then existing Authority shall be given representation on the Board of Directors by adding additional directors in proportion to their population according to the last preceding Federal Census.

Section 13. Participation of Municipalities and other Political Subdivisions in Establishment and Operation of Mental Health, Mental Retardation, or Public Health Services

Notwithstanding any other section of this article, the Legislature in providing for the creation, establishment, maintenance and operation of a hospital district, shall not be required to provide that such district shall assume full responsibility for the establishment, maintenance, support, or operation of mental health services or mental retardation services including the operation of any community mental health centers, community mental retardation centers or community mental health and mental retardation centers which may exist or be thereafter established within the boundaries of such district, nor shall the Legislature be required to provide that such district shall assume full responsibility of public health department units and clinics and related public health activities or services, and the Legislature shall not be required to restrict the power of any municipality or political subdivision to levy taxes or issue bonds or other obligations or to expend public moneys for the establishment, maintenance, support, or operation of mental health services, mental retardation services, public health units or clinics or related public health activities or services or the operation of such community mental health or mental retardation centers within the boundaries of the hospital districts; and unless a statute creating a hospital district shall expressly prohibit participation by any entity other than the hospital district in the establishment, maintenance, or support of mental health services, mental retardation services, public health units or clinics or related public health activities within or partly within the boundaries of any hospital district, any municipality or any other political subdivision or state-supported entity within the hospital district may participate in the establishment, maintenance, and support of mental health services, mental retardation services, public health units and clinics and related public health activities and may levy taxes, issue bonds or other obligations, and expend public moneys for such purposes as provided by law.

Section 14. County Facilities for Indigent Inhabitants

Each county in the State may provide, in such manner as may be prescribed by law, a Manual Labor Poor House and Farm, for taking care of, managing, employing and supplying the wants of its indigent and poor inhabitants.

ARTICLE 10. RAILROADS

Section 1. Repealed

Section 2. Railroads as Public Highways and Common Carriers; Regulation

Railroads heretofore constructed or which may hereafter be constructed in this state are hereby declared public highways, and railroad companies, common carriers. The Legislature shall pass laws to regulate railroad, freight and passenger tariffs, to correct abuses and prevent unjust discrimination and extortion in the rates of freight and passenger tariffs on the different railroads in this state, and enforce the same by adequate penalties; and to the further accomplishment of these objects and purposes, may provide and establish all requisite means and agencies invested with such powers as may be deemed adequate and advisable.

Section 3. Repealed

Section 4. Repealed

Section 5. Repealed

Section 6. Repealed

Section 7. Repealed

Section 8. Repealed

Section 9. Repealed

ARTICLE 11. MUNICIPAL CORPORATIONS

Section 1. Counties as Legal Subdivisions

The several counties of this State are hereby recognized as legal subdivisions of the State.

Section 2. Jails, Courthouses, Bridges, and Roads

The construction of jails, court-houses and bridges and the laying out, construction and repairing of county roads shall be provided for by general laws.

Section 3. County or Municipal Investment in or Donation or Loan to Private Corporation or Association Prohibited

No county, city, or other municipal corporation shall hereafter become a subscriber to the capital of any private corporation or association, or make any appropriation or donation to the same, or in anywise loan its credit; but this shall not be construed to in any way affect any obligation heretofore undertaken pursuant to law or to prevent a county, city, or other municipal corporation from investing its funds as authorized by law.

Section 4. Cities and Towns with Population of 5,000 or Less: Chartered by General Law; Taxes; Fines, Forfeitures, and Penalties

Cities and towns having a population of five thousand or less may be chartered alone by general law. They may levy, assess and collect such taxes as may be authorized by law, but no tax for any purpose shall ever be lawful for any one year which shall exceed one and one-half per cent of the taxable property of such city; and all taxes shall be collectible only in current money, and all licenses and occupation taxes levied, and all fines, forfeitures and penalties accruing to said cities and towns shall be collectible only in current money.

Section 5. Cities of More Than 5,000 Population: Adoption or Amendment of Charters; Taxes; Debt Restrictions

(a) Cities having more than five thousand (5000) inhabitants may, by a majority vote of the qualified voters of said city, at an election held for that purpose, adopt or amend their charters. If the number of inhabitants of cities that have adopted or amended their charters under this section is reduced to five thousand (5000) or fewer, the cities still may amend their charters by a majority vote of the qualified voters of said city at an election held for that purpose. The adoption or amendment of charters is subject to such limitations as may be prescribed by the Legislature, and no charter or any ordinance passed under said charter shall contain any provision inconsistent with the Constitution of the State, or of the general laws enacted by the Legislature of this State. Said cities may levy, assess and collect such taxes as may be authorized by law or by their charters; but no tax for any purpose shall ever be lawful for any one year, which shall exceed two and one-half per cent. of the taxable property of such city, and no debt shall ever be created by any city, unless at the same time provision be made to assess and collect annually a sufficient sum to pay the interest thereon and creating a sinking fund of at least two per cent. thereon, except as provided by Subsection (b). Furthermore, no city charter shall be altered, amended or repealed oftener than every two years.

(b) To increase efficiency and effectiveness to the greatest extent possible, the legislature may by general law authorize cities to enter into inter-local contracts with other cities or counties without meeting the assessment and sinking fund requirements under Subsection (a).

Section 6. Repealed

Section 7. Counties and Cities on Gulf of Mexico; Tax for Sea Walls, Breakwaters, and Sanitation; Bonds; Condemnation of Right of Way

(a) All counties and cities bordering on the coast of the Gulf of Mexico are hereby authorized upon a vote of the majority of the qualified voters voting thereon at an election called for such purpose to levy and collect such tax for construction of sea walls, breakwaters, or sanitary purposes, as may now or may hereafter be authorized by law, and may create a debt for such works and issue bonds in evidence thereof. But no debt for any purpose shall ever be incurred in any manner by any city or county unless provision is made, at the time of creating the same, for levying and collecting a sufficient tax to pay the interest thereon and provide at least two per cent (2%) as a sinking fund, except as provided by Subsection (b); and the condemnation of the right of way for the erection of such works shall be fully provided for.

(b) To increase efficiency and effectiveness to the greatest extent possible, the legislature may by general law authorize cities or counties to enter into interlocal contracts with other cities or counties without meeting the tax and sinking fund requirements under Subsection (a).

Section 8. Donation of Public Domain to Aid in Construction of Sea Walls or Breakwaters

The counties and cities on the Gulf Coast being subject to calamitous overflows, and a very large proportion of the general revenue being derived from those otherwise prosperous localities, the Legislature is especially authorized to aid by donation of such portion of the public domain as may be deemed proper, and in such mode as may be provided by law, the construction of sea walls, or breakwaters, such aid to be proportioned to the extent and value of the works constructed, or to be constructed, in any locality.

Section 9. County or Municipal Property Held for Public Purpose Exempt from Forced Sale and Taxation

The property of counties, cities and towns, owned and held only for public purposes, such as public buildings and the sites therefor, fire engines and the furniture thereof, and all property used, or intended for extinguishing fires, public grounds and all other property devoted exclusively to the use and benefit of the public shall be exempt from forced sale and from taxation, provided, nothing herein shall prevent the enforcement of the vendors lien, the mechanics or builders lien, or other liens now existing.

Section 10. Repealed

Section 11. Term of Office Exceeding Two Years in Home Rule and General Law Cities; Vacancies

(a) A Home Rule City may provide by charter or charter amendment, and a city, town or village operating under the general laws may provide by majority vote of the qualified voters voting at an election called for that purpose, for a longer term of office than two (2) years for its officers, either elective or appointive, or both, but not to exceed four (4) years; provided, however, that tenure under Civil Service shall not be affected hereby; provided, however, that such officers, elective or appointive, are subject to Section 65(b), Article XVI, of this Constitution, providing for automatic resignation in certain circumstances, in the same manner as a county or district officer to which that section applies.

(b) A municipality so providing a term exceeding two (2) years but not exceeding four (4) years for any of its non-civil service officers must elect all of the members of its governing body by majority vote of the qualified voters in such municipality.

(c) Any vacancy or vacancies occurring on such governing body shall not be filled by appointment but must be filled by majority vote of the qualified voters at a special election called for such purpose within one hundred and twenty (120) days after such vacancy or vacancies occur except that the municipality may provide by charter or charter amendment the procedure for filling a vacancy occurring on its governing body for an unexpired term of 12 months or less.

Section 12. Expenditures for Relocation or Replacement of Sanitation Sewer or Water Laterals on Private Property

The legislature by general law may authorize a city or town to expend public funds for the relocation or replacement of sanitation sewer laterals or water laterals on private property if the relocation or replacement is done in conjunction with or immediately following the replacement or relocation of sanitation sewer mains or water mains serving the property. The law must authorize the city or town to affix, with the consent of the owner of the private property, a lien on the property for the cost of relocating or replacing the laterals on the property and must provide that the cost shall be assessed against the property with repayment by the property owner to be amortized over a period not to exceed five years at a rate of interest to be set as provided by the law. The lien may not be enforced until after five years have expired since the date the lien was affixed.

Section 13. Classification of Municipal Functions

(a) Notwithstanding any other provision of this constitution, the legislature may by law define for all purposes those functions of a municipality that are to be considered governmental and those that are proprietary, including reclassifying a function's classification assigned under prior statute or common law.

(b) This section applies to laws enacted by the 70th Legislature, Regular Session, 1987, and to all subsequent regular or special sessions of the legislature.

ARTICLE 12. PRIVATE CORPORATIONS

Section 1. Creation of Private Corporations by General Laws Only

No private corporation shall be created except by general laws.

Section 2. General Laws for Creation of Private Corporations and Protection of Public and Stockholders

General laws shall be enacted providing for the creation of private corporations, and shall therein provide fully for the adequate protection of the public and of the individual stockholders.

Section 3. Repealed

Section 4. Repealed

Section 5. Repealed

Section 6. Repealed

Section 7. Repealed

ARTICLE 12. PRIVATE CORPORATIONS

Repealed

ARTICLE 14. PUBLIC LANDS AND LAND OFFICE

Section 1. General Land Office

There shall be one General Land Office in the State, which shall be at the seat of government, where all land titles which have emanated or may hereafter emanate from the State shall be registered, except those titles the registration of which may be prohibited by this Constitution. It shall be the duty of the Legislature at the earliest practicable time to make the Land Office self sustaining, and from time to time the Legislature may establish such subordinate offices as may be deemed necessary.

Section 2. Repealed

Section 3. Repealed

Section 4. Repealed

Section 5. Repealed

Section 6. Repealed

Section 7. Repealed

Section 8. Repealed

ARTICLE 15. IMPEACHMENT

Section 1. Impeachment by House of Representatives

The power of impeachment shall be vested in the House of Representatives.

Section 2. Trial of Impeachment of Certain Officers by Senate

Impeachment of the Governor, Lieutenant Governor, Attorney General, Commissioner of the General Land Office, Comptroller and the Judges of the Supreme Court, Court of Appeals and District Court shall be tried by the Senate.

Section 3. Impartial Trial by Senate; Concurrence of Two-Thirds Required

When the Senate is sitting as a Court of Impeachment, the Senators shall be on oath, or affirmation impartially to try the party impeached, and no person shall be convicted without the concurrence of two-thirds of the Senators present.

Section 4. Judgment to Remove and Disqualify; Punishment Under Other Law Permitted

Judgment in cases of impeachment shall extend only to removal from office, and disqualification from holding any office of honor, trust or profit under this State. A party convicted on impeachment shall also be subject to indictment, trial and punishment according to law.

Section 5. Suspension Pending Impeachment; Provisional Appointment

All officers against whom articles of impeachment may be preferred shall be suspended from the exercise of the duties of their office, during the pendency of such impeachment. The Governor may make a provisional appointment to fill the vacancy occasioned by the suspension of an officer until the decision on the impeachment.

Section 6. Removal of District Judges by Supreme Court

Any judge of the District Courts of the State who is incompetent to discharge the duties of his office, or who shall be guilty of partiality, or oppression, or other official misconduct, or whose habits and conduct are such as to render him unfit to hold such office, or who shall negligently fail to perform his duties as judge; or who shall fail to execute in a reasonable measure the business in his courts, may be removed by the Supreme Court. The Supreme Court shall have original jurisdiction to hear and determine the causes aforesaid when presented in writing upon the oaths taken before some judge of a court of record of not less than ten lawyers, practicing in the courts held by such judge, and licensed to practice in the Supreme Court; said presentment to be founded either upon the knowledge of the persons making it or upon the written oaths as to the facts of creditable witnesses. The Supreme Court may issue all needful process and prescribe all needful rules to give effect to this section. Causes of this kind shall have precedence and be tried as soon as practicable.

Section 7. Removal of Officers When Mode not Provided in Constitution

The Legislature shall provide by law for the trial and removal from office of all officers of this State, the modes for which have not been provided in this Constitution.

Section 8. Removal of Judges by Governor on Address of Two-Thirds of each House of Legislature

The Judges of the Supreme Court, Court of Appeals and District Courts, shall be removed by the Governor on the address of two-thirds of each House of the Legislature, for wilful neglect of duty, incompetency, habitual drunkenness, oppression in office, or other reasonable cause which shall not be sufficient ground for impeachment; provided, however, that the cause or causes for which such removal shall be required, shall be stated at length in such address and entered on the journals of each House; and provided further, that the cause or causes shall be notified to the judge so intended to be removed, and he shall be admitted to a hearing in his own defense before any vote for such address shall pass, and in all such cases, the vote shall be taken by yeas and nays and entered on the journals of each House respectively.

Section 9. Removal of Public Officer by Appointing Governor with Advice and Consent of Senate

(a) In addition to the other procedures provided by law for removal of public officers, the governor who appoints an officer may remove the officer with the advice and consent of two-thirds of the members of the senate present.

(b) If the legislature is not in session when the governor desires to remove an officer, the governor shall call a special session of the senate for consideration of the proposed removal. The session may not exceed two days in duration.

ARTICLE 16. GENERAL PROVISIONS

Section 1. Official Oath of Office

(a) All elected and appointed officers, before they enter upon the duties of their offices, shall take the following Oath or Affirmation:

"I, _____, do solemnly swear (or affirm), that I will faithfully execute the duties of the office of _____ of the State of Texas, and will to the best of my ability preserve, protect, and defend the Constitution and laws of the United States and of this State, so help me God."

(b) All elected or appointed officers, before taking the Oath or Affirmation of office prescribed by this section and entering upon the duties of office, shall subscribe to the following statement:

"I, _____, do solemnly swear (or affirm) that I have not directly or indirectly paid, offered, promised to pay, contributed, or promised to contribute any money or thing of value, or promised any public office or employment for the giving or withholding of a vote at the election at which I was elected or as a reward to secure my appointment or confirmation, whichever the case may be, so help me God."

(c) Members of the Legislature, the Secretary of State, and all other elected and appointed state officers shall file the signed statement required by Subsection (b) of this section with the Secretary of State before taking the Oath or Affirmation of office prescribed by Subsection (a) of this section. All other officers shall retain the signed statement required by Subsection (b) of this section with the official records of the office.

Section 2. Exclusions from Office for Conviction of High Crimes

Laws shall be made to exclude from office persons who have been convicted of bribery, perjury, forgery, or other high crimes.

Section 3. Repealed

Section 4. Repealed

Section 5. Disqualification from Office for Giving or Offering Bribe

Every person shall be disqualified from holding any office of profit, or trust, in this State, who shall have been convicted of having given or offered a bribe to procure his election or appointment.

Section 6. Appropriations for Private Purposes; Annual Accounting of Public Money; Acceptance and Expenditure of Certain Money for Persons With Disabilities

(a) No appropriation for private or individual purposes shall be made, unless authorized by this Constitution. A regular statement, under oath, and an account of the receipts and expenditures of all public money shall be published annually, in such manner as shall be prescribed by law.

(b) State agencies charged with the responsibility of providing services to those who are blind, crippled, or otherwise physically or mentally handicapped may accept money from private or federal sources, designated by the private or federal source as money to be used in and establishing and equipping facilities for assisting those who are blind, crippled, or otherwise physically or mentally handicapped in becoming gainfully employed, in rehabilitating and restoring the handicapped, and in providing other services determined by the state agency to be essential for the better care and treatment of the handicapped. Money accepted under this subsection is state money. State agencies may spend money accepted under this subsection, and no other money, for specific programs and projects to be conducted by local level or other private, nonsectarian associations, groups, and nonprofit organizations, in establishing and equipping facilities for assisting those who are blind, crippled, or otherwise physically or mentally handicapped in becoming gainfully employed, in rehabilitating and restoring the handicapped, and in providing other services determined by the state agency to be essential for the better care or treatment of the handicapped. The state agencies may deposit money accepted under this subsection either in the state treasury or in other secure depositories. The money may not be expended for any purpose other than the purpose for which it was given. Notwithstanding any other provision of this Constitution, the state agencies may expend money accepted under this subsection without the necessity of an appropriation, unless the Legislature, by law, requires that the money be expended only on appropriation. The Legislature may prohibit state agencies from accepting money under this subsection or may regulate the amount of money accepted, the way the acceptance and expenditure of the money is administered, and the purposes for which the state agencies may expend the money. Money accepted under this subsection for a purpose prohibited by the Legislature shall be returned to the entity that gave the money.

This subsection does not prohibit state agencies authorized to render services to the handicapped from contracting with privately-owned or local facilities for necessary and essential services, subject to such conditions, standards, and procedures as may be prescribed by law.

Section 7. Repealed

Section 8. Re-designated

Section 9. No Forfeiture of Residence by Absence on Public Business

Absence on business of the State, or of the United States, shall not forfeit a residence once obtained, so as to deprive any one of the right of suffrage, or of being elected or appointed to any office under the exceptions contained in this Constitution.

Section 10. Deductions from Salary of Public Officer for Neglect of Duty

The Legislature shall provide for deductions from the salaries of public officers who may neglect the performance of any duty that may be assigned them by law.

Section 11. Usury; Rate of Interest in Absence of Legislation

The Legislature shall have authority to define interest and fix maximum rates of interest; provided, however, in the absence of legislation fixing maximum rates of interest all contracts for a greater rate of interest than ten per centum (10%) per annum shall be deemed usurious; provided, further, that in contracts where no rate of interest is agreed upon, the rate shall not exceed six per centum (6%) per annum.

Section 12. Ineligibility of Members of Congress and Officers of United States or Foreign Power to Hold Another Office

No member of Congress, nor person holding or exercising any office of profit or trust, under the United States, or either of them, or under any foreign power, shall be eligible as a member of the Legislature, or hold or exercise any office of profit or trust under this State.

Section 13. Unopposed Candidate for Office

For an office for which this constitution requires an election, the legislature may provide by general law for a person to take the office without an election if the person is the only candidate to qualify in an election to be held for that office.

Section 13A. Unopposed Candidate for Office of Political Subdivision

For an office of a political subdivision for which this constitution requires an election, the legislature may provide by general law for a person to assume the office without an election if the person is the only candidate to qualify in an election to be held for that office.

Section 14. Civil Officers; Residence; Location of Offices

All civil officers shall reside within the State; and all district or county officers within their districts or counties, and shall keep their offices at such places as may be required by law; and failure to comply with this condition shall vacate the office so held.

Section 15. Separate and Community Property of Spouses

All property, both real and personal, of a spouse owned or claimed before marriage, and that acquired afterward by gift, devise or descent, shall be the separate property of that spouse; and laws shall be passed more clearly defining the rights of the spouses, in relation to separate and community property; provided that persons about to marry and spouses, without the intention to defraud pre-existing creditors, may by written instrument from time to time partition between themselves all or part of their property, then existing or to be acquired, or exchange between themselves the community interest of one spouse or future spouse in any property for the community interest of the other spouse or future spouse in other community property then existing or to be acquired, whereupon the portion or interest set aside to each spouse shall be and constitute a part of the separate property and estate of such spouse or future spouse; spouses also may from time to time, by written instrument, agree between themselves that the income or property from all or part of the separate property then owned or which thereafter might be acquired by only one of them, shall be the separate property of that spouse; if one spouse makes a gift of property to the other that gift is presumed to include all the income or property which might arise from that gift of property; spouses may agree in writing that all or part of their community property becomes the property of the surviving spouse on the death of a spouse; and spouses may agree in writing that all or part of the separate property owned by either or both of them shall be the spouses' community property.

Section 16. Corporations with Banking and Discounting Privileges

(a) The Legislature shall by general laws, authorize the incorporation of state banks and savings and loan associations and shall provide for a system of State supervision, regulation and control of such bodies which will adequately protect and secure the depositors and creditors thereof.
No state bank shall be chartered until all of the authorized capital stock has been subscribed and paid in full in cash. Except as may be permitted by the Legislature pursuant to Subsections (b), (d), and (e) of this Section 16, a state bank shall not be authorized to engage in business at more than one place which shall be designated in its charter; however, this restriction shall not apply to any other type of financial institution chartered under the laws of this state.
No foreign corporation, other than the national banks of the United States domiciled in this State, shall be permitted to exercise banking or discounting privileges in this State.

(b) If it finds that the convenience of the public will be served thereby, the Legislature may authorize State and national banks to establish and operate unmanned teller machines within the county or city of their domicile. Such machines may perform all banking functions. Banks which are domiciled within a city lying in two or more counties may be permitted to establish and operate unmanned teller machines within both the city and the county of their domicile. The Legislature shall provide that a bank shall have the right to share in the use of these teller machines, not situated at a banking house, which are located within the county or the city of the bank's domicile, on a reasonable, nondiscriminatory basis, consistent with anti-trust laws. Banks may share the use of such machines within the county or city of their domicile with savings and loan associations and credit unions which are domiciled in the same county or city.

(c) A state bank created by virtue of the power granted by this section, notwithstanding any other provision of this section, has the same rights and privileges that are or may be granted to national banks of the United States domiciled in this State.

(d) The Legislature may authorize a state bank or national bank of the United States domiciled in this State to engage in business at more than one place if it does so through the purchase and assumption of certain assets and liabilities of a failed state bank or a failed national bank of the United States domiciled in this State.

(e) The Legislature shall authorize a state bank or national bank of the United States domiciled in this State to establish and operate banking facilities at locations within the county or city of its domicile, subject to limitations the Legislature imposes. The Legislature may permit a bank domiciled within a city located in two or more counties to establish and operate branches within both the city and the county of its domicile, subject to limitations the Legislature imposes.

(f) A bank may not be considered a branch or facility of another bank solely because it is owned or controlled by the same stockholders as the other bank, has common accounting and administrative systems with the other bank, or has a name similar to the other bank's or because of a combination of those factors.

Section 17. Service of Public Officer Pending Qualification of Successor

(a) Except as provided by Subsection (b) of this section, all officers of this State shall continue to perform the duties of their offices until their successors shall be duly qualified.
\
(b) Following the expiration of a term of an appointive office

that is filled by appointment of the Governor with the advice and consent of the Senate and that is not an office for which the officer receives a salary, the period for which the officer shall continue to perform the duties of office under Subsection (a) of this section ends on the last day of the first regular session of the Legislature that begins after the expiration of the term.

Section 18. Repealed

Section 19. Repealed

Section 20. Regulation of Mixed Alcoholic Beverages and Intoxicating Liquors; Local Option Elections; Wineries

(a) The Legislature shall have the power to enact a Mixed Beverage Law regulating the sale of mixed alcoholic beverages on a local option election basis. The Legislature shall also have the power to regulate the manufacture, sale, possession and transportation of intoxicating liquors, including the power to establish a State Monopoly on the sale of distilled liquors. Should the Legislature enact any enabling laws in anticipation of this amendment, no such law shall be void by reason of its anticipatory nature.

(b) The Legislature shall enact a law or laws whereby the qualified voters of any county, justice's precinct or incorporated town or city, may, by a majority vote of those voting, determine from time to time whether the sale of intoxicating liquors for beverage purposes shall be prohibited or legalized within the prescribed limits; and such laws shall contain provisions for voting on the sale of intoxicating liquors of various types and various alcoholic content.

(c) In all counties, justice's precincts or incorporated towns or cities wherein the sale of intoxicating liquors had been prohibited by local option elections held under the laws of the State of Texas and in force at the time of the taking effect of Section 20, Article XVI of the Constitution of Texas, it shall continue to be unlawful to manufacture, sell, barter or exchange in any such county, justice's precinct or incorporated town or city, any spirituous, vinous or malt liquors or medicated bitters capable of producing intoxication or any other intoxicants whatsoever, for beverage purposes, unless and until a majority of the qualified voters in such county or political subdivision thereof voting in an election held for such purpose shall determine such to be lawful; provided that this subsection shall not prohibit the sale of alcoholic beverages containing not more than 3.2 per cent alcohol by weight in cities, counties or political subdivisions thereof in which the qualified voters have voted to legalize such sale under the provisions of Chapter 116, Acts of the Regular Session of the 43rd Legislature.

(d) The legislature may enact laws and direct the Alcoholic Beverage Commission or its successor to set policies for all wineries in this state, regardless of whether the winery is located in an area in which the sale of wine has or has not been authorized by local option election, for the manufacturing of wine, including the on-premises selling of wine to the ultimate consumer for consumption on or off the winery premises, the buying of wine from or the selling of wine to any other person authorized under general law to purchase and sell wine in this state, and the dispensing of wine without charge, for tasting purposes, for consumption on the winery premises, and for any purpose to promote the wine industry in this state.

Section 21. Contracts for Public Printing and Binding and for Repairs and Furnishings of Legislative Facilities

All stationery, printing, fuel used in the legislature and departments of the government other than the judicial department, printing and binding of the laws, journals, and department reports, and all other printing and binding and the repairing and furnishing of the halls and rooms used during meetings of the legislature and in committees, except proclamations and such products and services as may be done by handicapped individuals employed in nonprofit rehabilitation facilities providing sheltered employment to the handicapped in Texas, shall be performed under contract, to be given to the lowest responsible bidder, below such maximum price and under such regulations as shall be prescribed by law. No member or officer of any department of the government shall in any way have a financial interest in such contracts, and all such contracts or programs involving the state use of the products and services of handicapped individuals shall be subject to such requirements as might be established by the legislature.

Section 22. Repealed

Section 23. Regulation of Livestock; Protection of Stock Raisers; Inspections; Brands

The Legislature may pass laws for the regulation of live stock and the protection of stock raisers in the stock raising portion of the State, and exempt from the operation of such laws other portions, sections, or counties; and shall have power to pass general and special laws for the inspection of cattle, stock and hides and for the regulation of brands; provided, that any local law thus passed shall be submitted to the qualified voters of the section to be affected thereby, and approved by them, before it shall go into effect.

Section 24. Roads and Bridges

The Legislature shall make provision for laying out and working public roads, for the building of bridges, and for utilizing fines, forfeitures, and convict labor to all these purposes.

Section 25. Drawbacks and Rebatement Prohibited to Carriers, Shippers, Merchants, Etc.

That all drawbacks and rebatement of insurance, freight, transportation, carriage, wharfage, storage, compressing, baling, repairing, or for any other kind of labor or service of, or to any cotton, grain, or any other produce or article of commerce in this

State, paid or allowed or contracted for, to any common carrier, shipper, merchant, commission merchant, factor, agent, or middleman of any kind, not the true and absolute owner thereof, are forever prohibited, and it shall be the duty of the Legislature to pass effective laws punishing all persons in this State who pay, receive or contract for, or respecting the same.

Section 26. Homicide: Liability for Exemplary Damages

Every person, corporation, or company, that may commit a homicide, through wilful act, or omission, or gross neglect, shall be responsible, in exemplary damages, to the surviving husband, widow, heirs of his or her body, or such of them as there may be, without regard to any criminal proceeding that may or may not be had in relation to the homicide.

Section 27. Vacancies Filled for Unexpired Term

In all elections to fill vacancies of office in this State, it shall be to fill the unexpired term only.

Section 28. Garnishment of Wages

No current wages for personal service shall ever be subject to garnishment, except for the enforcement of court-ordered:

(1) child support payments; or

(2) spousal maintenance.

Section 29. Repealed

Section 30. Duration of Public Offices; Railroad Commission

(a) The duration of all offices not fixed by this Constitution shall never exceed two years.

(b) When a Railroad Commission is created by law it shall be composed of three Commissioners who shall be elected by the people at a general election for State officers, and their terms of office shall be six years. And one Railroad Commissioner shall be elected every two years. In case of vacancy in said office the Governor of the State shall fill said vacancy by appointment until the next general election.

(c) The Legislature may provide that members of the governing board of a district or authority created by authority of Article III, Section 48-e, Article III, Section 52(b)(1) or (2), or Article XVI, Section 59, of this Constitution serve terms not to exceed four years.

(d) The Legislature by general or special law may provide that members of the governing board of a hospital district serve terms not to exceed four years.

Section 30a. Members of State Boards; Terms of Office

The Legislature may provide by law that the Board of Regents of the State University and boards of trustees or managers of the educational, eleemosynary, and penal institutions of the State, and such boards as have been, or may hereafter be established by law, may be composed of an odd number of three or more members who serve for a term of six (6) years, with one-third, or as near as one-third as possible, of the members of such boards to be elected or appointed every two (2) years in such manner as the Legislature may determine; vacancies in such offices to be filled as may be provided by law, and the Legislature shall enact suitable laws to give effect to this section. The Legislature may provide by law that a board required by this constitution be composed of members of any number divisible by three (3) who serve for a term of six (6) years, with one-third of the members elected or appointed every two (2) years.

Section 30b. Duration of Municipal Civil Service Offices

Wherever by virtue of Statute or charter provisions appointive offices of any municipality are placed under the terms and provisions of Civil Service and rules are set up governing appointment to and removal from such offices, the provisions of Article 16, Section 30, of the Texas Constitution limiting the duration of all offices not fixed by the Constitution to two (2) years shall not apply, but the duration of such offices shall be governed by the provisions of the Civil Service law or charter provisions applicable thereto.

Section 31. Practitioners of Medicine

The Legislature may pass laws prescribing the qualifications of practitioners of medicine in this State, and to punish persons for malpractice, but no preference shall ever be given by law to any schools of medicine.

Section 32. Repealed

Section 33. Salary or Compensation Payments to Persons Holding More Than One Public Office

The accounting officers in this State shall neither draw nor pay a warrant or check on funds of the State of Texas, whether in the treasury or otherwise, to any person for salary or compensation who holds at the same time more than one civil office of emolument, in violation of Section 40.

Section 34. Repealed

Section 35. Repealed

Section 36. Repealed

Section 37. Liens of Mechanics, Artisans, and Material Men

Mechanics, artisans and material men, of every class, shall have a lien upon the buildings and articles made or repaired by them for the value of their labor done thereon, or material furnished therefor; and the Legislature shall provide by law for the speedy and efficient enforcement of said liens.

Section 38. Repealed

Section 39. Appropriations for Historical Memorials

The Legislature may, from time to time, make appropriations for preserving and perpetuating memorials of the history of Texas, by means of monuments, statues, paintings and documents of historical value.

Section 40. Holding More Than One Public Office; Exceptions; Right of Officeholder to Vote

(a) No person shall hold or exercise at the same time, more than one civil office of emolument, except that of Justice of the Peace, County Commissioner, Notary Public and Postmaster, Officer of the National Guard, the National Guard Reserve, and the Officers Reserve Corps of the United States and enlisted men of the National Guard, the National Guard Reserve, and the Organized Reserves of the United States, and retired officers of the United States Army, Air Force, Navy, Marine Corps, and Coast Guard, and retired warrant officers, and retired enlisted men of the United States Army, Air Force, Navy, Marine Corps, and Coast Guard, and officers and enlisted members of the Texas State Guard and any other active militia or military force organized under state law, and the officers and directors of soil and water conservation districts, unless otherwise specially provided herein. Provided, that nothing in this Constitution shall be construed to prohibit an officer or enlisted man of the National Guard, the National Guard Reserve, the Texas State Guard, and any other active militia or military force organized under state law, or an officer in the Officers Reserve Corps of the United States, or an enlisted man in the Organized Reserves of the United States, or retired officers of the United States Army, Air Force, Navy, Marine Corps, and Coast Guard, and retired warrant officers, and retired enlisted men of the United States Army, Air Force, Navy, Marine Corps, and Coast Guard, and officers of the State soil and water conservation districts, from holding at the same time any other office or position of honor, trust or profit, under this State or the United States, or from voting at any election, general, special or primary in this State when otherwise qualified.

(b) State employees or other individuals who receive all or part of their compensation either directly or indirectly from funds of the State of Texas and who are not State officers, shall not be barred from serving as members of the governing bodies of school districts, cities, towns, or other local governmental districts. Such State employees or other individuals may not receive a salary for serving as members of such governing bodies, except that:

(1) a schoolteacher, retired schoolteacher, or retired school administrator may receive compensation for serving as a member of a governing body of a school district, city, town, or local governmental district, including a water district created under Section 59, Article XVI, or Section 52, Article III; and

(2) a faculty member or retired faculty member of a public institution of higher education may receive compensation for serving as a member of a governing body of a water district created under Section 59 of this article or under Section 52, Article III, of this constitution.

(c) It is further provided that a nonelective State officer may hold other nonelective offices under the State or the United States, if the other office is of benefit to the State of Texas or is required by the State or Federal law, and there is no conflict with the original office for which he receives salary or compensation.

(d) No member of the Legislature of this State may hold any other office or position of profit under this State, or the United States, except as a notary public if qualified by law.

Section 41. Bribery and Solicitation or Acceptance of Bribes

Any person who shall, directly or indirectly, offer, give, or promise, any money or thing of value, testimonial, privilege or personal advantage, to any executive or judicial officer or member of the Legislature to influence him in the performance of any of his public or official duties, shall be guilty of bribery, and be punished in such manner as shall be provided by law. And any member of the Legislature or executive or judicial officer who shall solicit, demand or receive, or consent to receive, directly or indirectly, for himself, or for another, from any company, corporation or person, any money, appointment, employment, testimonial, reward, thing of value or employment, or of personal advantage or promise thereof, for his vote or official influence, or for withholding the same, or with any understanding, expressed or implied, that his vote or official action shall be in any way influenced thereby, or who shall solicit, demand and receive any such money or other advantage matter or thing aforesaid for another, as the consideration of his vote or official influence, in consideration of the payment or promise of such money, advantage, matter or thing to another, shall be held guilty of bribery, within the meaning of the Constitution, and shall incur the disabilities provided for said offenses, with a forfeiture of the office they may hold, and such other additional punishment as is or shall be provided by law.

Section 42. Repealed

Section 43. Repealed

Section 44. County Treasurer and County Surveyor

(a) Except as otherwise provided by this section, the Legislature shall prescribe the duties and provide for the election by the qualified voters of each county in this State, of a County Treasurer and a County Surveyor, who shall have an office at the county seat, and hold their office for four years, and until their successors are qualified; and shall have such compensation as may be provided by law.

(b) The office of County Treasurer or County Surveyor does not exist in those counties in which the office has been abolished pursuant to constitutional amendment or pursuant to the authority of Subsection (c) of this section.

(c) The Commissioners Court of a county may call an election to abolish the office of County Surveyor in the county. The office of County Surveyor in the county is abolished if a majority of the voters of the county voting on the question at that election approve the abolition. If an election is called under this subsection, the Commissioners Court shall order the ballot for the election to be printed to provide for voting for or against the proposition: "Abolishing the office of county surveyor of this county." If the office of County Surveyor is abolished under this subsection, the maps, field notes, and other records in the custody of the County Surveyor are transferred to the county officer or employee designated by the Commissioners Court of the county in which the office is abolished, and the Commissioners Court may from time to time change its designation as it considers appropriate.

Section 45. Repealed

Section 46. Repealed

Section 47. Repealed

Section 48. Existing State Laws to Continue in Force

All laws and parts of laws now in force in the State of Texas, which are not repugnant to the Constitution of the United States, or to this Constitution, shall continue and remain in force as the laws of this State, until they expire by their own limitation or shall be amended or repealed by the Legislature.

Section 49. Protection of Personal Property from Forced Sale

The Legislature shall have power, and it shall be its duty, to protect by law from forced sale a certain portion of the personal property of all heads of families, and also of unmarried adults, male and female.

Section 50. Protection of Homestead from Forced or Unauthorized Sale; Exceptions; Requirements for Mortgage Loans and other Obligations Secured by Homestead

(a) The homestead of a family, or of a single adult person, shall be, and is hereby protected from forced sale, for the payment of all debts except for:

(1) the purchase money thereof, or a part of such purchase money;

(2) the taxes due thereon;

(3) an owelty of partition imposed against the entirety of the property by a court order or by a written agreement of the parties to the partition, including a debt of one spouse in favor of the other spouse resulting from a division or an award of a family homestead in a divorce proceeding;

(4) the refinance of a lien against a homestead, including a federal tax lien resulting from the tax debt of both spouses, if the homestead is a family homestead, or from the tax debt of the owner;

(5) work and material used in constructing new improvements thereon, if contracted for in writing, or work and material used to repair or renovate existing improvements thereon if:

(A) the work and material are contracted for in writing, with the consent of both spouses, in the case of a family homestead, given in the same manner as is required in making a sale and conveyance of the homestead;

(B) the contract for the work and material is not executed by the owner or the owner's spouse before the fifth day after the owner makes written application for any extension of credit for the work and material, unless the work and material are necessary to complete immediate repairs to conditions on the homestead property that materially affect the health or safety of the owner or person residing in the homestead and the owner of the homestead acknowledges such in writing;

(C) the contract for the work and material expressly provides that the owner may rescind the contract without penalty or charge within three days after the execution of the contract by all parties, unless the work and material are necessary to complete immediate repairs to conditions on the homestead property that materially affect the health or safety of the owner or person residing in the homestead and the owner of the homestead acknowledges such in writing; and

(D) the contract for the work and material is executed by the owner and the owner's spouse only at the office of a third-party lender making an extension of credit for the work and material, an attorney at law, or a title company;

(6) an extension of credit that:

(A) is secured by a voluntary lien on the homestead created under a written agreement with the consent of each owner and each owner's spouse;

(B) is of a principal amount that when added to the aggregate total of the outstanding principal balances of all other indebtedness secured by valid encumbrances of record against the homestead does not exceed 80 percent of the fair market value of the homestead on the date the extension of credit is made;

(C) is without recourse for personal liability against each owner and the spouse of each owner, unless the owner or spouse obtained the extension of credit by actual fraud;

(D) is secured by a lien that may be foreclosed upon only by a court order;

(E) does not require the owner or the owner's spouse to pay, in addition to any interest or any bona fide discount points used to buy down the interest rate, any fees to any person that are necessary to originate, evaluate, maintain, record, insure, or service the extension of credit that exceed, in the aggregate, two percent of the original principal amount of the extension of credit, excluding fees for:

(i) an appraisal performed by a third party appraiser;

(ii) a property survey performed by a state registered or licensed surveyor;

(iii) a state base premium for a mortgagee policy of title insurance with endorsements established in accordance with state law; or

(iv) a title examination report if its cost is less than the state base premium for a mortgagee policy of title insurance without endorsements established in accordance with state law;

(F) is not a form of open-end account that may be debited from time to time or under which credit may be extended from time to time unless the open-end account is a home equity line of credit;

(G) is payable in advance without penalty or other charge;

(H) is not secured by any additional real or personal property other than the homestead;

(I) Repealed

(J) may not be accelerated because of a decrease in the market value of the homestead or because of the owner's default under other indebtedness not secured by a prior valid encumbrance against the homestead;

(K) is the only debt secured by the homestead at the time the extension of credit is made unless the other debt was made for a purpose described by Subsections (a)(1)-(a)(5) or Subsection (a)(8) of this section;

(L) is scheduled to be repaid:

(i) in substantially equal successive periodic installments, not more often than every 14 days and not less often than monthly, beginning no later than two months from the date the extension of credit is made, each of which equals or exceeds the amount of accrued interest as of the date of the scheduled installment; or

(ii) if the extension of credit is a home equity line of credit, in periodic payments described under Subsection (t)(8) of this section;

(M) is closed not before:

(i) the 12th day after the later of the date that the owner of the homestead submits a loan application to the lender for the extension of credit or the date that the lender provides the owner a copy of the notice prescribed by Subsection (g) of this section;

(ii) one business day after the date that the owner of the homestead receives a copy of the loan application if not previously provided and a final itemized disclosure of the actual fees, points, interest, costs, and charges that will be charged at closing. If a bona fide emergency or another good cause exists and the lender obtains the written consent of the owner, the lender may provide the documentation to the owner or the lender may modify previously provided documentation on the date of closing; and

(iii) the first anniversary of the closing date of any other extension of credit described by Subsection (a)(6) of this section secured by the same homestead property, except a refinance described by Paragraph (Q)(x)(f) of this subdivision, unless the owner on oath requests an earlier closing due to a state of emergency that:

(a) has been declared by the president of the United States or the governor as provided by law; and

(b) applies to the area where the homestead is located;

(N) is closed only at the office of the lender, an attorney at law, or a title company;

(O) permits a lender to contract for and receive any fixed or variable rate of interest authorized under statute;

(P) is made by one of the following that has not been found by a federal regulatory agency to have engaged in the practice of refusing to make loans because the applicants for the loans reside or the property proposed to secure the loans is located in a certain area:

(i) a bank, savings and loan association, savings bank, or credit union doing business under the laws of this state or the United States, including a subsidiary of a bank, savings and loan association, savings bank, or credit union described by this subparagraph;

(ii) a federally chartered lending instrumentality or a person approved as a mortgagee by the United States government to make federally insured loans;

(iii) a person licensed to make regulated loans, as provided by statute of this state;

(iv) a person who sold the homestead property to the current owner and who provided all or part of the financing for the purchase;

(v) a person who is related to the homestead property owner within the second degree of affinity or consanguinity; or

(vi) a person regulated by this state as a mortgage banker or mortgage company; and

(Q) is made on the condition that:

(i) the owner of the homestead is not required to apply the proceeds of the extension of credit to repay another debt except debt secured by the homestead or debt to another lender;

(ii) the owner of the homestead not assign wages as security for the extension of credit;

(iii) the owner of the homestead not sign any instrument in which blanks relating to substantive terms of agreement are left to be filled in;

(iv) the owner of the homestead not sign a confession of judgment or power of attorney to the lender or to a third person to confess judgment or to appear for the owner in a judicial proceeding;

(v) at the time the extension of credit is made, the owner of the homestead shall receive a copy of the final loan application and all executed documents signed by the owner at closing related to the extension of credit;

(vi) the security instruments securing the extension of credit contain a disclosure that the extension of credit is the type of credit defined by Subsection (a)(6) of this section;

(vii) within a reasonable time after termination and full payment of the extension of credit, the lender cancel and return the promissory note to the owner of the homestead and give the owner, in recordable form, a release of the lien securing the extension of credit or a copy of an endorsement and assignment of the lien to a lender that is refinancing the extension of credit;

(viii) the owner of the homestead and any spouse of the owner may, within three days after the extension of credit is made, rescind the extension of credit without penalty or charge;

(ix) the owner of the homestead and the lender sign a written acknowledgment as to the fair market value of the homestead property on the date the extension of credit is made;

(x) except as provided by Subparagraph (xi) of this paragraph, the lender or any holder of the note for the extension of credit shall forfeit all principal and interest of the extension of credit if the lender or holder fails to comply with the lender's or holder's obligations under the extension of credit and fails to correct the failure to comply not later than the 60th day after the date the lender or holder is notified by the borrower of the lender's failure to comply by:

(a) paying to the owner an amount equal to any overcharge paid by the owner under or related to the extension of credit if the owner has paid an amount that exceeds an amount stated in the applicable Paragraph (E), (G), or (O) of this subdivision;

(b) sending the owner a written acknowledgment that the lien is valid only in the amount that the extension of credit does not exceed the percentage described by Paragraph (B) of this subdivision, if applicable, or is not secured by property described under Paragraph (H) of this subdivision, if applicable;

(c) sending the owner a written notice modifying any other amount, percentage, term, or other provision prohibited by this section to a permitted amount, percentage, term, or other provision and adjusting the account of the borrower to ensure that the borrower is not required to pay more than an amount permitted by this section and is not subject to any other term or provision prohibited by this section;

(d) delivering the required documents to the borrower if the lender fails to comply with Subparagraph (v) of this paragraph or obtaining the appropriate signatures if the lender fails to comply with Subparagraph (ix) of this paragraph;

(e) sending the owner a written acknowledgment, if the failure to comply is prohibited by Paragraph (K) of this subdivision, that the accrual of interest and all of the owner's obligations under the extension of credit are abated while any prior lien prohibited under Paragraph (K) remains secured by the homestead; or

(f) if the failure to comply cannot be cured under Sub-paragraphs (x)(a)-(e) of this paragraph, curing the failure to comply by a refund or credit to the owner of $1,000 and offering the owner the right to refinance the extension of credit with the lender or holder for the remaining term of the loan at no cost to the owner on the same terms, including interest, as the original extension of credit with any modifications necessary to comply with this section or on terms on which the owner and the lender or holder otherwise agree that comply with this section; and

(xi) the lender or any holder of the note for the extension of credit shall forfeit all principal and interest of the extension of credit if the extension of credit is made by a person other than a person described under Paragraph (P) of this subdivision or if the lien was not created under a written agreement with the consent of each owner and each owner's spouse, unless each owner and each owner's spouse who did not initially consent subsequently consents;

(7) a reverse mortgage; or

(8) the conversion and refinance of a personal property lien secured by a manufactured home to a lien on real property, including the refinance of the purchase price of the manufactured home, the cost of installing the manufactured home on the real property, and the refinance of the purchase price of the real property.

(b) An owner or claimant of the property claimed as homestead may not sell or abandon the homestead without the consent of each owner and the spouse of each owner, given in such manner as may be prescribed by law.

(c) No mortgage, trust deed, or other lien on the homestead shall ever be valid unless it secures a debt described by this section, whether such mortgage, trust deed, or other lien, shall have been created by the owner alone, or together with his or her spouse, in case the owner is married. All pretended sales of the homestead involving any condition of defeasance shall be void.

(d) A purchaser or lender for value without actual knowledge may conclusively rely on an affidavit that designates other property as the homestead of the affiant and that states that the property to be conveyed or encumbered is not the homestead of the affiant.

(e) A refinance of debt secured by a homestead and described by any subsection under Subsections (a)(1)-(a)(5) that includes the advance of additional funds may not be secured by a valid lien against the homestead unless:

(1) the refinance of the debt is an extension of credit described by Subsection (a)(6) of this section; or

(2) the advance of all the additional funds is for reasonable costs necessary to refinance such debt or for a purpose described by Subsection (a)(2), (a)(3), or (a)(5) of this section.

(f) A refinance of debt secured by the homestead, any portion of which is an extension of credit described by Subsection (a)(6) of this section, may not be secured by a valid lien against the homestead unless either:

(1) the refinance of the debt is an extension of credit described by Subsection (a)(6) or (a)(7) of this section; or

(2) all of the following conditions are met:

(A) the refinance is not closed before the first anniversary of the date the extension of credit was closed;

(B) the refinanced extension of credit does not include the advance of any additional funds other than:

(i) funds advanced to refinance a debt described by Subsections (a)(1) through (a)(7) of this section; or

(ii) actual costs and reserves required by the lender to refinance the debt;

(C) the refinance of the extension of credit is of a principal amount that when added to the aggregate total of the outstanding principal balances of all other indebtedness secured by valid encumbrances of record against the homestead does not exceed 80 percent of the fair market value of the homestead on the date the refinance of the extension of credit is made; and

(D) the lender provides the owner the following written notice on a separate document not later than the third business day after the date the owner submits the loan application to the lender and at least 12 days before the date the refinance of the extension of credit is closed:

"YOUR EXISTING LOAN THAT YOU DESIRE TO REFINANCE IS A HOME EQUITY LOAN. YOU MAY HAVE THE OPTION TO REFINANCE YOUR HOME EQUITY LOAN AS EITHER A HOME EQUITY LOAN OR AS A NON-HOME EQUITY LOAN, IF OFFERED BY YOUR LENDER.

"HOME EQUITY LOANS HAVE IMPORTANT CONSUMER PROTECTIONS. A LENDER MAY ONLY FORECLOSE A HOME EQUITY LOAN BASED ON A COURT ORDER. A HOME EQUITY LOAN MUST BE WITHOUT RECOURSE FOR PERSONAL LIABILITY AGAINST YOU AND YOUR SPOUSE.

"IF YOU HAVE APPLIED TO REFINANCE YOUR EXISTING HOME EQUITY LOAN AS A NON-HOME EQUITY LOAN, YOU WILL LOSE CERTAIN CONSUMER PROTECTIONS. A NON-HOME EQUITY REFINANCED LOAN:

"**(1)** WILL PERMIT THE LENDER TO FORECLOSE WITHOUT A COURT ORDER;

"**(2)** WILL BE WITH RECOURSE FOR PERSONAL LIABILITY AGAINST YOU AND YOUR SPOUSE; AND

"**(3)** MAY ALSO CONTAIN OTHER TERMS OR CONDITIONS THAT MAY NOT BE PERMITTED IN A TRADITIONAL HOME EQUITY LOAN.

"BEFORE YOU REFINANCE YOUR EXISTING HOME EQUITY LOAN TO MAKE IT A NON-HOME EQUITY LOAN, YOU SHOULD MAKE SURE YOU UNDERSTAND THAT YOU ARE WAIVING IMPORTANT PROTECTIONS THAT HOME EQUITY LOANS PROVIDE UNDER THE LAW AND SHOULD CONSIDER CONSULTING WITH AN ATTORNEY OF YOUR CHOOSING REGARDING THESE PROTECTIONS.

"YOU MAY WISH TO ASK YOUR LENDER TO REFINANCE YOUR LOAN AS A HOME EQUITY LOAN. HOWEVER, A HOME EQUITY LOAN MAY HAVE A HIGHER INTEREST RATE AND CLOSING

COSTS THAN A NON-HOME EQUITY LOAN."

(f-1) A lien securing a refinance of debt under Subsection (f)(2) of this section is deemed to be a lien described by Subsection (a)(4) of this section. An affidavit executed by the owner or the owner's spouse acknowledging that the requirements of Subsection (f)(2) of this section have been met conclusively establishes that the requirements of Subsection (a)(4) of this section have been met.

(g) An extension of credit described by Subsection (a)(6) of this section may be secured by a valid lien against homestead property if the extension of credit is not closed before the 12th day after the lender provides the owner with the following written notice on a separate instrument:

"NOTICE CONCERNING EXTENSIONS OF CREDIT DEFINED BY SECTION 50(a)(6), ARTICLE XVI, TEXAS CONSTITUTION:

"SECTION 50(a)(6), ARTICLE XVI, OF THE TEXAS CONSTITUTION ALLOWS CERTAIN LOANS TO BE SECURED AGAINST THE EQUITY IN YOUR HOME. SUCH LOANS ARE COMMONLY KNOWN AS EQUITY LOANS. IF YOU DO NOT REPAY THE LOAN OR IF YOU FAIL TO MEET THE TERMS OF THE LOAN, THE LENDER MAY FORECLOSE AND SELL YOUR HOME. THE CONSTITUTION PROVIDES THAT:

"**(A)** THE LOAN MUST BE VOLUNTARILY CREATED WITH THE CONSENT OF EACH OWNER OF YOUR HOME AND EACH OWNER'S SPOUSE;

"**(B)** THE PRINCIPAL LOAN AMOUNT AT THE TIME THE LOAN IS MADE MUST NOT EXCEED AN AMOUNT THAT, WHEN ADDED TO THE PRINCIPAL BALANCES OF ALL OTHER LIENS AGAINST YOUR HOME, IS MORE THAN 80 PERCENT OF THE FAIR MARKET VALUE OF YOUR HOME;

"**(C)** THE LOAN MUST BE WITHOUT RECOURSE FOR PERSONAL LIABILITY AGAINST YOU AND YOUR SPOUSE UNLESS YOU OR YOUR SPOUSE OBTAINED THIS EXTENSION OF CREDIT BY ACTUAL FRAUD;

"**(D)** THE LIEN SECURING THE LOAN MAY BE FORECLOSED UPON ONLY WITH A COURT ORDER;

"**(E)** FEES AND CHARGES TO MAKE THE LOAN MAY NOT EXCEED 2 PERCENT OF THE LOAN AMOUNT, EXCEPT FOR A FEE OR CHARGE FOR AN APPRAISAL PERFORMED BY A THIRD PARTY APPRAISER, A PROPERTY SURVEY PERFORMED BY A STATE REGISTERED OR LICENSED SURVEYOR, A STATE BASE PREMIUM FOR A MORTGAGEE POLICY OF TITLE INSURANCE WITH ENDORSEMENTS, OR A TITLE EXAMINATION REPORT;

"**(F)** THE LOAN MAY NOT BE AN OPEN-END ACCOUNT THAT MAY BE DEBITED FROM TIME TO TIME OR UNDER WHICH CREDIT MAY BE EXTENDED FROM TIME TO TIME UNLESS IT IS A HOME EQUITY LINE OF CREDIT;

"**(G)** YOU MAY PREPAY THE LOAN WITHOUT PENALTY OR CHARGE;

"**(H)** NO ADDITIONAL COLLATERAL MAY BE SECURITY FOR THE LOAN;

"**(I)** Repealed

"**(J)** YOU ARE NOT REQUIRED TO REPAY THE LOAN EARLIER THAN AGREED SOLELY BECAUSE THE FAIR MARKET VALUE OF YOUR HOME DECREASES OR BECAUSE YOU DEFAULT ON ANOTHER LOAN THAT IS NOT SECURED BY YOUR HOME;

"**(K)** ONLY ONE LOAN DESCRIBED BY SECTION 50(a)(6), ARTICLE XVI, OF THE TEXAS CONSTITUTION MAY BE SECURED WITH YOUR HOME AT ANY GIVEN TIME;

"**(L)** THE LOAN MUST BE SCHEDULED TO BE REPAID IN PAYMENTS THAT EQUAL OR EXCEED THE AMOUNT OF ACCRUED INTEREST FOR EACH PAYMENT PERIOD;

"**(M)** THE LOAN MAY NOT CLOSE BEFORE 12 DAYS AFTER YOU SUBMIT A LOAN APPLICATION TO THE LENDER OR BEFORE 12 DAYS AFTER YOU RECEIVE THIS NOTICE, WHICHEVER DATE IS LATER; AND MAY NOT WITHOUT YOUR CONSENT CLOSE BEFORE ONE BUSINESS DAY AFTER THE DATE ON WHICH YOU RECEIVE A COPY OF YOUR LOAN APPLICATION IF NOT PREVIOUSLY PROVIDED AND A FINAL ITEMIZED DISCLOSURE OF THE ACTUAL FEES, POINTS, INTEREST, COSTS, AND CHARGES THAT WILL BE CHARGED AT CLOSING; AND IF YOUR HOME WAS SECURITY FOR THE SAME TYPE OF LOAN WITHIN THE PAST YEAR, A NEW LOAN SECURED BY THE SAME PROPERTY MAY NOT CLOSE BEFORE ONE YEAR HAS PASSED FROM THE CLOSING DATE OF THE OTHER LOAN, UNLESS ON OATH YOU REQUEST AN EARLIER CLOSING DUE TO A DECLARED STATE OF EMERGENCY;

"**(N)** THE LOAN MAY CLOSE ONLY AT THE OFFICE OF THE LENDER, TITLE COMPANY, OR AN ATTORNEY AT LAW;

"**(O)** THE LENDER MAY CHARGE ANY FIXED OR VARIABLE RATE OF INTEREST AUTHORIZED BY STATUTE;

"**(P)** ONLY A LAWFULLY AUTHORIZED LENDER MAY MAKE LOANS DESCRIBED BY SECTION 50(a)(6), ARTICLE XVI, OF THE TEXAS CONSTITUTION;

"**(Q)** LOANS DESCRIBED BY SECTION 50(a)(6), ARTICLE XVI, OF THE TEXAS CONSTITUTION MUST:

"**(1)** NOT REQUIRE YOU TO APPLY THE PROCEEDS TO ANOTHER DEBT EXCEPT A DEBT THAT IS SECURED BY YOUR HOME OR OWED TO ANOTHER LENDER;

338

"**(2)** NOT REQUIRE THAT YOU ASSIGN WAGES AS SECURITY;

"**(3)** NOT REQUIRE THAT YOU EXECUTE INSTRUMENTS WHICH HAVE BLANKS FOR SUBSTANTIVE TERMS OF AGREEMENT LEFT TO BE FILLED IN;

"**(4)** NOT REQUIRE THAT YOU SIGN A CONFESSION OF JUDGMENT OR POWER OF ATTORNEY TO ANOTHER PERSON TO CONFESS JUDGMENT OR APPEAR IN A LEGAL PROCEEDING ON YOUR BEHALF;

"**(5)** PROVIDE THAT YOU RECEIVE A COPY OF YOUR FINAL LOAN APPLICATION AND ALL EXECUTED DOCUMENTS YOU SIGN AT CLOSING;

"**(6)** PROVIDE THAT THE SECURITY INSTRUMENTS CONTAIN A DISCLOSURE THAT THIS LOAN IS A LOAN DEFINED BY SECTION 50(a)(6), ARTICLE XVI, OF THE TEXAS CONSTITUTION;

"**(7)** PROVIDE THAT WHEN THE LOAN IS PAID IN FULL, THE LENDER WILL SIGN AND GIVE YOU A RELEASE OF LIEN OR AN ASSIGNMENT OF THE LIEN, WHICHEVER IS APPROPRIATE;

"**(8)** PROVIDE THAT YOU MAY, WITHIN 3 DAYS AFTER CLOSING, RESCIND THE LOAN WITHOUT PENALTY OR CHARGE;

"**(9)** PROVIDE THAT YOU AND THE LENDER ACKNOWLEDGE THE FAIR MARKET VALUE OF YOUR HOME ON THE DATE THE LOAN CLOSES; AND

"**(10)** PROVIDE THAT THE LENDER WILL FORFEIT ALL PRINCIPAL AND INTEREST IF THE LENDER FAILS TO COMPLY WITH THE LENDER'S OBLIGATIONS UNLESS THE LENDER CURES THE FAILURE TO COMPLY AS PROVIDED BY SECTION 50(a)(6)(Q)(x), ARTICLE XVI, OF THE TEXAS CONSTITUTION; AND

"**(R)** IF THE LOAN IS A HOME EQUITY LINE OF CREDIT:

"**(1)** YOU MAY REQUEST ADVANCES, REPAY MONEY, AND REBORROW MONEY UNDER THE LINE OF CREDIT;

"**(2)** EACH ADVANCE UNDER THE LINE OF CREDIT MUST BE IN AN AMOUNT OF AT LEAST $4,000;

"**(3)** YOU MAY NOT USE A CREDIT CARD, DEBIT CARD, OR SIMILAR DEVICE, OR PREPRINTED CHECK THAT YOU DID NOT SOLICIT, TO OBTAIN ADVANCES UNDER THE LINE OF CREDIT;

"**(4)** ANY FEES THE LENDER CHARGES MAY BE CHARGED AND COLLECTED ONLY AT THE TIME THE LINE OF CREDIT IS ESTABLISHED AND THE LENDER MAY NOT CHARGE A FEE IN CONNECTION WITH ANY ADVANCE;

"**(5)** THE MAXIMUM PRINCIPAL AMOUNT THAT MAY BE EXTENDED, WHEN ADDED TO ALL OTHER DEBTS SECURED BY YOUR HOME, MAY NOT EXCEED 80 PERCENT OF THE FAIR MARKET VALUE OF YOUR HOME ON THE DATE THE LINE OF CREDIT IS ESTABLISHED;

"**(6)** IF THE PRINCIPAL BALANCE UNDER THE LINE OF CREDIT AT ANY TIME EXCEEDS 80 PERCENT OF THE FAIR MARKET VALUE OF YOUR HOME, AS DETERMINED ON THE DATE THE LINE OF CREDIT IS ESTABLISHED, YOU MAY NOT CONTINUE TO REQUEST ADVANCES UNDER THE LINE OF CREDIT UNTIL THE BALANCE IS LESS THAN 80 PERCENT OF THE FAIR MARKET VALUE; AND

"**(7)** THE LENDER MAY NOT UNILATERALLY AMEND THE TERMS OF THE LINE OF CREDIT.

"THIS NOTICE IS ONLY A SUMMARY OF YOUR RIGHTS UNDER THE TEXAS CONSTITUTION. YOUR RIGHTS ARE GOVERNED BY SECTION 50, ARTICLE XVI, OF THE TEXAS CONSTITUTION, AND NOT BY THIS NOTICE."

If the discussions with the borrower are conducted primarily in a language other than English, the lender shall, before closing, provide an additional copy of the notice translated into the written language in which the discussions were conducted.

(h) A lender or assignee for value may conclusively rely on the written acknowledgment as to the fair market value of the homestead property made in accordance with Subsection (a)(6) (Q)(ix) of this section if:

(1) the value acknowledged to is the value estimate in an appraisal or evaluation prepared in accordance with a state or federal requirement applicable to an extension of credit under Subsection (a)(6); and

(2) the lender or assignee does not have actual knowledge at the time of the payment of value or advance of funds by the lender or assignee that the fair market value stated in the written acknowledgment was incorrect.

(i) This subsection shall not affect or impair any right of the borrower to recover damages from the lender or assignee under applicable law for wrongful foreclosure. A purchaser for value without actual knowledge may conclusively presume that a lien securing an extension of credit described by Subsection (a)(6) of this section was a valid lien securing the extension of credit with homestead property if:

(1) the security instruments securing the extension of credit contain a disclosure that the extension of credit secured by the lien was the type of credit defined by Section 50(a)(6), Article XVI, Texas Constitution;

(2) the purchaser acquires the title to the property pursuant to or after the foreclosure of the voluntary lien; and

(3) the purchaser is not the lender or assignee under the extension of credit.

(j) Subsection (a)(6) and Subsections (e)-(i) of this section are not severable, and none of those provisions would have been enacted without the others. If any of those provisions are held to be preempted by the laws of the United States, all of those provisions are invalid. This subsection shall not apply to any lien or extension of credit made after January 1, 1998, and before the date any provision under Subsection (a)(6) or Subsections (e)-(i) is held to be preempted.

(k) "Reverse mortgage" means an extension of credit:

(1) that is secured by a voluntary lien on homestead property created by a written agreement with the consent of each owner and each owner's spouse;

(2) that is made to a person who is or whose spouse is 62 years or older;

(3) that is made without recourse for personal liability against each owner and the spouse of each owner;

(4) under which advances are provided to a borrower:

(A) based on the equity in a borrower's homestead; or

(B) for the purchase of homestead property that the borrower will occupy as a principal residence;

(5) that does not permit the lender to reduce the amount or number of advances because of an adjustment in the interest rate if periodic advances are to be made;

(6) that requires no payment of principal or interest until:

(A) all borrowers have died;

(B) the homestead property securing the loan is sold or otherwise transferred;

(C) all borrowers cease occupying the homestead property for a period of longer than 12 consecutive months without prior written approval from the lender;

(C-1) if the extension of credit is used for the purchase of homestead property, the borrower fails to timely occupy the homestead property as the borrower's principal residence within a specified period after the date the extension of credit is made that is stipulated in the written agreement creating the lien on the property; or

(D) the borrower:

(i) defaults on an obligation specified in the loan documents to repair and maintain, pay taxes and assessments on, or insure the homestead property;

(ii) commits actual fraud in connection with the loan; or

(iii) fails to maintain the priority of the lender's lien on the homestead property, after the lender gives notice to the borrower, by promptly discharging any lien that has priority or may obtain priority over the lender's lien within 10 days after the date the borrower receives the notice, unless the borrower:

(a) agrees in writing to the payment of the obligation secured by the lien in a manner acceptable to the lender;

(b) contests in good faith the lien by, or defends against enforcement of the lien in, legal proceedings so as to prevent the enforcement of the lien or forfeiture of any part of the homestead property; or

(c) secures from the holder of the lien an agreement satisfactory to the lender subordinating the lien to all amounts secured by the lender's lien on the homestead property;

(7) that provides that if the lender fails to make loan advances as required in the loan documents and if the lender fails to cure the default as required in the loan documents after notice from the borrower, the lender forfeits all principal and interest of the reverse mortgage, provided, however, that this subdivision does not apply when a governmental agency or instrumentality takes an assignment of the loan in order to cure the default;

(8) that is not made unless the prospective borrower and the spouse of the prospective borrower attest in writing that the prospective borrower and the prospective borrower's spouse received counseling regarding the advisability and availability of reverse mortgages and other financial alternatives that was completed not earlier than the 180th day nor later than the 5th day before the date the extension of credit is closed;

(9) that is not closed before the 12th day after the date the lender provides to the prospective borrower the following written notice on a separate instrument, which the lender or originator and the borrower must sign for the notice to take effect:

"IMPORTANT NOTICE TO BORROWERS RELATED TO YOUR REVERSE MORTGAGE

"UNDER THE TEXAS TAX CODE, CERTAIN ELDERLY PERSONS MAY DEFER THE COLLECTION OF PROPERTY TAXES ON THEIR RESIDENCE HOMESTEAD. BY RECEIVING THIS REVERSE MORTGAGE YOU MAY BE REQUIRED TO FORGO ANY PREVIOUSLY APPROVED DEFERRAL OF PROPERTY TAX COLLECTION AND YOU MAY BE REQUIRED TO PAY PROPERTY TAXES ON AN ANNUAL BASIS ON THIS PROPERTY.

"THE LENDER MAY FORECLOSE THE REVERSE MORTGAGE AND YOU MAY LOSE YOUR HOME IF:

"**(A)** YOU DO NOT PAY THE TAXES OR OTHER ASSESSMENTS ON THE HOME EVEN IF YOU ARE ELIGIBLE TO DEFER PAYMENT OF PROPERTY TAXES;

"(B) YOU DO NOT MAINTAIN AND PAY FOR PROPERTY INSURANCE ON THE HOME AS REQUIRED BY THE LOAN DOCUMENTS;

"(C) YOU FAIL TO MAINTAIN THE HOME IN A STATE OF GOOD CONDITION AND REPAIR;

"(D) YOU CEASE OCCUPYING THE HOME FOR A PERIOD LONGER THAN 12 CONSECUTIVE MONTHS WITHOUT THE PRIOR WRITTEN APPROVAL FROM THE LENDER OR, IF THE EXTENSION OF CREDIT IS USED FOR THE PURCHASE OF THE HOME, YOU FAIL TO TIMELY OCCUPY THE HOME AS YOUR PRINCIPAL RESIDENCE WITHIN A PERIOD OF TIME AFTER THE EXTENSION OF CREDIT IS MADE THAT IS STIPULATED IN THE WRITTEN AGREEMENT CREATING THE LIEN ON THE HOME;

"(E) YOU SELL THE HOME OR OTHERWISE TRANSFER THE HOME WITHOUT PAYING OFF THE LOAN;

"(F) ALL BORROWERS HAVE DIED AND THE LOAN IS NOT REPAID;

"(G) YOU COMMIT ACTUAL FRAUD IN CONNECTION WITH THE LOAN; OR

"(H) YOU FAIL TO MAINTAIN THE PRIORITY OF THE LENDER'S LIEN ON THE HOME, AFTER THE LENDER GIVES NOTICE TO YOU, BY PROMPTLY DISCHARGING ANY LIEN THAT HAS PRIORITY OR MAY OBTAIN PRIORITY OVER THE LENDER'S LIEN WITHIN 10 DAYS AFTER THE DATE YOU RECEIVE THE NOTICE, UNLESS YOU:

"(1) AGREE IN WRITING TO THE PAYMENT OF THE OBLIGATION SECURED BY THE LIEN IN A MANNER ACCEPTABLE TO THE LENDER;

"**(2)** CONTEST IN GOOD FAITH THE LIEN BY, OR DEFEND AGAINST ENFORCEMENT OF THE LIEN IN, LEGAL PROCEEDINGS SO AS TO PREVENT THE ENFORCEMENT OF THE LIEN OR FORFEITURE OF ANY PART OF THE HOME; OR

"**(3)** SECURE FROM THE HOLDER OF THE LIEN AN AGREEMENT SATISFACTORY TO THE LENDER SUBORDINATING THE LIEN TO ALL AMOUNTS SECURED BY THE LENDER'S LIEN ON THE HOME.

"IF A GROUND FOR FORECLOSURE EXISTS, THE LENDER MAY NOT COMMENCE FORECLOSURE UNTIL THE LENDER GIVES YOU WRITTEN NOTICE BY MAIL THAT A GROUND FOR FORECLOSURE EXISTS AND GIVES YOU AN OPPORTUNITY TO REMEDY THE CONDITION CREATING THE GROUND FOR FORECLOSURE OR TO PAY THE REVERSE MORTGAGE DEBT WITHIN THE TIME PERMITTED BY SECTION 50(k)(10), ARTICLE XVI, OF THE TEXAS CONSTITUTION. THE LENDER MUST OBTAIN A COURT ORDER FOR FORECLOSURE EXCEPT THAT A COURT ORDER IS NOT REQUIRED IF THE FORECLOSURE OCCURS BECAUSE:

"**(1)** ALL BORROWERS HAVE DIED; OR

"**(2)** THE HOMESTEAD PROPERTY SECURING THE LOAN IS SOLD OR OTHERWISE TRANSFERRED."

"YOU SHOULD CONSULT WITH YOUR HOME COUNSELOR OR AN ATTORNEY IF YOU HAVE ANY CONCERNS ABOUT THESE OBLIGATIONS BEFORE YOU CLOSE YOUR REVERSE MORTGAGE LOAN. TO LOCATE AN ATTORNEY IN YOUR AREA, YOU MAY WISH TO CONTACT THE STATE BAR OF TEXAS."

"THIS NOTICE IS ONLY A SUMMARY OF YOUR RIGHTS UNDER THE TEXAS CONSTITUTION. YOUR RIGHTS ARE GOVERNED IN PART BY SECTION 50, ARTICLE XVI, OF THE TEXAS CONSTITUTION, AND NOT BY THIS NOTICE.";

(10) that does not permit the lender to commence foreclosure until the lender gives notice to the borrower, in the manner provided for a notice by mail related to the foreclosure of liens under Subsection (a)(6) of this section, that a ground for foreclosure exists and gives the borrower at least 30 days, or at least 20 days in the event of a default under Subdivision (6)(D) (iii) of this subsection, to:

(A) remedy the condition creating the ground for foreclosure;

(B) pay the debt secured by the homestead property from proceeds of the sale of the homestead property by the borrower or from any other sources; or

(C) convey the homestead property to the lender by a deed in lieu of foreclosure; and

(11) that is secured by a lien that may be foreclosed upon only by a court order, if the foreclosure is for a ground other than a ground stated by Subdivision (6)(A) or (B) of this subsection.

(l) Advances made under a reverse mortgage and interest on those advances have priority over a lien filed for record in the real property records in the county where the homestead property is located after the reverse mortgage is filed for record in the real property records of that county.

(m) A reverse mortgage may provide for an interest rate that is fixed or adjustable and may also provide for interest that is contingent on appreciation in the fair market value of the homestead property. Although payment of principal or interest shall not be required under a reverse mortgage until the entire loan becomes due and payable, interest may accrue and be compounded during the term of the loan as provided by the reverse mortgage loan agreement.

(n) A reverse mortgage that is secured by a valid lien against homestead property may be made or acquired without regard to the following provisions of any other law of this state:

(1) a limitation on the purpose and use of future advances or other mortgage proceeds;

(2) a limitation on future advances to a term of years or a limitation on the term of open-end account advances;

(3) a limitation on the term during which future advances take priority over intervening advances;

(4) a requirement that a maximum loan amount be stated in the reverse mortgage loan documents;

(5) a prohibition on balloon payments;

(6) a prohibition on compound interest and interest on interest;

(7) a prohibition on contracting for, charging, or receiving any rate of interest authorized by any law of this state authorizing a lender to contract for a rate of interest; and

(8) a requirement that a percentage of the reverse mortgage proceeds be advanced before the assignment of the reverse mortgage.

(o) For the purposes of determining eligibility under any statute relating to payments, allowances, benefits, or services provided on a means-tested basis by this state, including supplemental security income, low-income energy assistance, property tax relief, medical assistance, and general assistance:

(1) reverse mortgage loan advances made to a borrower are considered proceeds from a loan and not income; and

(2) undisbursed funds under a reverse mortgage loan are considered equity in a borrower's home and not proceeds from a loan.

(p) The advances made on a reverse mortgage loan under which more than one advance is made must be made according to the terms established by the loan documents by one or more of the following methods:

(1) an initial advance at any time and future advances at regular intervals;

(2) an initial advance at any time and future advances at regular intervals in which the amounts advanced may be reduced, for one or more advances, at the request of the borrower;

(3) an initial advance at any time and future advances at times and in amounts requested by the borrower until the credit limit established by the loan documents is reached;

(4) an initial advance at any time, future advances at times and in amounts requested by the borrower until the credit limit established by the loan documents is reached, and subsequent advances at times and in amounts requested by the borrower according to the terms established by the loan documents to the extent that the outstanding balance is repaid; or

(5) at any time by the lender, on behalf of the borrower, if the borrower fails to timely pay any of the following that the borrower is obligated to pay under the loan documents to the extent necessary to protect the lender's interest in or the value of the homestead property:

(A) taxes;

(B) insurance;

(C) costs of repairs or maintenance performed by a person or company that is not an employee of the lender or a person or company that directly or indirectly controls, is controlled by, or is under common control with the lender;

(D) assessments levied against the homestead property; and

(E) any lien that has, or may obtain, priority over the lender's lien as it is established in the loan documents.

(q) To the extent that any statutes of this state, including without limitation, Section 41.001 of the Texas Property Code, purport to limit encumbrances that may properly be fixed on homestead property in a manner that does not permit encumbrances for extensions of credit described in Subsection (a)(6) or (a)(7) of this section, the same shall be superseded to the extent that such encumbrances shall be permitted to be fixed upon homestead property in the manner provided for by this amendment.

(r) The supreme court shall promulgate rules of civil procedure for expedited foreclosure proceedings related to the foreclosure of liens under Subsection (a)(6) of this section and to foreclosure of a reverse mortgage lien that requires a court order.

(s) The Finance Commission of Texas shall appoint a director to conduct research on the availability, quality, and prices of financial services and research the practices of business entities in the state that provide financial services under this section. The director shall collect information and produce reports on lending activity of those making loans under this section. The director shall report his or her findings to the legislature not later than December 1 of each year.

(t) A home equity line of credit is a form of an open-end account that may be debited from time to time, under which credit may be extended from time to time and under which:

(1) the owner requests advances, repays money, and reborrows money;

(2) any single debit or advance is not less than $4,000;

(3) the owner does not use a credit card, debit card, or similar device, or preprinted check unsolicited by the borrower, to obtain an advance;

(4) any fees described by Subsection (a)(6)(E) of this section are charged and collected only at the time the extension of credit is established and no fee is charged or collected in connection with any debit or advance;

(5) the maximum principal amount that may be extended under the account, when added to the aggregate total of the outstanding principal balances of all indebtedness secured by the homestead on the date the extension of credit is established, does not exceed an amount described under Subsection (a)(6)

(B) of this section;

(6) (repealed);

(7) the lender or holder may not unilaterally amend the extension of credit; and

(8) repayment is to be made in regular periodic installments, not more often than every 14 days and not less often than monthly, beginning not later than two months from the date the extension of credit is established, and:

(A) during the period during which the owner may request advances, each installment equals or exceeds the amount of accrued interest; and

(B) after the period during which the owner may request advances, installments are substantially equal.

(u) The legislature may by statute delegate one or more state agencies the power to interpret Subsections (a)(5)-(a)(7), (e)-(p), and (t), of this section. An act or omission does not violate a provision included in those subsections if the act or omission conforms to an interpretation of the provision that is:

(1) in effect at the time of the act or omission; and

(2) made by a state agency to which the power of interpretation is delegated as provided by this subsection or by an appellate court of this state or the United States.

(v) A reverse mortgage must provide that:

(1) the owner does not use a credit card, debit card, preprinted solicitation check, or similar device to obtain an advance;

(2) after the time the extension of credit is established, no transaction fee is charged or collected solely in connection with any debit or advance; and

(3) the lender or holder may not unilaterally amend the extension of credit.

Section 51. Size of Homestead; Uses; Release or Refinance of Existing Lien

The homestead, not in a town or city, shall consist of not more than two hundred acres of land, which may be in one or more parcels, with the improvements thereon; the homestead in a city, town or village, shall consist of lot or contiguous lots amounting to not more than 10 acres of land, together with any improvements on the land; provided, that the homestead in a city, town or village shall be used for the purposes of a home, or as both an urban home and a place to exercise a calling or business, of the homestead claimant, whether a single adult person, or the head of a family; provided also, that any temporary renting of the homestead shall not change the character of the same, when no other homestead has been acquired; provided further that a release or refinance of an existing lien against a homestead as to a part of the homestead does not create an additional burden on the part of the homestead property that is unreleased or subject to the refinance, and a new lien is not invalid only for that reason.

Section 52. Descent and Distribution of Homestead; Restrictions on Partition

On the death of the husband or wife, or both, the homestead shall descend and vest in like manner as other real property of the deceased, and shall be governed by the same laws of descent and distribution, but it shall not be partitioned among the heirs of the deceased during the lifetime of the surviving husband or wife, or so long as the survivor may elect to use or occupy the same as a homestead, or so long as the guardian of the minor children of the deceased may be permitted, under the order of the proper court having the jurisdiction, to use and occupy the same.

Section 53. Repealed

Section 54. Repealed

Section 55. Repealed

Section 56. Repealed

Section 57. Repealed

Section 58. Repealed

Section 59. Conservation and Development of Natural Resources; Development of Parks and Recreational Facilities; Conservation and Reclamation Districts; Indebtedness and Taxation Authorized

(a) The conservation and development of all of the natural resources of this State, and development of parks and recreational facilities, including the control, storing, preservation and distribution of its storm and flood waters, the waters of its rivers and streams, for irrigation, power and all other useful purposes, the reclamation and irrigation of its arid, semiarid and other lands needing irrigation, the reclamation and drainage of its overflowed lands, and other lands needing drainage, the conservation and development of its forests, water and hydro-electric power, the navigation of its inland and coastal waters, and the preservation and conservation of all such natural resources of the State are each and all hereby declared public rights and duties; and the Legislature shall pass all such laws as may be appropriate thereto.

(b) There may be created within the State of Texas, or the State may be divided into, such number of conservation and reclamation districts as may be determined to be essential to the accomplishment of the purposes of this amendment to the constitution, which districts shall be governmental agencies and bodies politic and corporate with such powers of government and with the authority to exercise such rights, privileges and functions concerning the subject matter of this amendment as may be conferred by law.

(c) The Legislature shall authorize all such indebtedness as may be necessary to provide all improvements and the maintenance thereof requisite to the achievement of the purposes of this amendment. All such indebtedness may be evidenced by bonds of such conservation and reclamation districts, to be issued under such regulations as may be prescribed by law. The Legislature shall also authorize the levy and collection within such districts of all such taxes, equitably distributed, as may be necessary for the payment of the interest and the creation of a sinking fund for the payment of such bonds and for the maintenance of such districts and improvements. Such indebtedness shall be a lien upon the property assessed for the payment thereof. The Legislature shall not authorize the issuance of any bonds or provide for any indebtedness against any reclamation district unless such proposition shall first be submitted to the qualified voters of such district and the proposition adopted.

(c-1) In addition and only as provided by this subsection, the Legislature may authorize conservation and reclamation districts to develop and finance with taxes those types and categories of parks and recreational facilities that were not authorized by this section to be developed and financed with taxes before September 13, 2003. For development of such parks and recreational facilities, the Legislature may authorize indebtedness payable from taxes as may be necessary to provide for improvements and maintenance only for a conservation and reclamation district all or part of which is located in Bexar County, Bastrop County, Waller County, Travis County, Williamson County, Harris County, Galveston County, Brazoria County, Fort Bend County, or Montgomery County, or for the Tarrant Regional Water District, a water control and improvement district located in whole or in part in Tarrant County. All the indebtedness may be evidenced by bonds of the conservation and reclamation district, to be issued under regulations as may be prescribed by law. The Legislature may also authorize the levy and collection within such district of all taxes, equitably distributed, as may be necessary for the payment of the interest and the creation of a sinking fund for the payment of the bonds and for maintenance of and improvements to such parks and recreational facilities. The indebtedness shall be a lien on the property assessed for the payment of the bonds. The Legislature may not authorize the issuance of bonds or provide for indebtedness under this subsection against a conservation and reclamation district unless a proposition is first submitted to the qualified voters of the district and the proposition is adopted. This subsection expands the authority of the Legislature with respect to certain conservation and reclamation districts and is not a limitation on the authority of the Legislature with respect to conservation and reclamation districts and parks and recreational facilities pursuant to this section as that authority existed before September 13, 2003.

(d) No law creating a conservation and reclamation district shall be passed unless notice of the intention to introduce such a bill setting forth the general substance of the contemplated law shall have been published at least thirty (30) days and not more than ninety (90) days prior to the introduction thereof in a newspaper or newspapers having general circulation in the county or counties in which said district or any part thereof is or will be located and by delivering a copy of such notice and such bill to the Governor who shall submit such notice and bill to the Texas Water Commission, or its successor, which shall file its recommendation as to such bill with the Governor, Lieutenant Governor and Speaker of the House of Representatives within thirty (30) days from date notice was received by the Texas Water Commission. Such notice and copy of bill shall also be given of the introduction of any bill amending a law creating or governing a particular conservation and reclamation district if such bill (1) adds additional land to the district, (2) alters the taxing authority of the district, (3) alters the authority of the district with respect to the issuance of bonds, or (4) alters the qualifications or terms of office of the members of the governing body of the district.

(e) No law creating a conservation and reclamation district shall be passed unless, at the time notice of the intention to introduce a bill is published as provided in Subsection (d) of this section, a copy of the proposed bill is delivered to the commissioners court of each county in which said district or any part thereof is or will be located and to the governing body of each incorporated city or town in whose jurisdiction said district or any part thereof is or will be located. Each such commissioners court and governing body may file its written consent or opposition to the creation of the proposed district with the governor, lieutenant governor, and speaker of the house of representatives. Each special law creating a conservation and reclamation district shall comply with the provisions of the general laws then in effect relating to consent by political subdivisions to the creation of conservation and reclamation districts and to the inclusion of land within the district.

(f) A conservation and reclamation district created under this section to perform any or all of the purposes of this section may engage in fire-fighting activities and may issue bonds or other indebtedness for fire-fighting purposes as provided by law and this constitution.

Section 60. Repealed

Section 61. Compensation of District, County, and Precinct Officers, Notaries Public, and Public Weighers; Salary or Fee Basis; Disposition of Fees

(a) All district officers in the State of Texas and all county officers in counties having a population of twenty thousand (20,000) or more, according to the then last preceding Federal Census, shall be compensated on a salary basis.

(b) In all counties in this State, the Commissioners Courts shall be authorized to determine whether precinct officers shall be compensated on a fee basis or on a salary basis, with the exception that it shall be mandatory upon the Commissioners Courts, to compensate all justices of the peace, constables, deputy constables and precinct law enforcement officers on a salary basis.

(c) In counties having a population of less than twenty thousand (20,000), according to the then last preceding Federal Census, the Commissioners Courts have the authority to determine whether county officers shall be compensated on a fee basis or on a salary basis, with the exception that it shall be mandatory upon the Commissioners Courts to compensate all sheriffs, deputy sheriffs, county law enforcement officers including sheriffs who also perform the duties of assessor and collector of taxes, and their deputies, on a salary basis.

(d) All fees earned by district, county and precinct officers shall be paid into the county treasury where earned for the account of the proper fund, provided that fees incurred by the State, county and any municipality, or in case where a pauper's oath is filed, shall be paid into the county treasury when collected and provided that where any officer is compensated wholly on a fee basis such fees may be retained by such officer or paid into the treasury of the county as the Commissioners Court may direct.

(e) All Notaries Public, county surveyors and public weighers shall continue to be compensated on a fee basis.

Section 62. Repealed

Section 63. Repealed

Section 64. Terms of Elective District, County, and Precinct Offices

The elective district, county, and precinct offices which have heretofore had terms of two years, shall hereafter have terms of four years; and the holders of such offices shall serve until their successors are qualified.

Section 65. Automatic Resignation on Becoming Candidate for Another Office

(a) This section applies to the following offices: District Clerks; County Clerks; County Judges; Judges of the County Courts at Law, County Criminal Courts, County Probate Courts and County Domestic Relations Courts; County Treasurers; Criminal District Attorneys; County Surveyors; County Commissioners; Justices of the Peace; Sheriffs; Assessors and Collectors of Taxes; District

Attorneys; County Attorneys; Public Weighers; and Constables.

(b) If any of the officers named herein shall announce their candidacy, or shall in fact become a candidate, in any General, Special or Primary Election, for any office of profit or trust under the laws of this State or the United States other than the office then held, at any time when the unexpired term of the office then held shall exceed one year and 30 days, such announcement or such candidacy shall constitute an automatic resignation of the office then held, and the vacancy thereby created shall be filled pursuant to law in the same manner as other vacancies for such office are filled.

Section 65A. Repealed

Section 66. Protected Benefits Under Certain Public Retirement Systems

(a) This section applies only to a public retirement system that is not a statewide system and that provides service and disability retirement benefits and death benefits to public officers and employees.

(b) This section does not apply to a public retirement system that provides service and disability retirement benefits and death benefits to firefighters and police officers employed by the City of San Antonio.

(c) This section does not apply to benefits that are:

(1) health benefits;

(2) life insurance benefits; or

(3) disability benefits that a retirement system determines are no longer payable under the terms of the retirement system as those terms existed on the date the retirement system began paying the disability benefits.

(d) On or after the effective date of this section, a change in service or disability retirement benefits or death benefits of a retirement system may not reduce or otherwise impair benefits accrued by a person if the person:

(1) could have terminated employment or has terminated employment before the effective date of the change; and

(2) would have been eligible for those benefits, without accumulating additional service under the retirement system, on any date on or after the effective date of the change had the change not occurred.

(e) Benefits granted to a retiree or other annuitant before the effective date of this section and in effect on that date may not be reduced or otherwise impaired.

(f) The political subdivision or subdivisions and the retirement system that finance benefits under the retirement system are jointly responsible for ensuring that benefits under this section are not reduced or otherwise impaired.

(g) This section does not create a liability or an obligation to a retirement system for a member of the retirement system other than the payment by active members of a required contribution or a future required contribution to the retirement system.

(h) A retirement system described by Subsection (a) and the political subdivision or subdivisions that finance benefits under the retirement system are exempt from the application of this section if:

(1) the political subdivision or subdivisions hold an election on the date in May 2004 that political subdivisions may use for the election of their officers;

(2) the majority of the voters of a political subdivision voting at the election favor exempting the political subdivision and the retirement system from the application of this section; and

(3) the exemption is the only issue relating to the funding and benefits of the retirement system that is presented to the voters at the election.

Section 67. State and Local Retirement Systems.

(a) General Provisions

(1) The legislature may enact general laws establishing systems and programs of retirement and related disability and death benefits for public employees and officers. Financing of benefits must be based on sound actuarial principles. The assets of a system are held in trust for the benefit of members and may not be diverted.

(2) A person may not receive benefits from more than one system for the same service, but the legislature may provide by law that a person with service covered by more than one system or program is entitled to a fractional benefit from each system or program based on service rendered under each system or program calculated as to amount upon the benefit formula used in that system or program. Transfer of service credit between the Employees Retirement System of Texas and the Teacher Retirement System of Texas also may be authorized by law.

(3) Each statewide benefit system must have a board of trustees to administer the system and to invest the funds of the system in such securities as the board may consider prudent investments. In making investments, a board shall exercise the judgment and care under the circumstances then prevailing that persons of ordinary prudence, discretion, and intelligence exercise in the management of their own affairs, not in regard to speculation, but in regard to the permanent disposition of their funds, considering the probable income therefrom as well as the probable safety of their capital. The legislature by law may further restrict the investment discretion of a board.

(4) General laws establishing retirement systems and optional retirement programs for public employees and officers in effect at the time of the adoption of this section remain in effect, subject to the general powers of the legislature established in this subsection.

(b) State Retirement Systems.

(1) The legislature shall establish by law a Teacher Retirement System of Texas to provide benefits for persons employed in the public schools, colleges, and universities supported wholly or partly by the state. Other employees may be included under the system by law.

(2) The legislature shall establish by law an Employees Retirement System of Texas to provide benefits for officers and employees of the state and such state-compensated officers and employees of appellate courts and judicial districts as may be included under the system by law.

(3) The amount contributed by a person participating in the Employees Retirement System of Texas or the Teacher Retirement System of Texas shall be established by the legislature but may not be less than six percent of current compensation. The amount contributed by the state may not be less than six percent nor more than 10 percent of the aggregate compensation paid to individuals participating in the system. In an emergency, as determined by the governor, the legislature may appropriate such additional sums as are actuarially determined to be required to fund benefits authorized by law.

(c) Local Retirement Systems. (1) The legislature shall provide by law for:

(A) the creation by any city or county of a system of benefits for its officers and employees;

(B) a statewide system of benefits for the officers and employees of counties or other political subdivisions of the state in which counties or other political subdivisions may voluntarily participate; and

(C) a statewide system of benefits for officers and employees of cities in which cities may voluntarily participate.

(2) Benefits under these systems must be reasonably related to participant tenure and contributions.

(d) Judicial Retirement System.

(1) Notwithstanding any other provision of this section, the system of retirement, disability, and survivors' benefits heretofore established in the constitution or by law for justices, judges, and commissioners of the appellate courts and judges of the district and criminal district courts is continued in effect. Contributions required and benefits payable are to be as provided by law.

(2) General administration of the Judicial Retirement System of Texas is by the Board of Trustees of the Employees Retirement System of Texas under such regulations as may be provided by law.

(e) Anticipatory Legislation. Legislation enacted in anticipation of this amendment is not void because it is anticipatory.

(f) Retirement Systems Not Belonging to a Statewide System. The board of trustees of a system or program that provides retirement and related disability and death benefits for public officers and employees and that does not participate in a statewide public retirement system shall:

(1) administer the system or program of benefits;

(2) hold the assets of the system or program for the exclusive purposes of providing benefits to participants and their beneficiaries and defraying reasonable expenses of administering the system or program; and

(3) select legal counsel and an actuary and adopt sound actuarial assumptions to be used by the system or program.
(g) If the legislature provides for a fire fighters' pension commissioner, the term of office for that position is four years.

Section 68. Assessments on Product Sales by Associations of Agricultural Producers

The legislature may provide for the advancement of food and fiber in this state by providing representative associations of agricultural producers with authority to collect such refundable assessments on their product sales as may be approved by referenda of producers. All revenue collected shall be used solely to finance programs of marketing, promotion, research, and education relating to that commodity.

Section 69. Prior Approval of Expenditure or Emergency Transfer of Appropriated Funds

The legislature may require, by rider in the General Appropriations Act or by separate statute, the prior approval of the expenditure or the emergency transfer of any funds appropriated to the agencies of state government.

Section 70. Expired

Section 71. Texas Product Development Fund; Small Business Incubator Fund

(a) The legislature by law may establish a Texas product development fund to be used without further appropriation solely in furtherance of a program established by the legislature to aid in the development and production of new or improved products in this state. The fund shall contain a program account, an interest and sinking account, and other accounts authorized by the legislature. To carry out the program authorized by this subsection, the legislature may authorize loans, loan guarantees, and equity investments using money in the Texas product development fund and the issuance of up to $25 million of general obligation bonds to provide initial funding of the Texas product development fund. The Texas product development fund is composed of the proceeds of the bonds authorized by this subsection, loan repayments, guarantee fees, royalty receipts, dividend income, and other amounts received by the state from loans, loan guarantees, and equity investments made under this subsection and any other amounts required to be deposited in the Texas product development fund by the legislature.

(b) The legislature by law may establish a Texas small business incubator fund to be used without further appropriation solely in furtherance of a program established by the legislature to foster and stimulate the development of small businesses in the state. The fund shall contain a project account, an interest and sinking account, and other accounts authorized by the legislature. A small business incubator operating under the program is exempt from ad valorem taxation in the same manner as an institution of public charity under Article VIII, Section 2, of this constitution. To carry out the program authorized by this subsection, the legislature may authorize loans and grants of money in the Texas small business incubator fund and the issuance of up to $20 million of general obligation bonds to provide initial funding of the Texas small business incubator fund. The Texas small business incubator fund is composed of the proceeds of the bonds authorized by this subsection, loan repayments, and other amounts received by the state for loans or grants made under this subsection and any other amounts required to be deposited in the Texas small business incubator fund by the legislature.

(c) The legislature may require review and approval of the issuance of bonds under this section, of the use of the bond proceeds, or of the rules adopted by an agency to govern use of the bond proceeds. Notwithstanding any other provision of this constitution, any entity created or directed to conduct this review and approval may include members, or appointees of members, of the executive, legislative, and judicial departments of state government.

(d) Bonds authorized under this section constitute a general obligation of the state. While any of the bonds or interest on the bonds is outstanding and unpaid, there is appropriated out of the first money coming into the treasury in each fiscal year, not otherwise appropriated by this constitution, the amount sufficient to pay the principal of and interest on the bonds that mature or become due during the fiscal year, less any amount in any interest and sinking account at the end of the preceding fiscal year that is pledged to payment of the bonds or interest.

Section 72. Temporary Replacement of Public Officer on Active Military Duty

(a) An elected or appointed officer of the state or of any political subdivision who enters active duty in the armed forces of the United States as a result of being called to duty, drafted, or activated does not vacate the office held, but the appropriate authority may appoint a replacement to serve as temporary acting officer as provided by this section if the elected or appointed officer will be on active duty for longer than 30 days.

(b) For an officer other than a member of the legislature, the authority who has the power to appoint a person to fill a vacancy in that office may appoint a temporary acting officer. If a vacancy would normally be filled by special election, the governor may appoint the temporary acting officer for a state or district office, and the governing body of a political subdivision may appoint the temporary acting officer for an office of that political subdivision.

(c) For an officer who is a member of the legislature, the member of the legislature shall select a person to serve as the temporary acting representative or senator, subject to approval of the selection by a majority vote of the appropriate house of the legislature. The temporary acting representative or senator must be:

(1) a member of the same political party as the member being temporarily replaced; and

(2) qualified for office under Section 6, Article III, of this constitution for a senator, or Section 7, Article III, of this constitution for a representative.

(d) The officer who is temporarily replaced under this section may recommend to the appropriate appointing authority the name of a person to temporarily fill the office.

(e) The appropriate authority shall appoint the temporary acting officer to begin service on the date specified in writing by the officer being temporarily replaced as the date the officer will enter active military service.

(f) A temporary acting officer has all the powers, privileges, and duties of the office and is entitled to the same compensation, payable in the same manner and from the same source, as the officer who is temporarily replaced.

(g) A temporary acting officer appointed under this section shall perform the duties of office for the shorter period of:

(1) the term of the active military service of the officer who is temporarily replaced; or

(2) the term of office of the officer who is temporarily replaced.

(h) In this section, "armed forces of the United States" means the United States Army, the United States Navy, the United States Air Force, the United States Marine Corps, the United States Coast Guard, any reserve or auxiliary component of any of those services, or the National Guard.

Section 73. Veterans Hospitals

The state may contribute money, property, and other resources for the establishment, maintenance, and operation of veterans hospitals in this state.

ARTICLE 17. MODE OF AMENDING THE CONSTITUTION OF THIS STATE

Section 1. Proposed Amendments; Publication; Submission to Voters; Adoption

(a) The Legislature, at any regular session, or at any special session when the matter is included within the purposes for which the session is convened, may propose amendments revising the Constitution, to be voted upon by the qualified voters for statewide offices and propositions, as defined in the Constitution and statutes of this State. The date of the elections shall be specified by the Legislature. The proposal for submission must be approved by a vote of two-thirds of all the members elected to each House, entered by yeas and nays on the journals.

(b) A brief explanatory statement of the nature of a proposed amendment, together with the date of the election and the wording of the proposition as it is to appear on the ballot, shall be published twice in each newspaper in the State which meets requirements set by the Legislature for the publication of official notices of offices and departments of the state government. The explanatory statement shall be prepared by the Secretary of State and shall be approved by the Attorney General. The Secretary of State shall send a full and complete copy of the proposed amendment or amendments to each county clerk who shall post the same in a public place in the courthouse at least 30 days prior to the election on said amendment. The first notice shall be published not more than 60 days nor less than 50 days before the date of the election, and the second notice shall be published on the same day in the succeeding week. The Legislature shall fix the standards for the rate of charge for the publication, which may not be higher than the newspaper's published national rate for advertising per column inch.

(c) The election shall be held in accordance with procedures prescribed by the Legislature, and the returning officer in each county shall make returns to the Secretary of State of the number of legal votes cast at the election for and against each amendment. If it appears from the returns that a majority of the votes cast have been cast in favor of an amendment, it shall become a part of this Constitution, and proclamation thereof shall be made by the Governor.

Section 2. Repealed

www.ingramcontent.com/pod-product-compliance
Lightning Source LLC
Chambersburg PA
CBHW071248220526
45468CB00001B/44